The Howe Estate
Halstead

It's History, Inhabitants and their Families 1750 to 1960
by Pam Corder-Birch

with photographic restoration by Christine Walker

An aerial view of The Howe circa 1954

Dedication: To my husband Adrian, an acknowledged local Historian and author for his love and support.

Front Cover: The Howe circa 1910.
Back Cover: Howe Ground Cottages in the snow circa 1910.

© Pam Corder-Birch 2012

Published by

Pam Corder-Birch
Rustlings
Howe Drive
Halstead
Essex CO9 2QL

All rights reserved. No part of this publication may be reproduced or transmitted in any form or by any means, electronic or mechanical, including photocopying, recording, or any information storage and retrieval system, without permission in writing from the publisher.

Every effort has been made to contact copyright holders of material reproduced in this book. If any have been inadvertently overlooked, apologies will be made at the earliest opportunity.

Printed by
The Lavenham Press Ltd
Arbons House
47 Water Street
Lavenham
Suffolk
CO10 9RN

ISBN - 978-0-9553537-1-0

Further copies of this book are available from the Author/Publisher as above.

Price: £14.95 plus P&P

Cheques and postal orders in English pounds sterling, payable to Mrs P Corder-Birch.

Contents

		Page
Introduction		4
Acknowledgements		6
Foreword		9
Chapters		
1	A History of The Howe	11
2	The Tweed Family	15
3	The Start Family	23
4	John Crump	33
5	John Sparrow	36
6	The May Family	41
7	Aaron Morritt, Nicholas Morritt, Nicholas Thomas Walter, Arthur Macnamara, William Gosset and Charles Walter	55
8	The Hornor Family	59
9	Fetes and Garden Parties held at The Howe during the Hornor years	85
10	The Hill Farm, Ridgewell, Essex	89
11	The Courtauld Family	99
12	Staff employed by Samuel and Edith Courtauld	125
13	Noel House, Palace Green, London and Eastry, Frinton on Sea, Essex	133
14	The Howe - Auction of 1953	137
15	The Development of The Howe Estate during the mid 1950s including Howe Chase, Howe Drive and Ashlong Grove	139
16	Ralph van Asch	153
17	The Howe Estate - Howe Ground Cottages and occupants	155
18	Howe Cottages and occupants	167
19	Howe Lodge and occupants	173
20	Bailiffs Cottage, North Lodge, Howe Gardens Gardeners Cottage or Howe Cottage	181
21	The Norman Family	183
22	Cottages in Box Mill Lane and the Old School House	189
23	Cottages at The Wash	199
24	Cottages at Does Corner	207
	Miscellany	213
	Glossary	228
	Appendix I	229
	Appendix II	230
	Appendix III	231
	Appendix IV	232
	Appendix V	234
	Appendix VI	236
	Appendix VII	238
	Bibliography	243
	Index	246
	The Author & Other Books by Pam and Adrian Corder-Birch	256

Introduction

My parents moved from Lancashire to Sible Hedingham in the 1930s and to Halstead in 1956. I went away to boarding school, which was followed by many years living and working in London, so I am not exactly what you would call a local lass! However I am extremely interested in local history and I like nothing better than looking at old photographs and postcards, or watching film and slide shows about 'Halstead and surrounding villages' of yesteryear. I have already written and published a book based on the life and work of a Lancashire artist, so I am not a novice when it comes to researching and gathering information for publication. I am also very fortunate that my husband Adrian and friend Doreen Potts are both very accomplished local historians and authors, who can point me in the right direction if the need arises.

Since moving back into the family home, built on land which was once part of the Howe Estate, I have wanted to know more about its history. Mention 'The Howe' and it is usually remembered as the house where Edward Hornor and Samuel Courtauld once lived. Both great benefactors to Halstead. However its history like its owners goes back much further in time and once I began my research, I became totally involved and found myself completely immersed in the fascinating eras of The Howe's history.

Documents show there was a farm, known as How Farm in Halstead for hundreds of years, but not necessarily on the spot where the present house stands. In the 1700s How Farm was described as a modest brick built farmhouse, but, by the mid 1820s, it had been replaced by a gault brick building known as The Howe. No earlier foundations have been found to suggest another house once stood in close proximity to the existing Howe. However there are strong indications that farm buildings were erected close to where the present dwelling stands today, some time before Edward May's arrival. Perhaps it is time to call in Time Team and Geophysics!

In 1759, one father stipulated that his daughter was forbidden from inheriting the estate if she married a clergyman and, in the 1830s, Edward May's daughter caused quite a scandal when she eloped from the house, with a local solicitor. However it was not only the owners of The Howe whose families were involved in romantic dalliances. Several workers on the estate as well as servants in The Howe married and raised families. Some of the cottages were home to several generations of the same families. Also, sons followed in their father's footsteps, taking over their job when the latter retired.

At the turn of the last century The Estate consisted of about 153 acres of land, woods and ponds, farm buildings and outbuildings. As well as the mansion house there was a lodge, and several cottages which were attached to The Estate. Horse power was slowly giving way to tractors; pony and trap, along with horses and carriages were being replaced by cars, and the old coachmen were being replaced by chauffeurs. England including The Howe Estate was being brought into the twentieth century.

The following chapters endeavour to follow the history of The Howe, its occupants and their families, as well as the families who lived at the lodge and in all the various cottages. Also incorporated is the development of the housing estate in the 1950s and early 1960s which was built on land that once formed part of the Howe Estate and is known as Ashlong Grove.

It is not my intention to invade anyone's privacy and therefore only brief references will be made to people connected to the Howe Estate after the mid 1950s. (Unless of course they have given me their consent).

Many hours of patient research has gone into creating this book. Looking at old documents and unravelling the past is very fascinating, but it can also be very frustrating too! Unfortunately the folk who went about their daily lives during the 1700, 1800 and even 1900s did not realise that, where they lived, or what they did, would be so interesting today! Many informative documents over the centuries have unfortunately been destroyed, so it is therefore inevitable that occasionally gaps may appear and questions remain unanswered.

I have enjoyed writing this book enormously, every minute spent on it has been a joy, and I am already contemplating my next project. Is there another book 'in me'? I sincerely hope so!

It is now my hope that some readers will be able to furnish me with further information regarding The Howe Estate or its employees, and any photographs would be most welcome. However small a piece of information or comment may be, please do contact me using my home or email address which is on page 246.

The Howe
(a watercolour)
Courtesy of David and Angela Kerrison

Acknowledgements

Without my friend and sister in law, Christine Walker, I doubt there would be any illustrations in this book. Chris is a whiz kid on the computer when it comes to photographic work and she has helped me enormously. She has transformed scruffy little faded photographs into good quality prints, as well as cropping and enlarging them to suit my every whim! She has also 'knitted' several sections of maps together to produce single illustrations. When Chris's computer was 'bursting at the seams' with over one hundred and thirty photographic images, she spent many hours preparing them for the printers. Chris has been extremely supportive and a very big heartfelt thank you hardly seems adequate enough.

I would like to thank the staff in the search room at the Essex Record Office for all their kind and valuable assistance. Not only those staff 'front of house', but the back room boys as well who have had the job of collecting and returning all the many ledgers, books, deeds and bundles of papers that I have searched through.

Although the Buckinghamshire Record Office at Aylesbury is tiny compared with the Essex Record Office, the staff are equally helpful and knowledgeable, and went out of their way to assist me, as have the staff in the West Suffolk Record Office at Bury St Edmunds.

The National Archive Office at Kew is vast and quite awesome, but, thanks to the helpful staff who work in the various departments, our days spent researching their records were most fruitful.

I thank, too, the staff at Colchester Library who have cheerfully assisted me on my visits to the Local Studies Section.

I would like to thank Glynis Morris very much indeed for all her helpful expertise, knowledge and advice, and for transcribing some of the Manorial Records of Halstead for me. They are some of the most difficult records to decipher and I am most grateful for her assistance. Nothing is ever too much trouble for Glynis.

I thank Michael and Mavis Portway, long standing family friends, for their continued support and encouragement. As the first people to buy land in the 1950s on The Howe Estate from the developer, Ralph van Asch, their contribution has been invaluable.

Ursula Darrell, Trevor and Brenda Hillier have also shown a keen interest in this project and helped me where possible, as have Gerry and Joan Martin, with their knowledge of events in Howe Chase. Elaine Pasfield and her late brother Bernard Turkentine, who once worked at The Howe, provided much valuable information.

Marjorie McAleese, Gem Rayner, Beryl and Eric Smith, Roslyn Taylor and Eunice Youngs have all contributed helpful information about the development of Ashlong Grove for which I am most grateful. Eunice, too, has very kindly read my chapter about Ashlong Grove to make sure that I have not missed anything out, and that I have correctly identified each house with its rightful owner!

I thank Barbara Hill and her sister in law Valerie Bulpitt from America, whose grandmother worked at The Howe, and Barbara's daughter and son in law Philippa and Ian Carruthers for their support and interest.

Doreen Potts, keeper of back issues of the Halstead Gazette, has kindly allowed me access to the newspapers ad lib, as well as looking out for anything 'Howe' related for me. Doreen has also helped me with general Halstead queries, and has read this book to ensure that to the best of her knowledge all Halstead data is correct. What Doreen doesn't know about Halstead isn't worth knowing! Thank you, Doreen.

I am grateful to Jim Davis, Curator of the Halstead Museum on behalf of the Halstead and District Local History Society for his time, help, loan of a photograph and for copying a couple of the Society's postcards for me. Also Dave Osborne, for answering questions both about his relation who once lived at the Bailiffs Cottage, later referred to as Howe Cottage, and the odd football query.

Malcolm Root, a very busy renowned artist, has most generously copied one or two interesting pieces of information for me, and has shown much interest in this project.

Glennis Sewell in Australia, who is descended from the Sewell family, has passed on some extremely helpful information regarding the May and Sewell families. Glennis who we have met on her visits to England is a most enthusiastic researcher and her knowledge of the World wide internet sites is amazing. Thank you Glennis for all your support.

Marcel Rayner's family moved to Howe Lodge in 1900 where they remained until 1919. I have spent several delightful and happy hours listening to his reminiscences and anecdotes, which, with his photographs have enhanced this book enormously.

Barry Sparke and his wife Veronica, who lived in Hedingham Road for many years before they moved to Norfolk, kindly sent me a copy of a much needed map. Barry also supplied photographs and information relating to his family's business in North Street/Hedingham Road for which I am very grateful.

Chatting to Angela Kerrison one day, I learnt that her husband David was the grandson of Victor George Cross, who was head gardener at The Howe for twenty years. I cannot thank them enough for their help and kindness in supplying information, photographs and copies of watercolours to enhance this book. Their enthusiasm to assist me is much appreciated.

John Steed has amused me with many tales over the years, and kindly allowed me to include a photograph of himself with friends, as 'the dashing young men' standing outside The Howe drawing room window! Many thanks John.

I thank Deborah Dumont in Canada for sending me information regarding the Norman family who emigrated to the Nipissing area of Ontario during the 1880s.

I met Richard Blackwell when he joined the Halstead and District Local History Society and soon established that he had lived at Howe Ground with his parents and siblings. The family had resided in the cottages which were erected c1825, and later in a bungalow built on the site. Richard's knowledge along with his sister Janet's, has been invaluable.

Malcolm Marjoram from Islington, London has gone out of his way to record items of interest he has found in London Repositories which have helped to 'add meat to the bones'. Thank you Malcolm.

I was absolutely delighted when David van Asch, who lives in Spain, contacted me after hearing from the 'van Asch Family History Society' in New Zealand, that I was seeking information regarding his father Ralph. David's photographs, help and support have been invaluable and he has given me a clear vision of his father's forward thinking. A man ahead of his time who was prepared to take on the challenge and risk of creating a private estate of houses long before it became popular in the United Kingdom.

I would also like to record my grateful thanks to the late Rosie Taylor of London, who kindly looked up one or two pieces of information for me. Rosie will be sorely missed.

Derek Reid and his sister Brenda have very kindly allowed me to reproduce a watercolour of one of the Howe Ground Cottages painted by their grandfather, for which I am most grateful.

I thank all my family and friends who have encouraged me throughout this project, especially my cousin Martin and his wife Angela, and my good friend, Penny Marks. Also thanks to Sally and Andrew Leech, and Christine and Ron Cooper, friends from Buckinghamshire who have kindly entertained us on our visits to their area and shown great interest in my research.

I thank Adrian, my husband, for all his loving support and encouragement. He has accompanied me on most of my visits to the various Record Offices and Libraries and, although busy with his own research, Adrian is always more than happy to give me a hand. His legal knowledge has also been of great assistance especially when looking at very old documents. We have travelled both locally and further afield to find answers to questions relating to The Howe and eaten our picnic lunches in some very odd places!

As Adrian is an author of several local history books, including a recent one about his ancestors involvement in the local brickmaking industry (published 2010), and his next book is in progress, I am never short of advice when I require it!

I wanted someone with a close family connection to The Howe to write the 'Foreword' for this book, so I was absolutely delighted when Julien Courtauld, a grandson of Samuel Augustine Courtauld, kindly agreed to my request. I would therefore like to thank Julien very much indeed for reading my book and, for providing me with such a kind, witty and thoughtful foreword. I would also like to thank his brother Stephen for providing some anecdotes.

Finally, I must thank Daphne Jones, a friend, who has painstakingly read my every word. Her comments and amendments have enhanced the text of this book enormously. I am also exceedingly grateful to Adrian who has also kindly proof read this book several times!

I have endeavoured to thank everyone who has made a valuable contribution to this book, if I have been remiss and left anyone out, I apologise most sincerely.

Pam Corder-Birch

Foreword
by Julien Courtauld

The more powerful the magnifying glass that is used to examine history, the more fascinating that story becomes. This is certainly true when applied to the story Pam Corder-Birch has told about a house on the edge of Halstead in Essex. The strands she has woven are as numerous as those of the Jacquard looms in Courtaulds Weaving sheds once in the town, and make fascinating reading as they connect the many families that have lived in the district over the past 400 years. The evolution of field names and areas given in acres and perches is particularly evocative.

I can only claim knowledge of two of the inhabitants of The Howe, my grandparents, and their staff. They were the sort of grandparents who followed the "children are better seen and not heard" school of thought, and we probably knew the staff better. I have memories of trailing along after the grown ups through interminable green houses full of the most exotic and highly coloured plants, for the "after tea" inspection of the garden. There was a dairy with Guernsey cows being milked and the warm cow smell comes back to me as I write. We would climb over the "expensive" iron park fencing as installed by Edward May in the early 1800s. Sometimes we would be allowed "off the lead" to explore the Rhododendrons and an exciting pond containing, to our eyes, colossal gold fish. When a little older we were able to play squash on the private court - an unheard of luxury for small boys. SAC's *(Samuel Augustine Courtauld)* love of English and Roman literature is referred to and the naming of the houses he built in Halstead from books by Jane Austen and the Fanny Burney. Sense and Sensibility are mentioned, but what the first tenants of Pride and Prejudice thought about the names of their homes when they moved in, is not recorded.

Three families, the high living hard drinking Mays, the completely temperance driven Hornors and the very "hum-drum" (SAC's words) Courtaulds, have occupied the house for a large part of this book and during their tenure some momentous changes came to The Howe and to Halstead. Edward May turned the house into a significant country estate. Edward Hornor bought the railway to Halstead and during Samuel Augustine Courtauld's time there, the business that started in Bocking, developed in Braintree, Halstead, Earls Colne and Chelmsford became the biggest textile company in the world and of course an important employer in Halstead.

This book will rightly become an important part of the archive of the history of north Essex.

Julien Courtauld
October 2012

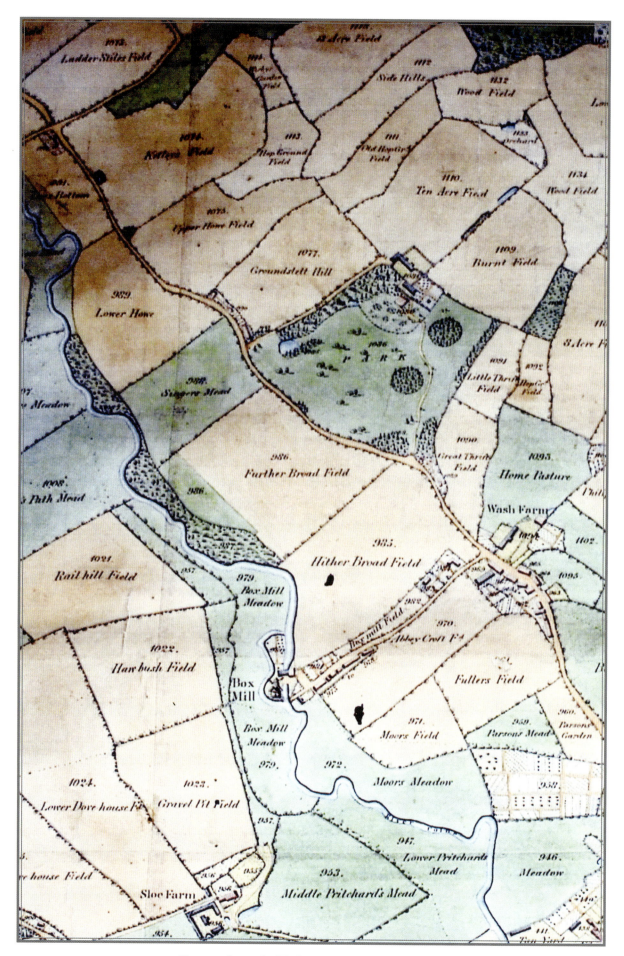

Extract from the Tithe Map of Halstead 1831

Chapter One
A History of The Howe

(Chapter one is a brief history of How Farm and The Howe and their owners, a more detailed account of the families who lived at the farm house, mansion house and on the estate follows in the next chapters).

Those who know the whereabouts of the present day property called The Howe, will picture a mansion house situated off the Hedingham Road, with its commanding views across the Colne Valley. However, take a step back in time and discover that the Howe Estate once consisted of a more modest farm house which was the centre of a busy working farm.

Over the centuries properties referred to as How Farm, How(e) Ground, How(e) House, Howe Park and today The Howe have stood near to, or where, the present house is situated. The buildings known as How Farm, The Howe, or above names, have been mentioned in deeds, marriage settlements, wills, newspapers and various documents with parts of the estate referred to as copyhold, freehold or leasehold. Research shows that How Farm was a freehold property, but several of the cottages and land on the estate were copyhold. Until more recent times, The Howe and its Estate comprised of messuages, appurtenances, cottages, tenements, hereditaments, farm buildings, woods and land, all of which were owned or occupied by many different families. Descendants of some of these families continue to live locally in Halstead and surrounding villages.

The earliest reference to The Howe appears in the Domesday Book which states, *"The Howe, a manor house near Halstead. Richard Fitzgilbert holds 32½ acres, 5 smallholders and 3 slaves. Woodland, 30 pigs; meadow, 8 acres. 8 cattle; 4 pigs; 83 sheep; 32 goats; Value 50 shillings"*. As Fitzgilbert c1031-1091 was a Norman Lord who participated in the Norman Conquest, he was granted one hundred and seventy six lordships and large areas of land throughout England including Clare, Suffolk. The Howe would have fallen into one of his many estates. Under the Manor of Hipworth Hall, today Hepworth Hall, dated 1547, reference is made to: *"Freeholders of certain land called The How, Sir Thomas Nevill, John Perry and some time of the Earl of Oxford"*.

According to William Evans - Old and New Halstead 1886; From at least the early 1700s The How or Hoo, from the Saxon word 'hou' meaning 'a hill' was a farm which consisted of arable and pasture land lying on either side of the road leading from Halstead towards Hepworth Hall. (Today this road forms part of Hedingham Road). From at least the mid 1700s How Farm was owned by Robert Tweed, a wealthy local gentleman, who also leased one or two of the cottages situated on an area of land known as 'How Ground'. On the 1838 Tithe Map, How Ground cottages were situated at the bottom end of a rough track, today called Howe Chase. This track ended in a dead end with a yard at the top and a barn which suggests that a farm house surrounded by farm buildings once stood there. Unfortunately no documentation exists to prove or deny this theory.

After Robert's death in 1759 the property was inherited by his only daughter and heir, Jane Tweed. In 1760 Jane married John Blatch Whaley Esquire, a merchant, from Colchester and, although they never lived in the farm house following their marriage, John retained a keen interest in the farm and its tenants which came to him via Jane's marriage settlement.

Shortly after John Whaley's death in 1788 the farm was purchased by William Start the younger, who owned Gissing Hall in Norfolk. John Crump was the tenant farmer until his death in 1801 when the farm was rented by John Sparrow, who leased it for some years before purchasing it from William Start in 1809.

In 1824 John Sparrow's executors sold the How(e) Estate to Edward May, a native of Halstead who had moved to London. In 1825 Edward was either responsible for making considerable alterations, additions and improvements to the original house, and incorporating it into the present house, or else he constructed a complete new building. The red brick farm house disappeared and in its place an elegant, modern and sumptuous mansion house was built using gault bricks. It was designed with a slate hipped roof, Doric portico and dentilled eaves and had a magnificent iron verandah, and a conservatory. The gardens were landscaped and delightful walks were created through the immaculate park land. The property became known as The Howe, the 'e' no longer being dropped from its spelling.

At the same time, a stable block was erected close to the house, which was possibly partly built with bricks from the old farm house. It is interesting to note that several of the buildings on the Howe Estate were constructed of brick and flint, which suggests there was a local source of flint in the area. It is quite likely too, that the first floor of the stable block was used as servants quarters. A lodge was built, using a similar style of architecture to The Howe, and stood at the bottom of the main drive which passed through parkland to the front of the house. Some of the farm land ran from Box Mill Lane, along the river bank towards Doe's Corner, and some was on the north east side of the road and ran behind The Howe almost as far as Wash Farm to the south east. The cottages which stood at Doe's Corner, since demolished for road widening and straightening, were also owned by Edward May, as were cottages and land in Box Mill Lane, Howe Ground, Thrifts Hill and The Wash.

An Essex Barn at Gestingthorpe
A barn, similar in design, was erected to the rear of The Howe, (see Tithe Map of 1838)

At the back of the house facing onto Howe Chase were farm buildings and a large barn in the style of a typical Essex Barn. The earlier surviving walls of the former Essex Barn and surrounding buildings are a mixture of brick and stone. This mainly applies to the remaining walls at the north west where some of the brickwork infill is of headers laid vertically. The wall along the north east elevation is mainly brick laid in header bond. It appears that other buildings, perhaps the dairy or an extension to the barn, were added onto the south west side. The brickwork is a mixture of English bond lower down and Flemish bond higher up. The various types of brickwork extend to about four or five foot high, although at the north west end, the mixture of brick and stone work is higher. Above the brickwork the barn was probably constructed of wood with a thatch or tile roof. The roof would not have been of slates because the barn was erected long before slates were transported to this area. There is little evidence of roofing tiles amongst the remaining building materials and therefore the roof was probably thatched. These barns also had doors on both sides of the building so that horses and carts could be driven in through one door of the barn and out the opposite side. It would have been built to thresh and store barley and wheat.

In 1844 the majority of The Howe Estate was sold to Arthur Macnamara and William Gosset for £10,260, it was definitely bought as part of a business arrangement and neither gentlemen occupied the house. Charles Walter, who was related to both Arthur Macnamara and William Gosset by marriage, was living there when it was purchased by Edward Hornor on the 5th December 1845.

Edward Hornor from Iver in Buckinghamshire obtained a mortgage of £8,000 from Robert Forster and Joseph Shewell, who were friends of his late father in law, Robert Moline, to buy the property. Once in Edward's ownership some of the older farm buildings were revamped, as the farm was updated and the old Essex Barn was retained. A new building was erected behind the stables, out of sight of The Howe, which was now referred to as Howe Park and extra accommodation was provided for farm workers. A gasometer, which served the house as well as the stables, was built near the Essex Barn. Gas mantels can still be seen over the doorways inside the stable block.

From 1868 Anne Hornor, Edward's widow, regularised the deeds relating to the copyhold properties on The Howe Estate when she applied for Awards of Enfranchisement to convert them to freehold.

In 1875 Joseph Shewell died and his executors were Joseph Talwin Shewell, Richard Bevington Shewell and Thomas Morland. In 1879 Thomas Morland disclaimed and renounced his interest in The Howe Estate. In 1881 Anne Hornor obtained another mortgage for £2000 from Joseph and Richard Shewell. Anne died in 1914 and on the 29th September 1914 The Howe Estate was sold to Samuel Augustine Courtauld for £17,500. The mortgages totalling £10,000 were repaid to the Shewells.

When Samuel Courtauld obtained The Howe Estate in 1914, he bought the house, yards, gardens, outbuildings, lodge, bailiffs cottage, several enclosures, pieces and parcels of land together with the sites of the cottages, tenements, and gardens amounting to approximately one hundred and fifty three acres. He also purchased the two Howe Cottages, situated on Wash Hill, and a further two hundred and five acres of land. Samuel Courtauld set about enlarging The Howe. He removed the conservatory and built a large extension onto the side of the house, which included a panelled dining room, and several bedrooms. Over time a piggery and more greenhouses were added. A pump house was built sometime after 1924, which covered the existing pump with the well below.

Samuel Courtauld owned The Howe until he died in January 1953. On the 26th May 1954 Ralph Gerrit van Asch*, an engineer from Colchester bought The Howe, consisting of the mansion house, bailiffs cottage and approximately forty two acres of land for £7,000.

The Howe was sold to the present owners towards the end of the 1950s and it continues to be a private residence. Today, the house is a listed building, which still stands in its commanding position overlooking the Colne valley, its views unhampered by modern development. A happy reminder of bygone days.

This introduction to The Howe ends with two quotes; The first made in 1848 when Edward Hornor was in residence: *'The Howe is a neat, modern mansion with pleasant grounds'*. While in his book, Man the Ropes, published in 1956 Augustine Courtauld, the son of Samuel Augustine Courtauld described The Howe as, *'a cold poor place to live'!*

*Ralph van Asch - Please note 'van Asch' with a lower case 'v' is correct.

Authors note:-
In addition to The Howe Estate, Samuel Augustine Courtauld also owned several other nearby farms, land and woods including Wash Farm, Hepworth Hall, Brook Street Farm, Sparrows Farm and Fitz John's Farm, to name but a few. Therefore when he died in 1953, he left a large estate. Please note this book does not endeavour to cover the history of these properties as they were not part of the original Howe Estate.

From Blackenham-Street to Henningham Lane to Hedingham Lane to North Street to Hedingham Road!

According to 'Holman's Halstead' a book printed in 1909 from a series of notes collected by William Holman 1700-1730, Hedingham Road was once known as Blackenham-Street. There was also a Blackenham Bridge over the Wash at the bottom of Henningham Lane. The Wash took its name from a nearby farm house called Wash Farm. The road eventually became known as Hedingham Lane and first appeared as North Street in 1863. It continued to alternate between the two names until 1869 when it was finally known as North Street. On the 5th January 1931 the Urban District Council agreed to change the name from North Street to Hedingham Road; The name it is still known by today.

The history of the last two name changes are explained in two letters which appeared in the Halstead Gazette in 1930. *(See appendix I for copies of these letters).*

Chapter Two
The Tweed Family

Ralph (1629-1688) and **Ann(e) Tweed (1636-1704)**. Ralph Tweed was born in 1629 and after his marriage he lived with his wife Ann(e) at Cooks Farm, Hartest, Suffolk. They also owned another farm called Sorrells situated in Hartest, which they leased out to tenants. Ralph and Ann(e) had at least two sons, John born in 1660 and Robert born in 1661, whose details follow below.

John Tweed (1660-1721) who was born at Hartest in 1660 married Katherine Bentall, a widow formerly Canham, in 1715.

Katherine Canham's first husband was John Bentall of Halstead, who she married in 1687. The Bentall family were involved in the brewing industry and owned breweries, malt houses, kilns and several ale houses and inns in the Halstead area. Katherine and John had two daughters who survived childhood, Katherine and Mary. When John died in 1700 shortly after he had made his will, Katherine was once again pregnant. John had hoped that she would safely deliver a son and made provision in his will for 'his son and heir'; sadly the baby did not survive. Katherine inherited their dwelling house and outbuildings in Town Street, which included a malt house. This property, which is known today as the White House in the High Street, was described as a customary freehold dwelling which adjoined the free school. Katherine also inherited other properties including a house with a tan yard, several inns, cottages and woods. Their two daughters were to receive a substantial amount of money when they came of age. In 1708, Katherine, John and Katherine's daughter, married Henry Potter, a woollen draper from Colchester. By 1722 both Katherine and Henry Potter, and Katherine's sister Mary, had all died.

Katherine Bentall married John Tweed in 1715 and they lived in Katherine's house in the High Street. Following their marriage, the Bentall Estate together with property purchased in 1695 passed into the Tweed family. As the eldest son, John had already inherited the bulk of his father Ralph's estate in 1688 and, combined with his marriage dowry, he became a wealthy gentleman.

As well as property and land in Hartest, John owned a farm in Walton, freehold and copyhold houses in the Manor of Prayors Glasscocks in Sible Hedingham, property in Castle Hedingham which included hop kilns, and three fields in Halstead which formed part of How Farm; Upper How and Lower How, which according to his will he had purchased from Mr and Mrs Jonathan Elford, and Ground letts which he had purchased from Nicholas Mearrott (sic).

John died in 1721 and was buried inside St Andrew's Church. In her will, made in 1728, with added codicils Katherine requested that she too be buried inside St Andrew's Church in the Chancel, near to her 'dear children'. She died in 1734.

Robert Tweed the elder (1661-1728), was the youngest son of Ralph and Ann(e). He too was born at Hartest in 1661, and married Sarah Spurgen in 1685 at Gedding in Suffolk. Robert and Sarah had five children, Robert the younger, Spurgen, Ann, Mary and Sarah. The family moved to Halstead where Robert owned a drapers shop. He died in 1726 and is buried in St Andrew's graveyard. In his will Robert left part of his estate to his wife, which included two of the best rooms in his dwelling house, together with the cellar and closet. These she could live in for the rest of her life provided she remained unmarried. His other houses and tenements with shop and yards, and a property in Parsonage Lane were left to his daughters Ann and Mary. Sarah died in 1740.

Robert Tweed 1687-1759
Courtesy of the Halstead and District Local History Society Museum

Robert Tweed the younger (1687-1759). Robert, the younger was born in 1687 at Hartest.

In 1721 Robert leased his Aunt Katherine Tweed's house in the High Street, with the brew house and all the out buildings. As John and Katherine had no surviving children, Robert, their much favoured nephew, was one of the main beneficiaries under his uncle's will. When John died in 1721, Robert inherited all his properties and lands in Halstead and Hartest, properties in Castle and Sible Hedingham, the farm at Walton and all his other real estate. He also inherited his Aunt's house in the High Street which he rented. As Robert had benefited under his Uncle's will, when his Aunt Katherine died in 1734 she left her estate to her nephew Robert Canham and six surviving nieces; Mary, Sarah, Elizabeth, Margaret, Katherine and Deborah, the son and daughters of her late brother Bartholomew Canham.

Robert Tweed married Jane Walford (1701- ?) of Bocking in 1722. Jane was the daughter of John Walford, a clothier and Jane formerly Desborrow. Robert and Jane had at least five children born between 1723 and 1738 and, although these children were baptised, only one daughter, Jane survived to adulthood.

Robert was obviously an astute business man as he continued to acquire property and lands in Halstead and surrounding district. He also owned How Farm which included a newly built farmhouse, farm buildings, gardens, orchards, meadows and pastures, and a couple of cottages on How Ground. Manorial Records for the Manor of Abels (later 'Abells') show that in 1729 'Robertus Tweed' was admitted to a cottage with a garden which had previously belonged to Sarah Younge, a spinster. This property was probably one of the How Ground cottages. However Robert and his family did not live on the farm as they preferred to reside in the High Street, therefore the farm was rented to tenants.

As well as the usual crops, hops were grown on the farm which were no doubt used in Robert's brew house. In 1745 Robert acquired The Kiln House with 8 rods or perches of ground from Robert Younge, a surgeon of Halstead. It was a freehold property built upon 'the Lords Waste Ground', which was situated near Hepworth Hall. The property abutted onto the field known as Upper How towards the North East, and onto Hedingham Road near Docs Corner. The Kiln House was erected before 1630, and had belonged to John Fookes and William Plumbe - Lords of the Manor of Hipworth (Hepworth).

The following properties were in Robert Tweed's possession when he made his will on the 29th December 1758:
Quote: *"Two freehold messuages now The Kings Arms private house and White Smiths shop Town Street near Market Place. Adjoining and standing in or upon or near the same spot were The Swan and Red Lion since pulled down and two messuages erected houses, outhouses, barns, stables etc. now in the tenure of John Crump and Charles Pratt.*
Two Brewers in Chappell Street.
The Bull/Black Bull, leading from Townford Bridge to Bocking.
Three Pigeons now divided into three tenements or dwelling houses.
Cock and Chequer, Town Street.
Three Crowns, Town Street.
Black Boy, upon or near the Causeway leading from Townford Mill towards Townford Bridge.
The Chequer.
Messuages and Barber shop, Town Street.
The Bear/White Bear, from Halstead Church to Sudbury.

The Dolphin, Town Street
The Three Feathers now The Angel, leading from Halstead Church to Sudbury.
Three Horse Shoes (formerly Goodall) Greenstead Green".

Also mentioned were: *'The Kiln House with ground adjoining, and his freehold messuage or tenement with brew house, storehouse, mill house, malt house, hop kiln, barns, stables, edifices, buildings, yards, gardens and appurtenances in or near the High Street of Halstead'.*

Robert died January 1759 and was buried in St Andrew's Church Graveyard on the 18th January 1759. He left his properties and land, both copyhold and freehold, to his daughter and heir Jane, with the proviso that his wife Jane should have a lifetime interest in them. In his will he also stipulated that if his daughter Jane married a clergyman, or a man whom his wife disapproved of, then she was to be disinherited! Presumably this was to protect Jane's inheritance from unscrupulous young gentlemen and the clergy, who were sometimes 'poor'. Alternatively he may have fallen out with the established Church.

After his death, Robert's wife Jane continued to live at their house in the High Street.

Jane, (daughter) made an Indenture for a Lease, which was dated April 1760 to Randolph Elkins of Pebmarsh (clerk) and William Walford, the younger of Bocking (clothier). The Indenture provided for:
Quote: *"All that capital messuage or tenement wherein the said Robert Tweed lately lived or dwelt, where Jane Tweed mother now lives together with brew house, stable and all other outbuildings whatsoever belonging to them etc. being in the Town Street in Halstead aforesaid, and doth abutt upon the free school of Halstead aforesaid towards the south west, and upon the messuage now or late of Nicholas Humfrey(sic) gentleman towards the north east, one head therefore abutting upon a croft, now or late of Catherine Tenner, widow, called Chapel Croft towards the north west, and the other head thereof abutting upon the said street called Town Street, which leads from Halstead towards Braintree toward the south east. Also all that capital messuage or tenement known as Cooks in Hartest with all the houses, barns, buildings, stables, yards, gardens and orchards. Also all those lands, meadows, pastures and feedings lying and being about the said last mentioned messuage formerly called Cooks Parmenters, and Potches (Potts), or otherwise. Also all that ground, messuage, tenement called Sorrell, lately stood which is since pulled down, with the yards and gardens, barns and stables, outhouses and all other lands, meadows, pastures, lands whatsoever belonging to the 30 acres lying and being in Hartest, adjoining to lands called Cooks. And two parcels of meadow ground commonly known as Cooks Meadow or otherwise 5 acres which belonged and is used with a customary messuage called Hedgefield in Hartest. And also all the appurtenances and premises in Hartest aforesaid now or late in the tenenture of James Firman. And also all other freehold messuages, lands and tenements and hereditaments whatsoever late of the said Robert Tweed in Hartest with appurtenances. And also all that messuage or tenement called Okins, alias Okeleys situate in Finchingfield and Wethersfield. And all that house and 18 acres in the occupation of Alexander Bright and now late Richard Gilby".*

The above were once again subject to the life interest of Jane Tweed the mother, who also leased How(e) Farm to Randolph Elkins and William Walford as follows:

Quote: *"All that farm commonly known by the name of The How, as well as Upper How and the Lower How or Nether How, or by whatsoever name or names the said is or hath been called and known. And also all the newly erected messuage or farm house with the outhouses, edifices, outbuildings, barns, stables, land, meadows, pastures and coppice woods feedings, profits and commodities whatsoever to the said messuage and farm belonging or in anyway appertaining situate lying in the Parish or Parishes there unto adjoining late in the possession of the said Robert Tweed or his tenants. And also all those three parrells (sic) of land and pasture with barn and shed built upon some part thereof commonly called or known as Gownsletts containing together 11 acres now planted with hops and being in Halstead or in any other town or town Parishes there unto adjoining late in the possession of the said Robert Tweed or his tenants".*

Also in 1760 Robert's widow, Jane received title deeds and writings to the following properties;

Angell(sic) Inn
Two tenements in Gatehouse Yard
Two Brewers and two tenements on How Ground
The Chequers Inn and Three Horse Shoes at Greenstead Green
A house bought from Christopher Carnall
Two tenements by Crow Bridge
Three Crowns and Black Boy
Dolphin Inn
Thatchers, Cooks and Sorells in Suffolk
Bull in Halstead
Finchingfield Estate
Edgware Estate

NB. Unfortunately a thorough search of the burial records has failed to prove conclusively exactly when Jane Tweed, Robert's widow died.

Jane Tweed (1738-1813) and John Blatch Whaley (1738-1788)
Jane, Robert and Jane Tweed's only surviving child was baptised 17th July 1738 at St Andrew's Church, Halstead. She married John Blatch Whaley, who was the son of Charles and Ann Whaley formerly Blatch at Colchester in 1760. Upon his marriage to Jane, John inherited a mansion with lands known as 'Aswells' or 'Israels' in Great Waltham and lands in Rainham, Essex, part of his family's marriage settlements dating back to 1708. These properties were later sold in 1771 and 1776.

John also acquired The Howe Estate as part of his marriage settlement with Jane. Although they never lived at The Howe, John ran the estate and like his father in law Robert Tweed, he rented out the farm house and land to tenants.

After their marriage John and Jane lived at Colchester where their children were born:
Jane Whaley   1761-1832
Ann Whaley   1762-1831
John Blatch Whaley   1764-1821

Another son Charles Blatch Whaley was baptised August 1770 at Holy Trinity Church, Colchester, he died four months later at Halstead and was interred in St Andrew's Churchyard.

John was a successful gentleman and the family lived in a brick built mansion house on East Hill in the parish of St James, Colchester. John had several business interests, properties and lands, which included Castle lands, houses in East Street with meadows and land with tithes. (Reference is given to rent of *four barrels of oysters* in lieu of cash)! He also owned barns, tenements, lands and tithes in St James and All Saints districts and a cottage with an orchard in St Mary at the Walls, plus a house in St James with two acres of Castle Land Meadow. He also owned Thern House in Harkstead, Suffolk.

In August 1775 the following notice appeared in the Ipswich Journal advertising the sale of a brewery and various public houses owned by John Blatch Whaley: *"BREWERY, To be sold by AUCTION at The Kings Arms Inn, Halstead in the County of Essex on Friday 1st of September next, at Ten in the Forenoon, (unless sooner disposed of by private contract. Notice will be given in this paper). ALL that good and well accustomed Brew-House; consisting of Brew-Office, millhouse, storehouses, cooperage, malt office, and chamber; hop kilns, ware houses, stables, cart lodge, dwelling house, yard and garden; formerly belonging to and in the occupation of ROBERT TWEED ESQ, deceased and now belonging to JOHN BLATCH WHALEY ESQ; and in the occupation of himself and of WILLIAM BIGG situate in Halstead aforesaid. Also at the same time will be SOLD by AUCTION in separate lots, 12 good and well accustomed PUBLIC HOUSES, commonly called or known by the several names or signs of the Two Brewers, the Black Bull, the Black Boy, the Three Crowns, the Cock and Chequer, the Dolphin, the Kings Head, the Angel, the White Bear, all in Halstead aforesaid; the Swan in Hedingham-Castle, the Three Horse Shoes at Greenstead Green, and the Blue Boar at Earls Colne in the said County of Essex; and several private houses and cottages in Halstead aforesaid, and all of which are also in the estates of the said JOHN BLATCH WHALEY. Mr William Bigg will show the premises."*

NB. The implements and utensils of the said Brew-House and the stock in trade were to be sold at the same time. Printed particulars and conditions of sale were available at the Horn Braintree, the Swan Sudbury, the Blue Posts Witham, the Black Boy Chelmsford, the White Hart Brentwood, the White Hart Colchester, the Great White Horse Ipswich and New York Coffee House, London, and from the printers of the newspaper. Further particulars were held by John Sealy, 53 Threadneedle Street or William Bullock, an attorney in Colchester.

In 1781 Osgood Gee of Oxford Street, London, was Lord of the Manor of Hepworth when John rented The Kiln House and adjoining land for five shillings per annum.

John Blatch Whaley died in April 1788 and The Howe Estate was sold to William Start.

Following John's death the Whaley family home at East Hill was advertised for sale by auction in August 1788. It was described as a capital brick mansion house, and consisted of a large hall, three good parlours and a drawing room on the ground floor. A large drawing room and five excellent bed-chambers were on the first floor and there was convenient servant accommodation. It also had an office both inside and outside the house, coach houses, a large stable yard, hog and poultry yard, large pleasure and kitchen gardens and a well stocked fish pond. There were 6 acres of land attached to the premises with beautiful views across the surrounding wooded countryside. Most of the furniture inside the house was for sale too. The property was considered suitable for a large genteel family.

The house evidently did not sell and was advertised again for sale by auction in June 1789 along with seven other lots of property owned by the late John Blatch Whaley. These included various pieces of meadow land and fields, a barn and barn yard, freehold houses and shops, an iron yard and a large mansion house with spacious wine vaults adapted for the residence and occupation of a wine merchant.

The Whaley family house was purchased by Benjamin Hall but was for sale again in May 1795 when he was declared bankrupt.

Jane died in 1813 and was buried in Holy Trinity Churchyard, Colchester. The Church is now redundant, although it has housed a museum and more recently a café. A white marble monument set into the north wall of the north aisle of the former Church has the following inscription:

Sacred to the Memory of
John Blatch Whaley Esq
who died April the 28th 1788
Aged 49 years

also of Jane his Wife
who died August the 5th 1813
Aged 75 years

also of John Blatch Whaley Esq
Son of the above
who died June the 16th 1821
and is buried at Margate in the County of Kent

also of Miss Ann Whaley
who died July 6th 1831

John and Jane Whaley's Children:
Jane Blatch Whaley was their eldest daughter who was baptised in 1761 at Colchester. She married Reverend John Weller Poley (1755-1799) in 1783 at St James Church, Colchester. John Weller Poley who was awarded a MA at Queen's College, Cambridge was descended from the Poley and Weller families who have owned Boxted Hall in Suffolk for over 600 years. In 1782 John purchased the Manor of Hartest, which included Hartest Farm, followed in 1783 by both Cooks and Sorrells Farms, when he married Jane. John was the Rector of Hartest and Boxted from 1791 until his death in 1799. His wife Jane died in 1832 and they are both buried in the family vault at Boxted.

John and Jane had one son, George Weller Poley who was born in 1783. He married Helen Sophia Fisher of Browston Hall, Suffolk in 1808 and they had at least thirteen children. In 1835 George was a Deputy Lieutenant for Suffolk. At the time of the Tithe Surveys for Hartest 1839-1841, George owned several farms and land, including: Kew Gardens Farm, Hill Farm, The Place Farm, Brick House Farm and Hartest Lodge, as well as land in Boxted, Stanstead, Somerton and Hawkedon, totalling 1,694 acres.

George Weller Poley died 5th November 1849.

Ann Whaley, John and Jane's second daughter Ann was born in 1762 and died a spinster in 1831. She is commemorated on her parents memorial inside Holy Trinity Church.

John Blatch Whaley, John and Jane's only surviving son was born in 1764. In 1786 when he was 22 years old, he was made a Freeman of the City of London by redemption in the Company of Wheelwrights. In 1788 John's address was 55 Threadneedle Street and he was probably a member of the South Seas Coffee House, which traded in goods from the East Indies. He apparently had no interest in brewing or farming and any properties he inherited from his father, with a Howe Estate connection, were disposed of. John died in 1821 and was buried in Margate, Kent. His sister Jane as next of kin applied to the Canterbury Prerogative Court as his Administratrix to settle his estate as he did not leave a will. John's memorial is included on his parents plaque in Holy Trinity Church.

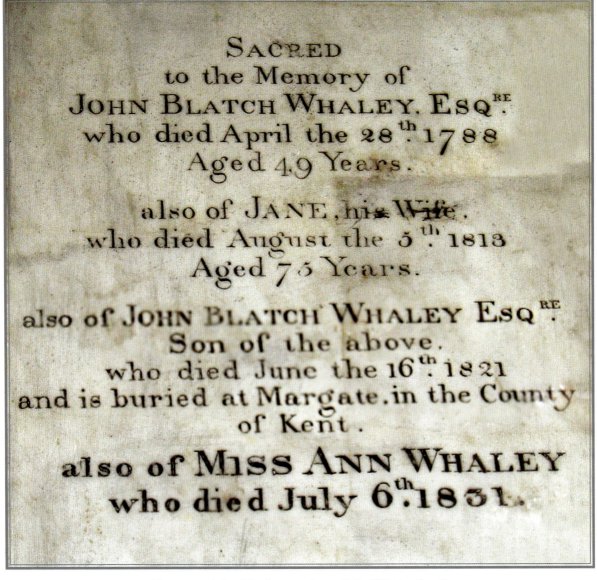

The memorial tablet for members of the Whaley family inside the redundant Holy Church at Colchester

Chapter Three
The Start Family

William Start the elder, was born in 1733 at Halstead into a Quaker family, the son of John and Elizabeth Start. He was a successful bay and say maker, often referred to as 'a clothier'. ('Bay' was a coarse cloth which was used to make many things, including habits for the clergy, cloaks for gentlemen and uniforms for soldiers. It was also used to make Quaker aprons. 'Say' was a more refined weave of cloth which, as it was thinner, was used for linings and more delicate items).

William lived with his wife Mary born c1738, in the house on the High Street which was formerly occupied by Robert and Jane Tweed.

They had five children:
1. Mary Start   1759-1839
2. John Start   1760-1818
3. Elizabeth Start   1763-1791
4. William Start, the younger   c1765-1827
5. Ann Start   1767-1824

Towards the end of the eighteenth century bay and say making began to slip into a decline and families in this cloth making industry sought other business interests such as farming, malting and milling. William was no exception and, in 1780 he purchased one hundred acres of land in the Halstead area from Charles Kent of Vauxhall, London, whose family had owned the land since at least 1745.

The land purchased by William Start as it appeared on the Indenture:
Blackenhins
Balsams
Little Groundsels
Little Woodfield
Calvesthys
Scots Croft
Broadfields
Broadfield meadow
Down hedge

The majority of this land was leased out to tenants; 'Broadfields', which abutted onto Hedingham Lane on one side and the River Colne on the other, was attached to The Howe Estate, while 'Broadfield Meadow' alias 'Box Mill Meadow', situated on the other side of the river by Box Mill, and ran towards Townford Bridge, was part of Wash Farm, Hedingham Lane. This meadow was leased to John Rayner.

Land Tax Assessments for Halstead dating from 1782 to 1787 show that William the elder, also occupied land on The Howe Estate, which he rented to tenants until his death in 1790.

Following his father's death, William inherited the land that he had owned in and around Halstead. This included Wash Farm with its seventy acres of land, which was leased to Stephen Church for fifty two pounds per annum and the land with appurtenances containing twenty eight acres on The Howe Estate, which was rented to Thomas Greenwood, his late father's cousin, for forty pounds per annum. There were also two tenements in the occupation of William Winterflood and George Nash which adjoined land on Wash Farm.

Wash Farm, just visible behind the farm buildings

Around this time William Start the younger, also purchased Howe Farm from John Whaley's Executors. As well as the farm and land, William inherited the tenants who occupied the fields. Owning both Howe Farm and Wash Farm, William decided to transfer some of the land from one farm to the other; therefore four acres and two rods of land from 'Great Thrift Field' which belonged to Wash Farm, passed into The Howe Estate.

As William the younger, a farmer and land owner lived at Gissing Hall in Norfolk, he did not wish to move to Halstead so, Howe Farm was leased to John Crump, who lived there until he died in 1801.

In 1809 The Howe Estate was divided into two unequal parts and sold. One part was bought by John Sparrow who had rented land and tenements on the estate for well over twenty years, and had latterly resided in the farm house. The other part, Wash Farm was bought by Thomas Smoothy of Bois Hall.

William and Mary Start's Children:
1. **Mary Start** was born in 1759 at Halstead and married James Corder (1756-1835), a farmer, in 1786 at the Quaker Meeting House at Tivetshall in Norfolk. At the time of her marriage Mary lived with her brother William, at Gissing Hall. James and Mary moved to Feering Bury Manor, a farm house in Feering, where their ten children were born:

Mary Corder	1788-1829
William Corder	1790-1863
Elizabeth Corder	1791-1869
Charles Corder	1793-1877
George Corder	1794-1881
Ann Corder	1796-1825
Richard Corder	1797-1813
Alfred Corder	1799-1825
James Corder	1802-1891
Emmaretta Corder	1804-1887

Feering Bury Manor - 1928

Following the marriage of their eldest daughter Mary in 1817, James and Mary left Feering Bury Manor and moved to Hornigalls Farm, Coggeshall.

James and Mary Corder's children:
Mary Corder, born 1788, married Thomas Catchpole of Colchester in 1817 and they moved into Feering Bury Manor where their five children were born.

William Start Corder, born 1790, succeeded his father at Feering Bury Manor, where he lived until 1844. He died at Kelvedon in 1863.

Elizabeth Corder, born 1791, was a very dedicated Quaker. She worked on a committee run by Elizabeth Fry which organised visits to female prisoners in Newgate Prison. Elizabeth married David Priestman of York in 1837. She died at Bocking.

Charles Corder, born 1793, was apprenticed to Thomas Howe of London in 1809 and later established himself as a draper in Charlotte Street, Cavendish Square. He married Rachel Atkinson in 1819. Thirty years later he retired to Purleigh, Essex where he died and was interred at Maldon.

George Corder, born 1794, was apprenticed to a miller in Earls Colne and followed in the trade for some years. He later lived on a small farm at Purleigh and married Phoebe Gibson in 1837. They both moved to Maldon where they died and are buried.

Ann Corder, born 1796, was educated at William and Ann Alexander's School at York, the first girl's school run by the Society of Friends. She married James Marriage at Coggeshall in 1823 and died of Consumption two years later. Ann, too, is buried at Maldon.

Richard Corder, born 1797, was apprenticed to an ironmonger in Chelmsford in 1813. Unfortunately he was taken ill soon afterwards and died at Feering Bury Manor.

Alfred Corder, born 1799, entered into business in Ipswich. He was also a devout Quaker and gave much of his spare time to the service of the Friends Society. When he suffered from Consumption he moved to Southampton as he hoped the sea air would be beneficial. Sadly this was not so and he returned home to his parents house where he died.

James Corder, born 1802, was apprenticed to his brother in law, Thomas Catchpole. He succeeded his brother Alfred in his business at Ipswich. James married Elizabeth Catchpole in 1828 and, following her death in 1830, he lived at Foxhall Lodge, Ipswich. He married again in 1836 Elizabeth Kersey at Levington in Suffolk. They moved to Ipswich where he lived for a further 25 years. He then moved to Old Hall at Claydon where he died.

Emmaretta Corder, born 1804, was James and Mary's youngest child. She was educated at Kelvedon and at Sarah Bevan's School in Croydon. Emmaretta lived with her brother William at Feering until her marriage to Allen Francis Clayton in 1839, which took place at the Coggeshall Meeting House. They eventually moved to Edgbaston, a suburb of Birmingham. Their son Francis Corder Clayton later became Mayor of Birmingham.

2. John Start, the eldest son of William the elder and Mary, was born in 1760 at Halstead. He married Sarah Tayspill Day in 1796 at the Coggeshall Meeting House. Sarah was the daughter of Samuel Day, a grocer, from Stansted Mountfitchet and his wife Sarah. John worked in the bay and say industry in Halstead.

John and Sarah had four children, who were baptised at the Quaker Meeting House:

1a.	John Start, the younger	1797-1859
1b.	Sarah Fulcher Start	1800-1871
1c.	William Start	1801-1893
1d.	Mary Anna Start	1812 ?

When his father died John inherited the real estate, copyhold, freehold and leasehold properties which were not already allocated to his brother William, the younger. He also received his father's personal estate, bills, bonds, mortgages, stock and trade goods. In 1808 John also inherited a legacy under his Uncle, John Start's will. After leaving his Ridgewell, Tilbury Juxta Clare and Little Yeldham properties to another nephew, Joseph Suiter, Uncle John left the residue of his manors, houses, farms, lands, tenements, hereditaments and real estate to John. These properties must have made him a wealthy gentleman.

John died in 1818, aged 58 years and, in his will he stipulated that his house in the High Street, which was currently unoccupied be refurbished and the garden fenced off, so that his wife Sarah could reside there for the rest of her life. Sarah died in 1829 at her daughter Sarah's house in Teffont Evias, Wiltshire. Both Sarah and John were buried in the Coggeshall Meeting House Graveyard, although according to the Quaker records John was no longer a member of the Friends Society.

1a. John Start the younger, who was born in 1797 was the eldest son of John and Sarah. Following the death of his father in 1818 he inherited houses, farms, lands, woods, groves, cottages, tenements, hereditaments, livestock, grain and farming equipment in Pebmarsh, Alphamstone and Lamarsh, plus £500 (today worth £365,000 using the average earnings formula). This money was to enable John to continue his farming businesses.

In 1828 John married Emma Newman born c1809, at St Martins in the Field, London, and his brother in law, John Mayne, and friend James Brewster were two of the witnesses.

In 1841 John and his wife Emma lived at Moat Farm, Cross End, Pebmarsh, with four of their surviving children:
Ellen Jane Start	1829-1865
Louisa Emma Start	1831-1926
Charles William Start	1832-1908
Augusta Sarah Start	1833-1849

Two sons had died; John Creswall Start 1835-1836 and John Creswall Newman Start 1841-1841.

Emma died in June 1845, followed in 1849 by her youngest daughter Augusta. John moved to Sparlings Farm, also in Pebmarsh where he died in 1859. It would appear that John had broken away from the Quaker faith, as all his children's baptisms and two youngest son's burials were at St John the Baptist Church, Pebmarsh, where Emma and Augusta's interments also took place.

Charles William Start, John and Emma's son, continued to live at Moat Farm after his father moved to Sparlings Farm and, by the time he was 28 years old, Charles employed 29 men and 15 boys on the 646 acre farm. In 1867 Charles married Emily Margaret Brewster of Maplestead Hall. Emily who was born in 1846, was the daughter of James and Mary Anne Brewster formerly Gepp. Charles and Emily lived at Moat Farm until around 1900 when they moved into The Cottage, Pebmarsh. Charles died in 1908 in the Ipswich area and Emily died in 1938 aged 91 in the Deben area.

1b. Sarah Fulcher Start was born in 1800 at Halstead. She married John Thomas Mayne, a barrister and Fellow of the Royal Society, who lived at Teffont Manor, a large estate in Teffont Evias, near Salisbury. John, who was born in 1792, was the last of the Mayne line to live at the manor which had been in his family since 1679. John had a tendency to 'enhance' his lineage and had a reputation for being a bit of 'a scallywag'!

John and Sarah Mayne had four children, a son, John Augustus, who was unmarried when he died before his father, and three daughters, Emily, Margaret and Ellen Flora. John died in 1843 and Sarah continued to live with her daughters at the manor until 1852. In 1861 Sarah was in Weston Super Mare with three of her grandchildren but by 1871 she had moved to Clifton, Bristol, with her unmarried daughter Margaret. Teffont Manor passed successively to Emily, Margaret and Ellen. Following Sarah's death in 1871 Margaret moved to Weston Super Mare, and died in 1905.

In 1859 Emily Mayne married William Andrew Fane De Salis (1813-1896), a landed gentleman. Educated at Eton, Heidelberg University and Oriel, Oxford, William was a successful businessman, colonialist and barrister. Following their marriage, Emily and William lived at both Dawley Court, a large house in the Hillingdon area of Middlesex, and Teffont Manor. They both died in 1896.

Ellen Flora Mayne married Maurice Keatinge, who was born in Ireland in 1816, at Teffont Evias in 1848, and they moved to Ireland where Maurice was employed as a civil servant. By 1881 they had returned to England and lived in Marylebone. They were back in Teffont Evias in 1891 with two of their children and Maurice died there in 1896. Ellen died in Oxfordshire in 1907. Teffont Manor was inherited by Maurice Keatinge, Ellen and Maurice's son, and it remained in the Keatinge family until it was sold in the 1980s. The manor house has since been converted into flats.

1c. William Start was born c1802. In 1818 he inherited his father's farms, houses, lands, grounds, meadows and properties in Halstead and Colne Engaine. However, it would appear that William was not interested in farming and by 1826 he had moved to Teffont Evias where he was the Stipendiary Curate at the Parish Church. He received £60 a year plus free use of the Rectory house, garden and offices.

In August 1837 William sold some of his property at an auction arranged by Joseph Surridge. The sale took place at the George Inn, Halstead and was very well attended. There were nine lots, which included part of Rook Tree Farm, Colne Engaine, which was both copyhold and freehold, and let to John Boyer Brown for £100 per annum. This was bought by Thomas Sewell for £2,005. Various meadows and pasture land were sold which included a 7 acre freehold meadow near Box Mill, let to Jonathan Nash for £25 per annum, which was purchased by James G Sparrow for £115.

This was followed by another sale in November 1837 arranged by William Kirkham, an auctioneer from Braintree. This was a large sale to dispose of the rest of William's remaining Estates and again it was held at the George Inn. Sale details were available seven days prior to the auction at The White Hart Bocking, Saracen's Head Chelmsford, Three Cups Colchester, Chapel Inn Coggeshall and Crown at Sudbury, as well as the George Inn.

Sale details extracted from The Chelmsford Chronicle, October 1837. *"For Sale - a very large and commodious Dwelling House, replete with every convenience for a respectable family, with the extensive and nearly-new Silk Factories and Premises, all adjoining, well and conveniently fitted up, having a Frontage of almost 125 feet, abutting on a good road, from which it is entered by a Carriageway. A pair of close folding gates completely enclose the Premises, thereby rendering them more advantageous to those who wish to conduct their business with retirement and privacy. Almost forty six freehold, leasehold and copyhold houses, the major part of which being contiguous to the dwelling house and factories, would form a valuable appendage. The whole of the above are at present occupied, and are let, at very low rents."* These properties in Globe Yard which were behind the Globe Public House were demolished. (The Globe is now a private house).

William was a widower by 1851 and had moved to Weston Super Mare before 1861, where he was a clergyman for 'The Church of England, Seceder, Without Cure of Souls'. (Seceder was the name for those who followed the 18th Century Secession Movement from the Church of Scotland). From at least 1871 William's niece Louisa Emma, daughter of John Start, accompanied him, and they lived at Clifton. In about 1881 they moved to Minehead in Somerset, where they lived on their private incomes. William died in 1893 aged 92 years and by 1901 Louisa had returned to Essex where she was a lodger on a farm at Birch. She died in the Ipswich area in 1926.

1d. Mary Anna Start - born in 1812, was mentioned in her father's will made in 1818. No further information found.

3. Elizabeth Start - 1763-1791 Halstead.

4. William Start the younger, was William and Mary's youngest son who was born about 1765. He married Maria Howlett, who was descended from the Howlett family of Pulham Hall, Pulham Market in Norfolk, and they lived at Gissing Hall, near Diss, Norfolk.

William and Mary had five children:
Maria Sophia Start	1788 (married Samuel Bond in 1809)
William Start	1789-1820
Ann Start	1791
John Start	1792-1877
Samuel Start	1794

It would appear that all was not as harmonious as it could have been between William and his Howlett relations! In a letter dated 1815 sent by Samuel Howlett from Philadelphia, America to William, who was his brother in law, William was accused of ingratitude, inexcusable conduct, and was 'ticked off' for not replying to Samuel's letters. In fact this was the last letter he intended writing to him! Unfortunately what happened next was not documented.

Maria, a Quaker, died in 1797 and was buried at Tivetshall, Norfolk. William died in August 1827 and was buried in St Lawrence Church Graveyard at Thorpe, near Norwich. John Start and his wife Mary (1808-1879) inherited Gissing Hall after his father's death in 1827, and remained at Gissing for the rest of their lives. They are interred in Gissing Parish Churchyard.

5. Ann Start who was born in 1767 married James Hill Hooper in 1785. James was born in 1759 and was the son of Joseph and Rachel Hooper, who were also Quakers. James was a surgeon in London and, according to the Medical Register of 1783, had a practice in Tooley Street, Southwark, where he and Ann lived. In 1787 James was one of the Secretary's of the Medical Society, and owned other freehold and leasehold properties in London.

Ann and James had seven children:
Mary Hooper	1786	(married William Howe in 1807)
Ann Hooper	1788	
Joseph Hooper	1792	
James Hooper	1793	
William Start Hooper	1795-1795	
Emily Hooper	1796	
Alfred Hooper	1798	

When James died in 1821 he and Ann lived at 'Paragon', New Kent Road, Surrey. Ann died in 1824 and was buried at Whitechapel.

The Tweed and Start family house when it was the Doctor's house
Right hand side, foreground

Information regarding The White House, 32 High Street, Halstead.
The Bentall, Tweed and Start families successively owned The White House in the High Street, then known as Town Street. They played a significant role in the history of The Howe and its inhabitants. Although still recognisable from the 1700s, the White House has undergone building alterations since the days when it had a brew house, malt house, kiln, stables, large garden and orchards, which abutted onto meadow land.

In 1818 together with Box Meadow, the house was leased by Foyster and Company, before it became the Doctor's house and surgery. Over the years from the mid 1840s, several medical practitioners resided and held surgeries at the house including:- Duncan Sinclair, James Hines, James Henry Ashworth, Charles Stewart Wink, George Robert Leslie Jordan, William Percival Ker, Sybil Muriel Richards and lastly, Archie Herbert Rae.

William Start and his family

Generation No 1
1. William Start was born 1733 and died 1790. He married Mary ? Born 1738 and died 1787.

Children of William Start and Mary:
2.	i.	Mary Start	b.1759 d.1839
3.	ii.	John Start	b.1760 d.1818
	iii.	Elizabeth Start	b.1763 d.1791
4.	iv.	William Start	b.1765 d.1827
5.	v.	Ann Start	b.1767 d.1825

Generation No 2
2. Mary Start (2) was born 1759 and died in 1839.   She married James Corder born in 1756 and died 1835.

Children of James Corder and Mary Start:
i.	Mary Corder	b.1788 d.1829	She married Thomas Catchpole in 1817.
ii.	William Start Corder	b.1790 d.1863	
iii.	Elizabeth Corder	b.1791 d.1869	She married David Priestman in 1837.
iv.	Charles Corder	b.1793 d.1877	He married Rachel Atkinson in 1819.
v.	George Corder	b.1794 d.1881	He married Phoebe Gibson in 1837.
vi.	Anna Corder	b.1796 d.1825	She married James Marriage in 1823.
vii.	Richard Corder	b.1797 d.1813	
viii.	Alfred Corder	b.1799 d.1825	
ix.	James Corder	b.1802 d.1891	He married 1) Elizabeth Catchpole in 1828 who died in 1830. 2) Elizabeth Kersey in 1836.
x.	Emmaretta Corder	b.1804 d.1887	She married Allen Francis Clayton in 1839.

3. John Start (2) was born in 1760 and died in 1818.   He married Sarah Tayspill Day in 1796.

Children of John Start and Sarah Day:
i.	John Start	b.1797 d.1859	He married Emma Newman in 1828.
ii.	Sarah Fulcher Start	b.1800 d.1871	She married John Mayne of Teffont Evias Manor.
iii.	William Start	b.1801 d.1893	
iv.	Mary Anna Start	b.1812	

4. William Start (2) was born 1765 and died 1827.   He married Maria Howlett born in 1768 and died 1797.

Children of William Start and Maria Howlett:
i.	Maria Sophia Start	b.1788	She married Samuel Bond in 1809.
ii.	William Start	b.1789 d.1820.	
iii.	Ann Start	b.1791	
iv.	John Start	b.1792 d.1877	He married Mary b.1808 d.1879.
v.	Samuel Start	b.1794	

5. Ann Start (2) was born 1767 and died in 1825.   She married James Hill Hooper who was born in 1759 and died in 1821.

Children of James Hill Hooper and Ann Start:
i.	Mary Hooper	b.1786 d.1881.	She married William Howe b.1785 d.1848.
ii	Ann Hooper	b.1788	
iii.	Joseph Hooper	b.1792	
iv.	James Hooper	b.1793	
v.	William Start Hooper	b.1795 d1795.	
vi	Emily Hooper	b.1796	
viii.	Alfred Hooper	b.1798	

32 | *The Howe Estate Halstead*

An extract taken from the 1831 Tithe Map of Halstead showing the High Street and surrounding area. Listed below are some Tithe Award details which correspond with the numbers on the map.

Plot number		Owner	Occupier
425	House	Robert Greenwood	Robert Greenwood
428	House & Garden	John Start	Decimus Sewell
429	House & Garden	John Start	John Sperling
434	House	Christ's Hospital	James Flavell
440	Garden	John Start	William Root
450	House of Correction	County of Essex	
453	Church Yard	Reverend William Adams (glebe)	Reverend Adams (glebe)
462	Burial Ground	Quaker Society	
470	Silk Factory	William Little	Rayne, Cable, Bush, Wicker
476a	Independent Chapel	Independent Chapel	
490	Three Crowns Inn	James Cook	William Moye
499	Meeting House	The Quaker Society	
502	Malting	Isaac Walford	Isaac Walford

Chapter Four
John Crump

John Crump the elder was born c1735. He was married firstly to Elizabeth and they had a son John who was born in 1771 and, probably a daughter Jane born c1773. They also had several other children born between 1772 and 1778 who did not survive. No baptisms appear in the Parish Registers for St Andrew's Church, although the burials are recorded.

John Crump the elder was the licensee of the Kings Arms in Halstead from at least 1772 until 1787 and the Red Lion Public House from 1794 until he died. He was a tenant farmer on the Howe Estate from about 1782 when he rented the land from John Blatch Whaley and, later from William Start. Land Tax records indicate that the rentals included Groundsletts, How Ground and Thrifts Hill. From 1786 to 1792 he also rented Abbey Croft, a field attached to Wash Farm, which bordered Box Mill Lane.

Elizabeth died in October 1798 following a long illness and was buried in St Andrew's Churchyard. John married secondly Mary Ann Phillips in February 1800 when according to the Chelmsford Chronicle he was sixty five years old and Mary Ann was eighteen years old! Whether this is true or not is open to speculation as Mary Ann did not state that she was a minor on their marriage certificate.

John continued to live at How Farm with his new wife until he died in July 1801. He left a will, under which Mary Ann and her heirs or assigns inherited all his property which included the copyhold cottage on Thrifts Hill, which he had purchased from John Blatch Whaley the younger in 1789 and was leased to Anthony Moul. He also left her a further three dwellings which were leased to William Norman, 'Widow' Root and John Root, the lease on How Farm, which John referred to as How Ground, held under William Start and the lease on another farm at Whitehouse Green held under James Goodeve Sparrow, together with the lease on cottages and tenements, malting house, malt kilns and appurtenances with 7 acres of land which were held under John De Horne.

Mary Ann did not remain a widow for long as in December 1802 she married William Argent, a widower, at St Andrew's Church. It would appear that she either sold or transferred some of her inheritance to her stepson, John Crump the younger.

John Crump the younger, the only son of John and Elizabeth was born in1771 and records indicate that he was 'a bit of a rascal'! In 1791 when he was a minor, he married Susanna Brunwin at St Andrew's Church. Susanna was the daughter of John Brunwin, an inn keeper in Halstead, and his wife Jane. John and Susanna had two children, a son John, *(baptism date unknown)* and a daughter Jane baptised in 1804. Jane's age and date of birth appeared to fluctuate between 1804 and 1816. *(Possibly because the family were not adverse to being 'uneconomical' with the truth at times)!*

Following his father's death in 1801, John did not inherit anything. The lease on the Red Lion public house where John and Susanna lived and, the five acre meadow which was occupied by John the elder, held under Sir James Long, along with the lease on the cottage opposite the Red Lion with the brew house and appurtenances and all the equipment, held under Mr Wise were left to John and Susanna's son, John the elder's grandson, also named John. From 1812 until 1815 records show that John Crump continued as the licensee of the Red Lion. He appeared to own the copyhold cottage on Thrifts Hill, which was originally left to Mary Ann by his father and sold it to Rebecca Cutts for £52 10s.

In 1822, an early census return recorded that John and Susanna had moved to *"Bridge"* (Street).

John Crump was evidently not adverse to obtaining goods by deception! January 9th 1822 - Bury and Norwich Post. *"Several tradesmen of this town have been imposed upon by a fellow who represented himself as Mr Cousins of Cockfield and thus obtained goods from them; but it appears no such person resides in the village. One of the shopkeepers whom he attempted to cozen on Wednesday by introducing himself as an old acquaintance, although a total stranger, had him taken into custody, and after undergoing an examination next day at the Guildhall, he was remanded until Thursday. It seems Mister Cousins real name is Crump, and that he comes from South Halstead."*

In 1823 John and Susanna attended the Manorial Court for the Manor of Abells to dispose of a double tenement which Susanna had owned in equal shares with her sister Jane since 1790. Half the building was now owned by Jane's husband, John May, and let to William Brown. The other half which was owned by the Crump's was untenanted as it was in such a bad state of repair. The tenement was sold to Orbell Hustler for £15.

A further census taken in 1827 showed that John and Susanna still lived at *"Bridge"* (Street) where they had been joined by their daughter Jane. John received 4/6d parish relief, so evidently the family had fallen on hard times. Susanna died in 1838 and was interred in St Andrew's Churchyard.

In 1841 John and Jane resided at the Causeway, John was a labourer and Jane a charwoman. John died in 1850 and was buried in Holy Trinity Churchyard.

Jane, who was growing increasingly eccentric, continued to live at the Causeway and in 1851 declared she was born in Ireland and worked as a laundress, and in 1861 that she was born in Halstead and was a nurse!

In June 1864, the following report appeared in the Bury and Norwich Newspaper: *"Halstead - Great excitement was caused in this town by the death of an old woman, Jane Crump. It appears that the deceased who has for several years past been receiving parish relief lived in a secluded hovel in the town, in an entry near the Causeway, Halstead, never allowing anyone to enter and always keeping the door locked. She was a very eccentric person and about a month ago, it being discovered she was in possession of property, the parish discontinued her relief. This appeared to pray on her mind and she appeared to become everyday more anxious, and she fell down dead on her bed last Monday morning whilst in the act of dressing. A more decided act falsely obtaining sympathy could never have been, for whilst going about begging from day to day was her usual custom, winning the sympathy of all with her heart-rending tales of poverty and starvation, it appears that on searching her house the following articles were discovered: 40 to 50 pairs of stockings, as many good silk shawls; 50 dresses and a quarter not made up; many dozens of pairs of gloves; bounteous other articles. 50lbs of tea, several pounds of soap and candles; more than 100 reels of cotton and handkerchiefs etc. A curious worked motto was found, which appears to have been her study, as follows:- 'Jane Crump, aged 10 years, 1814. Economy is no disgrace; It is better to live on a little than to outlive a great deal'. On Wednesday an inquest was held upon the body by William Codd Esq when the jury returned a verdict of Death by Natural Causes."*

Another Newspaper report for the 10th June 1864, reported much as above, with the heading: *"Death of a miser"*, and added, *"In addition about £12 in gold and silver was discovered and it is not improbable that a further search may reveal more hidden treasure. The Police took possession of the property, the deceased being without a relative whose address is known."*

In 1864 Letters of Administration of the personal estate and effects of the late Jane Crump of Halstead were granted at the Principal Registry to Elizabeth Worthington, wife of Leonard Worthington, master mariner of Commercial Road East, Middlesex, the niece and only next of kin of the said deceased.

Leonard Worthington was born in 1836 at Port Louis, Mauritius, the son of Edward Worthington a master mariner. Leonard married Elizabeth Susannah Hutchinson in 1858 at Stepney, Middlesex. Elizabeth born in 1829 was the daughter of John Hutchinson, also a master mariner. Leonard died at sea in 1868 and Elizabeth died in 1873 leaving two young, sons Leonard born 1862 and John in 1866. According to an 1881 census return the children were adopted by William G Jones.

Research has failed to ascertain where the Crump family lived before they moved to Halstead or what became of John Crump junior following the death of his grandfather in 1801. It appears that during the late 1700s to the mid 1860s that the above Crump family were the only residents in Halstead with this surname, although research has been hampered by the lack of registered baptisms. No family connection linking the Crump and Worthington families has been found either.

Following the death of John Crump, William Start continued to own How(e) Farm and the lease passed to John Sparrow.

Chapter Five
John Sparrow

John Sparrow the younger was born in 1766, the son of John Sparrow the elder (1746-1826), a say maker, and his wife Elizabeth (1744-1791). They lived at The Chace, today known as The Chase in Head Street, Halstead. Both John the elder and Elizabeth were Quakers who attended the Coggeshall meeting. Following their deaths they were interred in the Friends Burial Ground at Halstead.

John Sparrow the younger, like others in the cloth industry turned to farming, and for a number of years he rented land on The How(e) Estate from William Start the younger. This included Groundsells (sic) and How Ground. After the death of John Crump in 1801 John Sparrow moved into How farm with his wife and children. In 1809 both John Sparrow and, Thomas Smoothy of Bois Hall, purchased land on The How(e) Estate and Wash Farm, which totalled about one hundred acres. Thomas Smoothy bought around sixty four acres, and John Sparrow about four acres, which when added together, were approximately the seventy acres leased to Stephen Church at Wash Farm in the 1780s. John purchased How Farm and a further twenty eight acres of land from William Start.

As well as How Farm, John owned copyhold and freehold property and land in Great and Little Maplestead, which he had purchased from his brother Jeremiah who was a farmer at Blankets Farm, Childerditch, Essex. These properties were occupied by John and Edward Piper. John Sparrow also rented Phidgeons, (Pidgeons), today known as Fitz Johns Farm, Dynes Hall Road, Great Maplestead, whose land adjoined How Farm.

New farming methods were being introduced and William Start was one of those responsible for bringing threshing machines to the district. Unfortunately not all the labourers welcomed them and riots occurred in Halstead in 1815. The Military based at Colchester were summoned to quell the angry mob after windows were smashed in the High Street. Whether farm labourers who worked for John Sparrow on The How(e) Estate joined these riots is not known!

John married twice. He had children by his first wife, the youngest son being Jeremiah. John was widowed and married secondly Elizabeth Totman in 1810 at St Andrew's Church, Halstead. Elizabeth, who was born in 1770 at Halstead, was the daughter of Abraham, a farmer, and Elizabeth Totman, formerly Poole. John and Elizabeth Sparrow had one child, a daughter Elizabeth who was born in 1812. After his death in 1816, John left How(e) Farm, which included the farm house, land, cottages, tenements and hereditaments, Gownsletts, (sic) Further Broadfield, Hither Broadfield, Great Frith *(Thrift)* Field and Rush or Duck Meadow to his wife Elizabeth. He left instructions for his Executors to run his farming businesses so that the monies raised would provide an income for Elizabeth and any of his unmarried children. John also stipulated that only his children who were under twenty one years of age and who did not own a business or work, were to benefit from this money. When these arrangements were no longer required the farms were to be sold and the interest on the money paid to his widow until her death. Once both his wife had died and Jeremiah was twenty one years old, the money was to be divided equally between all his children.

How(e) Farm was eventually sold to Edward May by John Sparrow's Executors in 1824.

John's widow Elizabeth, moved to Sudbury and by 1841 she resided at Burkitt's Lane. Their daughter Elizabeth had married Samuel Joscelyne, a cabinet maker, in 1832 at Christ's Church,

Spitalfields, Tower Hamlets, London, and they lived on Market Hill in Sudbury. Samuel and Elizabeth Joscelyne had at least three children, Samuel born c1833 who died in childhood, Emma Elizabeth born in 1834 and Charles Walter born in 1844. By 1851 when Elizabeth Sparrow was nearly eighty years old she had moved and lived with her daughter and family on Market Hill. Elizabeth died in 1856 at Braintree aged 86 years.

In July 1854 Samuel, Elizabeth, and Charles Walter Joscelyne emigrated to Tasmania, Australia. They left London on the SS Potentate and arrived in Launceston four months later in November. For the Joscelynes it was a successful move. Samuel worked as a cabinet maker and by 1855 he had taken over an upholstery business. The company prospered and he became an established cabinet maker, upholsterer and undertaker. Samuel died in 1877 and Elizabeth in 1882.

Charles Walter Joscelyne married Mary Ann Gould and they had ten children born between 1869 and 1892. He worked with his father Samuel and eventually inherited the business. Charles died in 1911 and Mary died in 1914.

Unfortunately Samuel and Elizabeth's daughter, Emma Elizabeth, did not have such a happy time. Emma met Archibald Hamilton when the family visited her father's relatives at Tower Hamlets and they were married in 1853 at St Mary's Church in the Strand, London. Within two weeks of their marriage, Archibald who had a violent temper, started to ill treat Emma. They moved frequently and lived in a number of different places including Chelmsford, Colchester, Oxford and Banbury. In 1854 Archibald and Emma joined Emma's parents and brother and emigrated to Launceston. On the passage out Archibald became so abusive that when they landed in Tasmania Emma left him and went to live with her parents. Later, Archibald who was a phrenologist and lecturer met Emily Ellis who he bigamously married in 1864. Emily became suspicious about Archibald's past and they separated when she found out that he was already married, albeit to a wife that he seldom saw. In 1871 Emma divorced Archibald citing adultery and bigamy, coupled with cruelty. She never married again and died in 1920 at Launceston.

(Several 'John Sparrow's', both Anglican and Non Conformist, married, had children and lived in and around Halstead in the mid to late 1700s and early 1800s. Unfortunately 'sketchy' documentation has made it impossible to construct an accurate family tree for the above John Sparrow, which includes his first wife and their children).

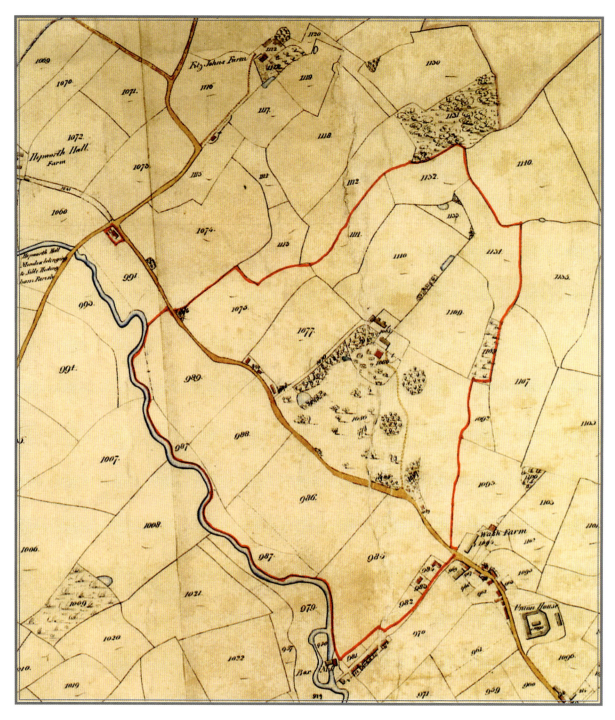

Extract from the Tithe Map of Halstead 1838
Reproduced by courtesy of Essex Record Office

The Howe and its Estate are within the areas edged in red, which includes the tenenments at Doe's Corner, number 992.

Tithe Award - Halstead
Dated 6th September 1838

The numbers and descriptions correspond with those on the Tithe Award and form The Howe Estate when it was in Edward May's possession in 1838

Number	Description	Type of land
982	Box Mill Field	arable
983	Tenements	
984	Tenements	
985	First Broad Field	arable
986	Second Broad Field	arable and grass
987	Alder Field	grass
988	Singers Meadow	arable
989	Lower Howe	arable
990	Three Cottages	
992	Tenements	
1075	Upper Howe	arable
1076	Plantation	wood
1077	Groundless Hill	arable
1078	Plantation	wood
1079	Cart Park and Chase	grass
1080	Mansion Pleasure Ground	
1081	Farm Yard	
1082	Plantation	wood
1083	Orchard	grass
1084	Plantation	wood
1085	Plantation	wood
1086	Flu Park	grass
1087	Plantation	wood
1088	Plantation	wood
1089	Cottage	
1108	Ash Ground	wood
1109	Burnt Field	arable
1110	Ten Acre Field	
1111	Old Hop Ground	arable
1132	Woodfield	arable
1133	Orchard	arable
1134	Woodfield	arable

NB. Before the Tithe Map of 1838 was printed, Edward May had taken Great and Little Thrift Fields, arable land, which abutted onto his east boundary, (Field numbers 1090 and 1091 on the 1831 Tithe Map), and incorporated them into grounds/parkland which surrounded The Howe. Part of this land was later developed in the 1950s, and is today known as Ashlong Grove.

*Extract from the Tithe Map of Halstead 1838
Showing The Howe Estate and surrounding area
Reproduced by courtesy of Essex Record Office*

Chapter Six
The May Family

Edward May was the youngest son of John May, a farmer and his wife Sarah (c1741-1815). Edward was baptized 24th May 1785 at St Andrew's Church, Halstead and lived at Gladfen Hall, Greenstead Green with his parents and siblings: Mary 1775, Abraham 1777-1842, Isaac 1780-1830, John, Samuel 1782, William and Sarah. John May made a will in 1803 in which he left £350 each to most of his children and his grand daughter, Sarah Argent. Gladfen Hall passed to John's two sons, John and Abraham, upon his death in 1810. Sarah died in 1815. John and Sarah May with their son Isaac are interred in St Andrew's Graveyard.

Perhaps wishing to seek his fortune elsewhere Edward moved to London and lived in the Parish of St. Marylebone. He married Elizabeth Roberts, born 1786, the daughter of John and Ann Roberts formerly Aldwin, at St Mary's Church, Harrow, Middlesex, on the 6th July 1809. By 1811 Edward traded as an ironmonger at 25 Davies Street, Berkeley Square, before he joined his father in law, John Roberts, who was a well established and respected Furnishing Ironmonger, at his premises at 66 & 67 Oxford Street in 1813. The business was renamed J. Roberts, May & Co. and they were Ironmongers, Braziers and Smiths.

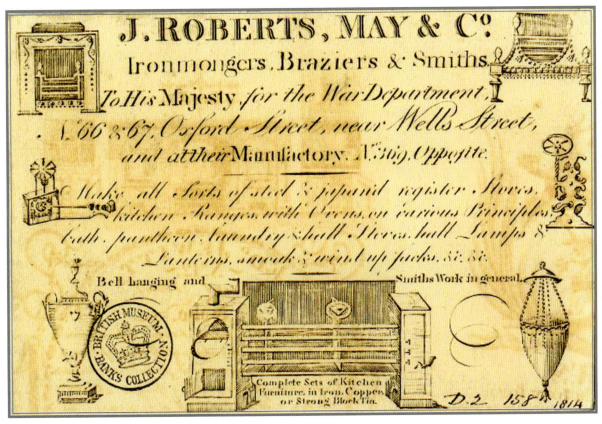

Draft design of a trade card for J. Roberts, May & Co. 1814
Courtesy of the British Museum, London

By 1815 Edward was a widower and he married Keren Happuch Michell Ching (c1792-1862) at Christ Church, Surrey, on the 15th February 1815. Keren Happuch, who was originally from Cornwall was the daughter of John and Rebecca Ching formerly Michell. John Ching, an apothecary invented and patented 'Ching's Worm Lozenges' in 1796. *(see note 1)*.

½ Penny Token circa 1795

Obverse: John Ching (?)
Outer Legend: I. Ching Patentee The Best Medicine in the World
Inner Legend: Sold in Boxes at 3/6, Packets 1s and in small packets at 6d each

Reverse: The Royal Coat of Arms
Legend: By Every Principal Medicine Vendor in the Kingdom

Edward and Keren Happuch May had four children:
1. Keren Amelia May   born 29th December 1815
2. Edward John May   born 20th June 1817
3. Augusta May   born 18th October 1819
4. Emily Ching May   born 31st January 1825

Edward and Keren Happuch had their children baptised at both St. Mary's Church, Marylebone and at Lady Huntingdon's Chapel, Southwark, Middlesex *(see note 2)*.

By 1817 John Roberts had retired from the Ironmongery business and Edward formed a new partnership with Aaron Morritt (1786-1858). They traded under the name of May and Morritt. In 1824 they provided the furnishings for two late Georgian terraces which were built at Bedford Terrace, by the Hall family, who offered Edward and Aaron the opportunity to purchase a lease on one of these houses. At about the same time they also leased a house in Holland Park Avenue which was part of the Ladbroke building development. Edward and Aaron rented out these properties to tenants which provided them with another source of income. Today the exterior of the houses in Bedford Terrace have not changed, although I'm sure the plumbing arrangements will have been updated! However the houses in Holland Park Avenue have undergone considerable alteration and rebuilding.

Edward and Aaron also supplied furnishings to another developer, Thomas Cubitt, who was an archetypal entrepreneur. Thomas, once a penniless carpenter, became one of the greatest speculative developers of his time. He built properties to suit all incomes and only employed high class workmen and used the best materials possible. To save on capital expenditure Thomas persuaded builders to take on the sites, therefore he only invested in the ground and site works.

In 1828 he went one step further when he leased six houses in Eaton Square to four of his most important builders and suppliers. One of these suppliers were May and Morritt, who more than likely took a lease on one of these houses in settlement of their account.

In 1824 Edward May bought The Howe and some land from John Sparrow's Executors, and set about completely rebuilding, renovating and modernising the house, creating a large, magnificent and impressive country mansion. Owning an ironmongery business must have been invaluable as the house was built with a stylish iron verandah and the grounds were enclosed with expensive iron fences. A conservatory was built on to the South East side of the house. Once building work was completed Edward furnished The Howe with the most expensive and elegant furniture available. He had rich satin damask sets of curtains, beautiful pendant lamps, marble topped washing tables and he filled his greenhouses with rare plants. Along with the house Edward built an imposing stable block which incorporated a dove cote. This building faced onto the main drive and was therefore seen by all visitors to The Howe. This was very unusual, as stables were usually modest affairs, hidden out of sight; it was as though Edward wanted to show off his opulence and wealth and give the impression that 'money was no object'. According to an early census return dated 1827 Edward employed eleven labourers on The Howe Estate. They would have worked on the land, kept his barn filled with oats, barley, wheat, hay and straw, and looked after the cows, pigs, poultry, and horses. Other staff were employed to work in the house and gardens.

The Howe
On the left hand side is the stable block with dove cote above

Over the next few years Edward acquired land, cottages and tenements, enlarging the estate. Manorial records for the Manor of Abells show that in 1829 he purchased copyhold cottages in Box Mill Lane, for £159 3s 8d from James Digby. He also paid £110 16s 4d for a customary and copyhold parcel of arable land which abutted onto the garden of Box Mill and the above cottages and gardens.

Which year Edward and his family started to stay at The Howe is a little uncertain, as in 1826 and 1827 'Mr Hanbury' was in residence, so, Edward either rented out the house to him or he was engaged in a 'care taking' capacity. Pigot's Commercial Directory for London 1832-1834 listed Edward twice, once under 'May and Morritt, ironmongers, Oxford Street', followed by 'Edward May, The How'. In 1839 his son Edward, while at University in Oxford, referred to his father as 'Edward May of Marylebone'.

With his business commitments in London, Edward did not live at The Howe permanently. He bought it as an investment as well as a country seat and retreat. This however did not stop his family from spending time at the house or from entertaining friends and visitors lavishly when he came down to Halstead. It was on one such evening in 1834 that the inhabitants of Halstead were to be scandalised by the elopement of Edward's daughter Keren Amelia with Decimus Sewell, a local solicitor. *(see page 50 for details).*

In 1836 'The Halstead Board of Guardians' decided that a Union Workhouse was required, and one of the sites which they considered was a 2 acre plot offered for sale by Edward at £200 per acre. However his offer was declined and the Workhouse was erected on land at Bois Field.

In 1839 having ensured that all legal documentation relating to The Howe Estate was correct, Edward, suffering from financial difficulties, was forced to take out a loan/mortgage against The Estate for £3,000, with an annual interest rate of £5 in every £100 (5%). He also had the ability to raise this with additional advances to £5,000 if the need arose. The money was to be paid back monthly within six months to John Taylor*, a solicitor, practising from Grays Inn Square, London, who had acted for Edward and Aaron Morritt on previous occasions. The monies were repaid.

The 1841 census return for The Howe showed that the May family were absent, and only James Maxim, husbandman, and Sophie, his wife, the housekeeper, both of Halstead, were in residence. Edward and his family's whereabouts remain unknown.

On 17th June 1842 Edward May and Aaron Morritt dissolved their partnership in the ironmongery business by mutual consent. Pigot's London Directory listed only Edward May as an ironmonger at 66, 67 and 370 Oxford Street from 1843 until the last entry in 1847.

By the beginning of 1843 things were far from good for Edward and he was forced to put The Howe, together with one hundred and thirty two acres of land on the market.

One 'For Sale advertisement' appeared in the Reading Mercury dated Saturday 13th May 1843: *"THE HOWE, within half a mile of the Town of HALSTEAD, an elegant and most Complete FREEHOLD RESIDENCE, on a beautiful and gravely(sic) spot, commanding highly picturesque scenery, in the centre of about ONE HUNDRED and THIRTY TWO ACRES of rich park-like land, bounded by the river Colne, between Braintree and Sudbury, only three and a half hour's journey from Town. MESSRS DANIEL SMITH and SON will SELL by AUCTION, in June next, (unless previously disposed of by Private Contract) the above truly-desirable and perfect RESIDENCE situated in the vicinity of Gosfield Hall, only half a mile from the church and town of Halstead, and with easy distance of the several other towns of Braintree, Sudbury, Bury, Colchester and Chelmsford. It comprises a modern mansion, with stone portico, elegant iron verandah, and beautiful conservatory, containing rooms of excellent dimensions, and finished in the best style; capital and substantial stabling, double coach-house, walled gardens, with spacious hot-house, heated with hot water, melon ground, superior and well arranged farm buildings, beautiful pleasure grounds, admirably laid out, and richly dressed with clumps and belts of plantations, enclosed by expensive iron fences, and studded with fine timber, with handsome carriage drive, and extensive walks, terminated by a neat lodge, and surrounded by the remainder of the land, forming a delightful farm, divided into ornamental undulating paddocks, nearly all sloping with south aspects to the river. Also several superior Neat Cottages, for bailiff, gardener, and labourers. The whole of the Estate is in the most perfect order, and altogether a most complete and enviable property. The greater part of the fitted and appropriate furniture may be had at a fair valuation, and immediate possession. Descriptive Particulars, with plans, are preparing, and may be had, when the day of the sale is fixed, at the chief Inns in the neighbourhood; at the Auction Mart; and Messrs. Smith's Offices in Waterloo Place, Pall Mall, and Windsor".*

1844 was another sad and miserable year for the May Family; Edward and Keren Happuch's daughter, Keren Amelia Sewell, died at Halstead shortly after giving birth to a daughter and Edward still suffered from cash flow problems. He had sold The Howe and was then forced to sell all the contents of the house at another auction at the end of August 1844.

Further notices of sale were issued by Messrs Daniel Smith and Son's to dispose of the valuable household effects at The Howe. Notice of Sale taken from the Chemlsford Chronicle 30th August 1844. *"Notice of Sale of the Elegant and Valuable House Effects at THE HOWE. Close to the town of Halstead; also of the Live and Dead Stock, Corn and Hay. The property of EDWARD MAY, Esq. Messrs Daniel Smith and Son beg to announce that having sold the above Estate, the whole of the superior and elegant furniture of the mansion, and also the valuable Farming Stock and crops, will be sold by auction, on the Premises, on Thursday, the 12th and Friday, the 13th September next, at Eleven o'clock. The Furniture (a great part from the manufactories of Messrs. Dowbiggin and Mr Bott) comprises an elegant suite of Drawing Room Furniture, of solid rosewood, in couches, tables and chairs; handsome dining table, modern sideboard and chairs, capital Turkey and Brussels carpets; also, rich satin damask sets of curtains, superb chimney glasses, elegant pendant and table lamps, a piano by Voraum (sic), an eight dial clock, alabaster figures, etc. Also a variety of most excellent Bedroom Furniture, handsome bedsteads and hangings, winged and other wardrobes, chests of drawers, washing tables, with marble tops; glasses, carpets, curtains and chairs, kitchen, dairy and brewing utensils; a large collection of rare and choice green-house plants, garden lights, tools and seats, iron roller etc. Also, the Live and Dead Stock, consisting of four cart horses, a handsome pony, Alderney and other cows, pigs, poultry, and a Newfoundland dog; wagons, carts, ploughs, harrow, large iron park roller, with several ricks of oats and barley, some wheat in the barn, two ricks of hay, straw,...feed etc. The Stock of Corn will be sold on Thursday 12th, and the Furniture on Friday 13th. Catalogues 1s., each (to be returned to the purchasers) will admit to view on Thursday, 12th, and may be had on the Premises, at all the principal Inns at Halstead, Braintree, Coggeshall, Chelmsford, Witham and Sudbury, and at Messrs. Daniel Smith and Son's offices in Pall Mall, London".*

On the 31st October 1844 Arthur Macnamara and William Matthew Gosset paid £10,260 for The Howe Estate including the house, lodge and copyhold cottages on Thrift Hill and Box Mill Lane. However this apparently did not solve Edward's financial problems.

Sale Notice for The Howe
Reading Mercury May 1843

Sale Notice of Household Effects
Chelmsford Chronicle August 1844

Another sale took place on the 3rd December 1844, presumably on the instruction of Messrs Macnamara and Gosset. *"At Halstead. SALE OF TIMBER. To be sold by Auction, by J S Surridge, on Tuesday, the 3rd December 1844, at The White Hart Inn, at three o'clock in the Afternoon. Nearly 200 Oak, Elm, Ash and Poplar TIMBER TREES, some of large dimensions and of Excellent quality, growing on THE HOWE ESTATE Halsted. They are numbered with white paint in convenient Lots, and may be viewed on application to (Thomas) Norman, the Bailiff, either on Tuesday, 26th inst., or the day of Sale. The tops will be included and purchasers are to stub and clear the Timber before Christmas Day next. Deposits and approved joint Bills will be taken as usual, if required. Descriptive Catalogue may be had at Carter's Printing Offices in Halsted and Hedingham, and of the Auctioneer, Coggeshall".*

Edward had also taken a lease on a house in Holland Park Avenue, London which was owned by Charles Richardson, a solicitor who had unsuccessfully speculated on the property market. The 1840s ended in a depression within the building industry, which prevented the sale of houses and caused serious problems for builders and their tradesmen.

On the 6th May 1847, Edward, now in severe financial difficulty was declared bankrupt after he appeared at The Court of Bankruptcy, London Division. The petitioning creditors were Henry Elliott Hoole, trading as Henry E. Hoole of Sheffield, a merchant and Thomas Nicholson, Merchants and Stove-Grate Manufacturers. Another creditor was George Lacey May, his nephew, who was owed £2,000. He was represented by his attorney Stephen Williams. Following Edward's bankruptcy several notices appeared in The Law Times and London Gazette which invited both Edward May's creditors and debtors to contact the Official Assignee at Old Jewry Chambers. Several more creditors came forward and in November 1847 Edward appeared once again at The Court of Bankruptcy. His business accounts were produced which showed that Edward's accounts were up to date, and that he was not actually a reckless trader, although it was suggested that his personal expenditure was excessive and that he was an extravagant man. Another meeting of his creditors was called in April 1851, this time no doubt, to allot monies raised from his debtors and by the sale of any assets Edward may have possessed, for example his ironmongery business in Oxford Street. In 1851 Edward and his family left Oxford Street and moved into a house at 1 Tavistock Square, St. Pancras.

May and Morritt's Shop front, 66 & 67 Oxford Street
A sketch taken from John Tallis's 'London Street Views 1838-1840'

Edward May died on the 2nd September 1856 whilst visiting his friend, Richard Lacey** at his house in the High Street, Braintree. Richard was also related to Edward May as Sarah Lacey had married Abraham May, Edward's brother and their son, George Lacey May was living with Richard at the time of Edward's death. No will or administration has been found for Edward, which is hardly surprising as he was a bankrupt, he had no estate to leave. A rather sad end for a once prosperous, colourful and flamboyant gentleman.

Edward's widow, Keren Happuch, continued to live at Tavistock Square until she moved in 1861 with her daughters, Augusta and Emily, and lived with her son Edward at Abbey Wood College, Erith, Kent, where she died on the 5th April 1862.

Employees of Edward May on the 1827 Census Return for Halstead

Name	Age	Married	Home	Occupation
Thomas Chapman	41 yrs	yes	Hedingham Lane	Labourer
Mary Clemment	60 yrs	---	Wash	Labourer
James Evans	40 yrs	yes	Hedingham Lane	Labourer
William Fincham	33 yrs	yes	Mount Hill	Labourer
James Kemp	46 yrs	yes	How Ground	Labourer

James Nokes	62 yrs	yes	Box Mill Lane	Labourer
Thomas Norman	24 yrs	yes	Howe Ground	Labourer
William Norman	29 yrs	yes	Field	Labourer
William Norman	55 yrs	yes	Wash	Labourer
John Parker	52 yrs	yes	Howe Ground	Labourer

For the names of other labourers who appeared on the 1827 Census Return and lived at Howe Ground, but did not work for Edward May, *(See Appendix II)*.

*John Taylor a Solicitor and friend of Edward May's had qualified in 1829 and was in partnership with James Quilter until 1868. His son, also John Taylor, joined the practice when he qualified in 1866 and remained with his father until 1874. John Taylor the elder retired in 1880 and lived at Hampton Court, Middlesex.

**Richard Lacey (c1781-1867), was a maltster and farmer who lived in the High Street, Braintree. He died a bachelor, leaving an estate of around £3000, made up of copyhold, freehold and real estate. He left several legacies which included money to install a memorial or ornamental stained glass window at the east end of the Parish Church, Braintree, and money towards a new organ, or for the repair of ornaments in the church. He also left £100 to be given to a Church School in Braintree, to help with their expenses. Richard's nephew, George Lacey May (c1811-1885) also received a legacy, as did George May the son of William May of Gowers Farm, Stisted, and Edward and Keren Happuch's children; Edward John, Augusta and Emily May.

High Street, Braintree circa 1920

Edward and Keren Happuch May's children:
1. Keren Amelia May (1815 - 1844)

Keren Amelia May, known as Amey was born 29th December 1815, at St Marylebone, London. She was the eldest child and daughter of Edward and Keren Happuch, and during her teenage years came into contact with her father's friends and business acquaintances when staying at The Howe. This was probably how she came to meet her future husband, Decimus Sewell, who as a solicitor, practised in Halstead. Although he was seventeen years older than Amey, it was not long before friendship blossomed into love and Decimus requested Amey's hand in marriage. Edward was not at all pleased and would not give his blessing, so Decimus and Amey ran away to Gretna Green and married on 16th October 1834.

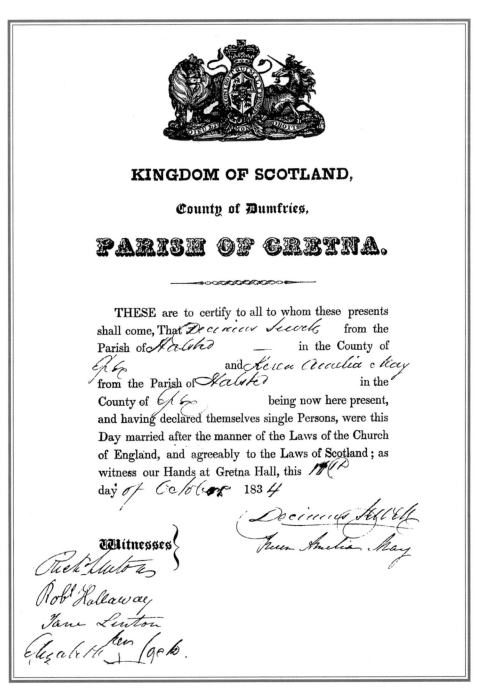

The Marriage certificate of Decimus Sewell and Keren Amelia (Amey) May

The elopement of Decimus and Amey has been well documented over the years, so just a brief resume of the event follows: One evening in October 1834 Edward entertained some of his friends at The Howe. Renowned for his generous hospitality, all the guests slept soundly once they had retired to bed and therefore did not hear Amey when she crept downstairs and slipped quietly out of the library window. Decimus was waiting with a gig and together they rushed to Gosfield where they changed to post horses and set off for Scotland. The following morning when Edward realised his daughter was missing, he searched for her everywhere before he learnt that she had eloped with Decimus. Edward was so outraged that despite the couple's seventeen hour head start, he chased after them intending to stop the wedding and to punish them for disobeying his wishes. However on arrival at Gretna Green, Edward discovered he was too late as they were already married. Undefeated, he tried to order his newly married daughter to return home with him at once! Needless to say Amey refused and Edward journeyed back to The Howe alone.

We presume all was eventually forgiven as Decimus and Amey returned to Halstead shortly after their marriage and had three children:

Percy Sewell	1835-1923
Edith Sewell	1841-died aged 3 months old.
Amy Constance Sewell	1844-died abroad

Sadly Amey died 26th September 1844 following the birth of her second daughter, Amy Constance, who survived. Amey and her first born daughter Edith who died in 1841, aged 3 months, were interred in the Old Independent Meeting Burial Ground, Halstead. (When the New Congregational Church was built behind the burial ground in 1865, the gravestones were removed and placed around the boundary wall. The church closed in 1997 when the structure of the building became unsafe). Shortly after Amey's death, Decimus left Halstead and moved around the country for some years before remarrying, and having a second family.

Decimus Sewell (1799-1886)
Decimus Sewell was born May 1799 at Little Maplestead Hall, the tenth child of John Sewell (1756-1843) and Elizabeth Sewell nee Smoothy (1763-1833) formerly of Birdbrook Hall. Decimus, a solicitor, practised in Halstead from 1822 to 1849, before he moved to Cheshire and then Gloucestershire. In 1856 he married his second wife, Eliza Maria Lawrence at St. Phillip's Church, Dalston, Hackney, Middlesex. By 1861 they had moved to Halstead and lived in Colchester Road where Decimus had a practice. During the 1860's he was a solicitor to the Colne Valley and Halstead Railway and no doubt came into contact with Edward Hornor, the owner of The Howe and a director of the railway. Decimus and Eliza had two children born at Halstead, a son, Alleine (1865-1962) and a daughter, Helen Elizabeth (1868-1960). In the 1880s Decimus and family returned to Gloucestershire where Decimus died 5th August 1886 at Nailsworth.

A brief obituary in the Halstead Gazette stated:
"Mr Sewell was married twice, his first marriage being an old-fashioned runaway match, the stern parent pursuing in hot haste".

Decimus and Keren Sewell's children:
Percy Sewell, also known in later life as Edward May Sewell.
Percy, the eldest child, was baptised 7th August 1835 at Halstead. He was only nine years old when his mother died, and about four years later left Halstead to live in Altrincham, Cheshire

with his father and sister. He studied Law and was an Attorney's clerk in 1851, perhaps under the pupilage of Decimus. This was probably the only time he was on 'the right side of the law' as his life certainly became more colourful as he grew older!

Percy married Elizabeth Docker Servier (1837-1903) at the Parish Church, St. Dunstan's Ward, London on March 8th 1853, and they had three children:

Percy Servier Sewell	1855 - 1890	died in Colney Hatch Asylum
Florence Sewell	1857 - 1941	married Charles Ingelby Palmer
Ernest Aveling Sewell	1859 - 1931	married Georgette Frances Beckett

Percy and Elizabeth's marriage was not a happy one, and Percy 'fell foul of the law'. One misdemeanour followed another and he became not only a conman but a bigamist too.

His 'first bigamist wife' was Anne Girdlestone Currie who he married in 1865. They had one daughter, May Sewell who was born in 1866, who sadly died in 1873 from phthisis. This 'marriage' did not last too long and in a bid to put the past behind him and escape his persecutors Percy changed his name to Edward May Sewell.

His 'second bigamist wife' was Amelia Lucy Penny who he married in 1870. It was a very short lived marriage, as in March 1871 Percy was in custody charged with two counts of bigamy. He was sentenced to 18 months hard labour for these offences. Percy and Amelia had a daughter, Edith Lucy Sewell, who was born whilst Percy was in prison in September 1871. Brought up by her mother, Edith was known as Edith Penny. She never married and died in 1961.

Once out of prison it was not long before Percy set 'up house' with Harriett Sarah Porter in about 1874. Harriett referred to herself as his wife, although this time no marriage had taken place, legally or otherwise! This union proved to be a happy one and between 1875 and 1894 they had twelve children, eleven of which survived. Percy though was still up to all his old tricks. He appeared in court on more than one occasion accused of carrying out various insurance scams. Several prison sentences did not deter him from his criminal activities and the family constantly moved to different locations within Essex.

Children born to Percy and Harriett:

Maud Daisy Sewell	1874-1949	emigrated to America and married George Alexander McDonell
Arthur Edward William Sewell	1877-1901	killed in action during the Boer War
Charles Bertie Sewell	1878-1959	married Jane Florence Kelsey and lived in Surrey
Rhoda Susannah Sewell	1880-1962	married Albert Thomas Coumbe
Mark Luke Sewell	1882-1960	married Louisa Hadley
Reuben John Sewell	1884-1914	unmarried - Died in 1914 in the sinking of HMS Hogue
Benjamin Leonard Sewell	1885- 1962	unmarried
Lionel Isaac Sewell	1887- ?	went to America in 1909, on a ticket paid for by George McDonell
Decimus Reginald Sewell	1890-1964	married Dora Farrington
Harriett Amelia Blanche Sewell	1892-1894	died in infancy
Robert Claude Sewell	1894-1981	married Marian Lewis

Percy's first and legal wife, Elizabeth, died at the beginning of 1901 and he finally married Harriett in the summer of 1903 at Ipswich, Suffolk, where they now lived. Percy died in 1921 and Harriett in 1922, both are interred at St. Margaret's cemetery, Ipswich.

Percy, the black sheep of the family; A lovable rogue…..who knows!

Edith May, born 1841 died three months later

Amy Constance Sewell was born in 1844 at Halstead and her mother Amey died shortly afterwards. As a girl she lived with her father but later moved to Hackney and resided with her brother Percy and his first wife Elizabeth. She returned home and worked as a music teacher until she married William Knibb Collings, a commercial traveller, in about 1871. William's father was Reverend William Collings, a well known Evangelical Baptist Minister in Gloucester. William and Amy had three children: Constance Sewell (1873-1881), Gertrude May (1875-1885) and Harold William (1880-1942). Shortly after 1886 the Colling's family travelled to Africa and on to Paraguay where William and Amy worked as missionaries. Presumably Harold accompanied his parents, and returned to England at a later date as he married Madelon Katie Langley in 1908 in the Birmingham area and moved to Worcestershire. William died c1908 in South America, Amy's date of death is unknown.

2. Edward John May (1817-1902)
Edward was the only son of Edward and Keren Happuch May. He was born 20th June 1817 and baptised 21st November 1817. He studied at Worcester College, Oxford, where in 1842 he obtained a Bachelor of Arts degree with honours. A religious young man he was destined to follow his beliefs and devoted his entire life to the Church of England. In 1843 he was a Curate at Litcham Parish Church, Norfolk, before moving to Kentish Town to be Head Master of the College School. Edward changed churches frequently. He was Curate at St Lawrence's Reading, and later Curate at Christ's Church, Clapham. From 1852 to 1858 he was Head Master of the Brewer's School, Tower Hill, London.

After his father Edward's death in 1856, he was both Clergyman and Warden at Abbey Wood College, Erith, Kent, and his mother and two sisters lived with him. He left the college to become Head Master of Nottingham College School. Later he was Curate in Charge of Strelley and Bilborough Parish Churches, Nottinghamshire, before he eventually moved to Hastings where he remained from 1868 to 1882. Edward acquired some land in Hastings and built St Andrew's Church, which was constructed from corrugated iron. All similar churches were commonly known as 'tin tabernacles'. A limited number of Church of England Ceremonies were held at the Church, which Edward was licensed to conduct. After Edward left Hastings, William Booth leased the building for the Salvation Army.

Edward married Caroline Susan Lancaster, at Kensington, London, in 1886, when they were both over sixty years of age. Caroline was born in 1818. They lived at Ivy House, Chertsey, Surrey, for the rest of their lives, where Edward was Curate at the Parish Church. Edward died in 1902 aged 85 years of age. Caroline died in 1909 aged 91 years.

According to Edward's will, despite his father's bankruptcy, he apparently owned several original notable paintings which had been in the possession of the May family for many years, as well as several antiques. Of course, Edward could have inherited these items from other members of the

May family. Some antiquities had been purchased by Edward during his travels abroad. He also appeared to have lavished furs and jewellery on his wife during their marriage. Some paintings included in his will were by the following artists:

Bartoleme Esleban Murillo	circa	1617-1682	Spanish painter
Carlo Maratti		1625-1713	Italian baroque artist
Nicolaas Berchem		1620-1683	Dutch Master
Adriaen Van Ostade		1610-1658	Dutch realist painter
Philips Wouvermans		1619-1668	Dutch artist
Jean-Baptiste-Camille Corot		1796-1875	French realist painter
Richard Cosway		1742-1821	English Rococo Era Miniaturist

Edward referred to a miniature of his grandmother Rebecca, painted by Corot in her younger days, when she was the celebrated 'Beautiful Miss Grant'. He also owned a portrait of Rebecca painted when she was 76 years old. If Edward's wishes were adhered to then the pictures are now the property of The National Portrait Gallery, The National Museum of Pictures, The Ashmolean and Bodleian Museums, or with The Chancellor, Masters and Scholars of the University of Oxford.

3. Augusta May (1820-1896)
Augusta was baptised 20th November 1820 at St Mary's Church, St Marylebone and 2nd February 1821 at Lady Huntingdon's Chapel, Southwark, Middlesex. Augusta died 1896.

4. Emily Ching May (1825-1888)
Emily was baptised 26th February 1825 at St Mary's Church, St Marylebone and 30th March 1825 at Lady Huntingdon's Chapel, Southwark, Middlesex. Emily died 1888.

Augusta and Emily, the second and third daughters of Edward and Keren Happuch May, spent most of their lives together. They lived with their parents in London and moved to Abbey Wood College, Erith to live with their brother Edward, after their father's death. By 1871 the three siblings lived at St. Leonards, Hastings and to earn a little money, they had taken in three lodgers; scholars, whose parents lived overseas. By the early 1880s the two sisters had moved within Hastings, to Wellington Square, where they lived quietly together with a housemaid. They finally moved one more time to Eastbourne, where Emily died in 1888 and Augusta died 1896. Two spinsters, whose prospects of wedding dowries and marriage to suitable young gentlemen had probably floundered when they were in their early twenties, casualties of their father's bankruptcy.

Note 1. John Ching was descended from one of the Ching families of Launceston, Cornwall. (Ching being an old Cornish surname, without any connection to the Chinese 'Q'ng' spelt today 'Ching'). John married Rebecca Michell (1760-1837) at St Mewan, Cornwall on 2nd October 1786, and they had six children. (Keren Happuch Michell Ching, their second child, married Edward May). John Ching, an apothecary, invented and patented 'Ching's Worm Lozenges' in 1796. These lozenges were extremely popular and were used by people from all walks of life, including King George III! The Ching's moved to London about 1798 and opened a shop in New Bond Street. John Ching died in 1800, and Rebecca continued to run the business with the help of their partner. In 1808 Rebecca Ching of Rush Common, Lambeth, Surrey, renewed the patent, to include improvements made to the lozenges, now called 'Ching's Worm Destroying Lozenges'. When Rebecca died in 1837, the secret recipe and patent for the lozenges was left to her surviving children, to either use or sell as they wished. In 1902 the recipe and patent, which belonged to their grandson, Edward John May, were given to a family friend and therefore left the possession of the Ching/May family.

Note 2. Selina, Countess of Huntingdon (1707-1791) played a prominent part in the religious revival of the eighteenth century, including the Methodist Movement in England and Wales, which promoted the work of John Wesley. 'Countess of Huntingdon's Connexion', was a Calvinistic Movement with the Methodist Church.

John May and his family

Generation No 1

1. Edward May's father was John May (1) who was born ? and died 1810, and his mother was Sarah who was born c1741 and died 1815.

Children of John and Sarah May:
2.	i	Mary May	b.1775 d. ?
	ii	Abraham May	b.1777 d.1842
	iii	Isaac May	b.1780 d.1830
	iv	John May	b. ? d. ?
	v	Samuel May	b.1782 d. ?
	vi	William May	b. ? d. ?
	vii	Sarah May	b. ? d. ?
	viii	Edward May (2)	b.1785 d.1856

Generation No 2

2. **Edward May (2)** (viii) was born 1785 and died in 1856. He married 1) Elizabeth Roberts born 1786 and died c1814 in 1809. 2) Keren Happuch Michell Ching born c1792 and died 1862 in 1815.

Children of Edward and Keren Happuch Michell May:
3.	i	Keren Amelia May	b.1815 d.1844	
4.	ii	Edward John May	b.1817 d.1902	
5.	iii	Augusta May	b.1820 d.1896	unmarried
6.	iv	Emily Ching May	b.1825 d.1888	unmarried

Generation No 3

3. Keren Amelia May (3), known as Amey, *Edward May (2), John May (1)* was born 1816 and died 1844. She married Decimus Sewell in 1834.

Children of Keren May and Decimus Sewell
i	Percy May Sewell	b.1835 d.1923 married:
		1) Elizabeth Docker Servier in 1853.
		2) bigamist marriage to Anne Girdlestone Currie in 1865.
		3) bigamist marriage to Amelia Lucy Penny in 1870.
		4) Harriett Potter in 1903.
ii	Edith Sewell	born and died in 1841.
iii	Amy Constance Sewell	b.1844 d. ? married William Collings c1875.
iv	Alleine Sewell	b.1866 d.1962 married Alice Wiggins in 1902.
v	Helen Elizabeth Sewell	b.1863 d.1960

4. Edward John May (3), *Edward May (2), John May (1)* was born 1817 and died 1902. He married Caroline Susan Lancaster in 1886. No issue.

5. Augusta May (3), *Edward May (2), John May (1)* was born 1820 and died 1896. Unmarried.

6. Emily Ching May (3), *Edward May (2), John May (1)* was born 1825 and died 1888. Unmarried.

Chapter Seven
Aaron Morritt, Nicholas Morritt, Nicholas Thomas Walter, Arthur Macnamara, William Gosset and Charles Walter

(Oh what a tangled web we weave! Research has proved that the Morritt and Walter families were related several times over by marriage, and that Arthur Macnamara and William Gosset had a family connection with the Walter's too! Therefore it makes it easier to understand how and why, they all became involved with The Howe Estate and Edward May, in both a business and personal capacity).

Aaron Morritt was born in 1785 and baptised at St Pancras Parish Church, Camden, London (then called Middlesex). He was the son of Aaron and Elizabeth Morritt formerly West and had at least five brothers and sisters, plus a half brother, Nicholas Morritt.

Aaron was involved in the ironmongery business from an early age, learning his trade with Robert Lewis of 'Lewis R & B, Platers, Founders & Ironmongers' at 107 Long Acre, London. In November 1807 Aaron was 'admitted free, by service to Robert Lewis' to The Worshipful Company of Ironmongers. As Aaron and Edward were business partners in May and Morritt for many years and bought property together in the London area, one assumes they were very good friends. Aaron would have been nearing sixty years of age when he and Edward dissolved their long standing partnership by mutual consent in 1842. Perhaps he simply wanted to retire, or did he foresee that Edward's cash flow problems and high living would be ruinous for their business?

> NOTICE is hereby given, that the Partnership heretofore subsisting between us the undersigned, Edward May and Aaron Morritt, carrying on the trade of Ironmongers, at No. 66, Oxford-street, in the county of Middlesex, has this day been dissolved by mutual consent.—Dated this 17th day of June 1842.
> *Edward May.*
> *A. Morritt.*

The end of Edward May and Aaron Morritt's business partnership
Courtesy of The London Gazette, 8th July 1842

In 1847 Edward surrendered the copyhold cottages he owned at The Wash, Hedingham Lane, to Aaron, which he let to tenants.

Aaron lived at Clarence Cottage, Regents Park, with his sister Elizabeth Morritt. Following Elizabeth's death in 1844, Keren Happuch May, Edwards wife, received a £100 legacy from her Executors. Aaron moved in the mid 1850s to Ladbroke Square, Notting Hill Gate where he died in 1858. He was buried at All Souls Cemetery, Kensal Green. Aaron left an exceedingly complex will which would have kept his Executors, Nicholas Thomas Walter, his great nephew, and John Taylor, his solicitor and friend very busy! Aaron left various trust funds to be financed by income received from his properties and a few legacies to family and friends. As a bachelor, he left most of his estate, approximately £30,000, (a fortune in 1858), to his relations. There was no specific property named in his will and the late Edward May's family were not mentioned. However shortly after Aaron's death his Executors did sell one of his London properties, namely number 97 Eaton Square, which was occupied by Edward Divett Esq. MP for Exeter, (styled Marquess of Hartington), and held on a 99 year lease from the Marquess of Westminster at £62 per annum ground rent. Aaron's houses were evidently sited at prime locations in London.

Nicholas Morritt, Aaron's half brother was a pawnbroker, who with his wife Ann fathered five daughters. Elizabeth, his eldest child married John Walter. They had a son, **Nicholas Thomas Walter** born in 1823 at Clerkenwell, London. He married Susanna Wyatt in 1847 and they had several children. After Nicholas Thomas Walter died in 1862, John Taylor, as joint executor of Aaron's will, surrendered the copyhold cottages at The Wash, which formed part of Aaron's estate, to Edward Hornor and he was admitted the tenant.

Hester Morritt (1811-1846), Nicholas and Ann's youngest daughter married Charles Walter, who was John Walter's brother. In 1833 Charles worked for Nicholas Morritt, his father in law, before he had his own pawnbroker's business in Marylebone High Street.

Arthur Macnamara and William Matthew Gosset purchased most of The Howe Estate from Edward May in October 1844 for £10,260. The £260 being payment due on the copyhold cottages and land, although the estate was not in their possession for long, as Edward Hornor purchased the property fourteen months later.

Arthur Macnamara, of Llangoed Castle, in the county of Brecon, Wales was a wealthy man. As well as Llangoed Castle, which his father was reputed to have won in a card game, he had a house in Grosvenor Street, London, a country house, Caddington Hall in Hertfordshire, and another estate at Eaton Bray, Bedfordshire. Sadly he died in 1846 when his heir also named Arthur was a boy. Llangoed Castle was sold in 1847 and Caddington Hall became the main family residence.

William Matthew Gosset was born c1794 in Jersey and married Louisa Walter, who was born in 1802, at Teddington, Middlesex, the daughter of William and Ann Walter. The family had moved to Devonshire Place before William and Louisa married in June 1830 at Marylebone Parish Church. Their two witnesses were Louisa's brother Charles Walter, and her sister Mary. In 1844 William was a Major in the Corps of Royal Engineers when he and Arthur purchased The Howe. By 1851 William had retired from the Royal Engineers having achieved the rank of Colonel and lived with Louisa in Teignmouth, Devon. He died in 1856 at the Walter family home, 9 Devonshire Place, Marylebone. Louisa moved to Cheltenham but later returned to London where she lived with her great niece, Adelaide Evelyn Louisa De Noual Ramas, in Devonshire Place, until she died in 1879.

Charles Walter, Louisa's elder brother, was born 1797 at Teddington. He married Elizabeth Lee Macnamara, who was originally from Alton, Hampshire, in 1829 and they had two daughters, Ellen and Elizabeth. A retired Captain in the Indian Army, Charles lived at The Howe for a year (1845), acting as its caretaker until it was sold in December. During this time he was a Magistrate sitting at Halstead Petty Sessions. By 1851 Charles and family were at a lodging house in Hastings, Sussex, where Charles was described as a fund holder and annuitant on the census return.

A section of the 1874 Ordnance Survey Map First Edition showing The Howe, stables and farm buildings. Number 56 = How(e) ground Cottages and number 89 = The Lodge and Howe cottages.

Edward Hornor
3rd June 1811 to 16th June 1868

Chapter Eight
The Hornor Family

Benjamin and Alice Hornor
Benjamin Hornor (1771-1836), married Alice Birkbeck (1774-1850), the daughter of William Birkbeck of Settle. Both families were devout members of the Society of Friends (Quakers).

Benjamin and Alice had three children:
Sarah Jane Hornor   1808-1827
Edward Hornor   1811-1868
Charles Birkbeck Hornor   1817-1858

Benjamin was a dental surgeon and in 1822 owned a practice in Coney Street, York, called 'Hornor and Turner', while Alice spent much of her time helping those who were less fortunate in life. She was one of the founder members of an elementary school for underprivileged girls, known as The British Girls School, in York. With around one hundred pupils the school prospered from the early 1800s until it closed in about 1891. Benjamin died in 1836 and Alice married Robert Waller in 1839. They continued to live in York. Robert died in 1847 and Alice, who suffered from ill health, moved to The Howe where she lived with her eldest son Edward, his wife Anne and their family. Alice died at The Howe on 25th June 1850 and was buried in Halstead.

Edward and Anne Hornor
Edward Hornor was born 3rd June 1811 at York, spending his childhood and school days in the York area. He followed his father into the dentistry profession and, in 1836 after Benjamin's death, Edward placed an advertisement in several Yorkshire newspapers to inform his friends and clients that he intended to continue as a Surgical Dentist, asking for their support. Another advertisement, in 1838, announced the formation of a partnership with his late father's principal assistant John King. The dental practice was named 'Hornor and King'.

Exactly when Edward left York is unclear, but it would have been some time during the latter part of 1830s when he moved to Iver in Buckinghamshire. An indenture drafted by Edward Harper, a solicitor, in 1838, showed that Edward, along with some other (unnamed) gentlemen, established an institution or asylum for *"the reception of invalids affected with insanity"* at Denham, Buckinghamshire. The private asylum was situated in a mansion house, with grounds, known as Denham Park. The indenture also stated that the institution was to be run for the profit of the partners and that the lease would be for twenty one years. In May 1838 Denham Park was opened as a private licensed asylum for up to seventeen paying patients by Sir William Charles Ellis and Edward Hornor. However, out of over fifty patients who were admitted in a six year period, only one, a farmer's wife, actually resided in Buckinghamshire. Others were from Durham, Yorkshire, Kent, Essex and London.

According to the Tithe Map and Award of 1840, Edward leased a house and orchard from the executors of Mr. Burrows. The property was situated on the Chequers Farm Estate, off the High Street in Iver. Edward also rented a field on the opposite side of the road called Chequer's Meadow.

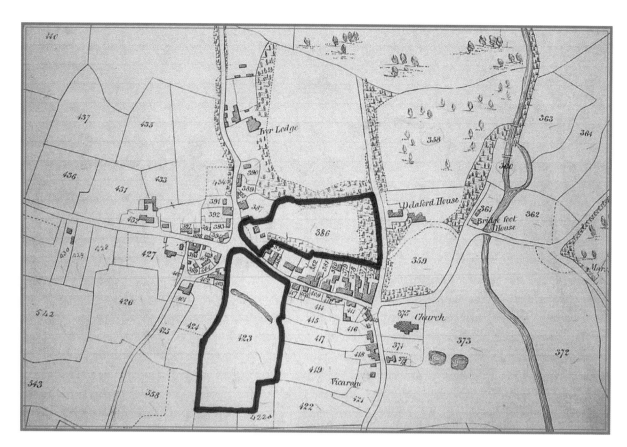

An extract from the Tithe Map of Iver, Buckinghamshire - 1840
Reproduced by courtesy of Buckinghamshire Record Office

The house, garden, orchard and field known as Chequers Meadow, which were on the Chequers Farm Estate are outlined in bold. Edward Hornor leased these properties circa 1840

Iver High Street: Edward Hornor's house was half way down the street on the right hand side

Edward Hornor married Anne Moline on the 26th August 1842 at Uxbridge Parish Church, Middlesex. Anne, who was born on 12th January 1821 at Stoneham, Kent, was the daughter of Robert Moline, a cheesemonger, and Elizabeth Moline formerly Gorham, who were also Quakers. Elizabeth died in 1831 and Robert died in 1836. At the time of his death, Robert owned properties in Gracechurch Street, London, and Loam Pit Hill, Deptford. In 1841 Anne lived with her Aunt, Ruth Gorham, sister Lydia, and cousins in Merton Cottage, which overlooked Uxbridge Common.

After their marriage Edward and Anne continued to live at Iver, where their first child and son, Francis, was born in 1843. Later they travelled abroad, probably on 'A Grand Tour,' as their second son, Lewis, was born in Rome in 1845.

Edward bought The Howe Estate in December 1845 from Arthur Macnamara and William Gosset. His younger brother Charles acted as his Attorney and the family moved into the house when Francis was a toddler and Lewis a baby. Edward and Charles continued to hold property in Iver and by 1848 they were both partners in the asylum at Denham Park. In 1852 the brothers were described as bankers, resident at The Howe. Edward, who had many business interests was a director of the Halstead District Provident Building Society.

Between 1846 and 1857 Edward and Anne had six more children:
Alice Hornor	1846-1939
Allan Moline Hornor	1848-1911
Charles Ernest Hornor	1849-1896
Edith Anne Hornor	1851-1925
Florence Hornor	1853-1931
Beatrice Hornor	1857-1949

Brought up in the Quaker faith, the young children soon learnt, from their parents, to be kind and friendly, to show humility and to dedicate themselves to the welfare of others. They were expected to find pleasure from the simple things in life and to be well behaved at all times. Their every day schooling was provided by a governess who lived with the family at The Howe. Henrietta Corlet, their first governess, was followed by Isabella Leslie.

Edward was a placid, benevolent man with a courteous manner. He was social and hospitable, a good conversationalist who avoided contentious issues and looked for the best in people. These qualities would certainly have helped Edward in his role as a Justice of the Peace. He was appointed a Magistrate in 1851 and sat on the South Hinckford Bench, which held its hearings at the Station House, Halstead, every alternate Tuesday.

Edward and Anne were staunch supporters of the Quaker and Temperance Movements. When Samuel Bowly, a popular temperance speaker from Gloucester addressed a meeting on social reform at Halstead Town Hall, Edward was in the chair. Because of their involvement with these societies, the Hornors were soon acquainted with a like minded local family, the Greenwoods, who became frequent visitors at The Howe.

In 1851 Edward built the Meeting House for the Society of Friends in Colchester Road. There was a burial ground to the rear of the building where some members of the Hornor family were later interred. This was cleared in the 1960s to make way for a car park. The headstones which were removed and sited along the Meeting House wall have long since disappeared too. The Meeting House was recently demolished to make way for a housing development.

The Meeting House for the Society of Friends in Colchester Road - 1967

At the end of December 1852 Edward bought The Hill Farm, Ridgewell, Essex. It was farmed for the Hornor family by tenant farmers for many years until the mid 1880s, when a succession of farm bailiff's were appointed to manage the farm. *(See Chapter 10)*.

A train on the Halstead to Hedingham line near Hepworth Hall Bridge

In 1855 Edward with several other distinguished and influential gentlemen, formed a company whose aim was to bring a railway to Halstead, and eventually the Colne Valley and Halstead Railway was born. Edward became the reluctant chairman of the Board of Directors, a position he held for only six months, although he continued to be a director of the company and a significant shareholder, for a number of years. Royal Assent was granted for the railway to be built in 1856, and the Chappel to Halstead line was the first phase to be constructed. However when it opened for traffic in 1860 it was not met with a great deal of enthusiasm! Edward, no doubt, took a great interest in the railway's progress as he watched the construction of the Halstead to Hedingham line from The Howe. This section was operational from 1861 until the last train ran on it in December 1964 when the line closed.

Edward Hornor – 1855
Reproduced by courtesy of Essex Record Office

On 31st October 1858, Edward's brother Charles died at The Howe. He left a will, but apart from a few legacies to the Consumption Hospital, Brompton, Middlesex, the Convalescent Hospital, London and the Royal Orthopaedic Hospital, Bloomsbury, Middlesex, Charles left the bulk of his estate, valued at around £30,000 to Edward.

Christmas 1860 was celebrated with a winter festival hosted by the Band of Hope Society, whose president was Edward. It was a grand affair and included recitations and music. There was a large illuminated Christmas tree and over two hundred toys were donated by ladies interested in the movement. The event was also used to create, *"an urgent and affectionate appeal to both parents and children to practice total abstinence"*.

In 1861 Edward built a school and master's house at the junction of Hedingham Road and Box Mill Lane. Known as The Howe School, it was built primarily for the education of his employee's children, who lived in the cottages and tenements on The Howe Estate and in Box Mill Lane. In 1874 the school was classed as a 'British School' and received a Parliamentary Grant of £49 18s. The School was closed in 1881 by Anne Hornor. Children's education was of paramount importance to Edward and, before he built the Howe School, he was already the proprietor of 'a schoolroom' in King's Arms Yard from around 1855 until his death in 1866.

Edward, true to his humanitarian beliefs as a Quaker was always ready to help those not so fortunate as himself, therefore in 1862, when the mill workers in the North of England were suffering great hardship due to the Lancashire cotton famine, it came as no surprise to find Edward organising collections of unwanted clothing. With George Harris, a solicitor who lived at Nether Priors, he supervised at depots where the garments were sorted into appropriate bundles and sent to the workers and their families.

Edward apparently had a good eye when it came to buying horses. In an 1862 edition of the Farmers Magazine he received a 'commended' in the Hunting class for Geldings. When he lived at Iver, Edward invented a guard which prevented crib-biting in horses. The device, allowed horses to eat normally without suffering from colic and received favourable comments. It was placed in the Mechanics Society repository in London, an Institute for the encouragement of arts, manufacturers and commerce.

In 1866 Edward found himself on the wrong side of the law! The Essex Standard reported *"Conviction of a Magistrate"*. Apparently Edward had unwittingly broken the 'Cattle Plague Orders' and allowed a cow from Howe Farm to be driven to Blamster's Farm, at the other end of Halstead. Unfortunately, County papers which referred to *"the restrictions on the movement of cattle"* had been delivered to Edward when he was out, and he was, therefore, unaware of their existence. He regretted the offence and made it known that he was pleased that the police had treated him like any other member of the public! However, the presiding Magistrate considered that the order was well publicised and therefore *"Ignorance would not be taken for an excuse"*! Edward was fined 20 shillings.

Also in 1866 Halstead suffered a smallpox epidemic, and with Edward's aid, Lucy Greenwood, a friend of the family, opened a small hospital in an old building in Bois Field where she nursed some of the victims. Edward was a frequent visitor to the hospital and it was very lucky for him and his family that he was not infected with the contagious disease. Following the epidemic,

Lucy with more financial assistance from Edward, established a school for poor and destitute girls, within the same building. It was known firstly as the Industrial School and later as the Greenwood School. The Hornor family continued to take immense interest in the school and Anne Hornor was on the management committee for many years. (The school closed in 1999 and has since become part of a housing development). Edward, who was a keen supporter for the education of children, was also a trustee of Halstead Grammar School.

The Hornor family enjoyed themselves within their own circle of friends and would often be seen out riding together on horseback with 'old Stammas', the groom in livery following discreetly behind! One friend who visited the Hornors at least once a year, especially during the 1850s, was the pre-eminent poet, teacher and critic, Matthew Arnold (1822-1888). He is particularly remembered for a collection of almost four thousand letters, which he wrote during the second half of the nineteenth century. Some of the letters, were written to Anne Hornor. *(See Appendix III for a transcript of a letter written to Anne dated 1872).* William Forster, a former Secretary for Ireland, and a Quaker, was also another regular visitor, often accompanied by his sisters. The Forsters were related to the Hornors as Anne's Grandfather, John Moline, married Deborah Forster, a relation of William.

Edward and Anne were gracious hosts and their grounds at The Howe were opened for garden parties and fetes, which were always well attended. Many local adults and children from various organisations were welcomed over the years - a real treat for them. The Hornor children must have thoroughly enjoyed these events too, especially as they usually had to amuse themselves. When garden parties were held at other large houses in and around Halstead, the entire family would attend and make it into a splendid day out.

The Howe was considered to be one of the principal mansions in the area and it was stated that a great deal of the parish belonged to Edward Hornor. He owned several other properties in Halstead, leased to tenants, which were not part of The Howe Estate.

Edward Hornor died at The Howe on 16th June 1868 aged 57 years. He was buried in the graveyard behind the Friends Meeting House in Colchester Road. The service was very well attended by the Friends and watched by many others who mourned his passing.

A report in the Essex Standard of Edward's funeral stated that: *"The mortal remains of this gentleman were interred in the Friends burial ground, Halstead on Saturday last. All shops in the town were closed and the funeral was attended by a large body of the inhabitants as well as by numerous friends from a distance. These included Messrs Richard Barrett, John Broomhall, Thomas Cash, James Christy, John Taylor and Robert Warner of the Temperance Provident Institution and Messrs Hugh Owen and Robert Rae of the National Temperance League. Addresses were delivered at the grave by Joseph Shewell Esquire of Colchester, and in the Friends Meeting House by William Mathews Esquire of Earls Colne".*

The Reverend Thomas Given Wilson preached a sermon on Sunday 21st June 1868 at the New Congregational Church, Halstead. He praised Edward's virtues and reminded the congregation of all the good things Edward had achieved in his lifetime, and referred to him as *"a dear friend, a most distinguished man".* Edward was no doubt a much loved husband, father and benefactor, kind to the employees on his estates and respected by all those lucky enough to cross his path.

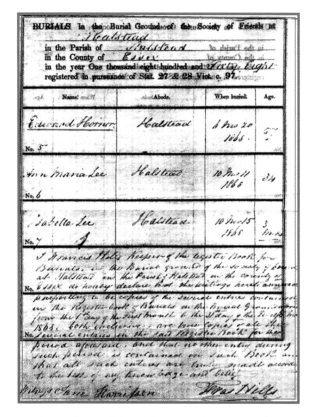 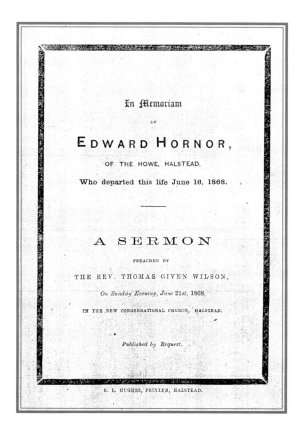

*Burial record for Edward who died 16th June 1868, and the In Memoriam of Edward Hornor
Reproduced by courtesy of Essex Record Office*

The Annual Monitor, or Obituary of the Members of the Friends Society published the following report: *"It has been suggested that many of the friends of the late Edward Hornor would be glad to see some details of his latter days, and his relatives incline to accede to the request, in the hope that his firm reliance on his Saviour and his calmness and composure in the prospect of death may be strengthening to others.*

For the greater part of his life to the will of his Heavenly Father, and careful that, even the smallest matters his example and influence should be in accordance with his Christian profession. In his own neighbourhood he took an active part in every movement which he thought calculated to promote the welfare of others, and was diligent in visiting the poor, and seeking to help any who were in trouble or distress. His advice was very frequently sought by persons in all ranks of life; and as he would spare no time or pains to master all the details submitted to him, he was often able to be of essential service to those applying to him. At the same time he thoroughly realised, that in all things he was still an unprofitable servant, and that it was only by the help and strength granted him by his Heavenly Father, that he was able to accomplish any good.

Though holding the position of County Magistrate he was regular and diligent as a Sabbath school teacher, in a school house which he had erected near to his own residence. He also took an active part in holding religious meetings with the poor. Years ago he adopted on principle the rule of total abstinence from all intoxicating drinks; and not only by his personal example and the arrangements of the household, but in public also, he gave a clear and emphatic testimony to the advantages of such a course. He was Vice President of the National Temperance League, and during the last winter was earnestly engaged in visiting many meetings of Friends in furtherance of the Temperance cause. In this he was united with Samuel Bowly, Jonathan Grubb, and others, as a deputation from the 'Friends' Temperance Union.

Early in the spring of 1868, Edward Hornor was sensible of a pain in the back, which was the indication of the malady that subsequently proved so distressing; but he went about as usual for some weeks till he was obliged to give way, and remain in recumbent posture. He had had a similar attack some years before, which having yielded to quiet and rest; his family were hopeful that such would be the case again. By the end of the fifth month, however the pain was so excruciating, that it was concluded to call in a special medical advisor, in whom he had great confidence. Some relief was obtained; but from that time the family were much discouraged, and he himself fully convinced he had but a short time to live. As the disease advanced he spoke fully and openly of his feelings in the prospect of his removal. At one time he said "I am the most religious unworthy sinner, and it is in God's grace that I have been led this way." (Then followed several religious declarations by Edward Hornor).

On the 3rd of the sixth month when reminded it was his birthday, he said "Yes, I had hoped that I should have spent my birthday in Heaven". When fearfully racked with pain he constantly cried out in prayer to God. He sent many kind messages to his friends and to those who had laboured with him in his efforts to benefit his poor neighbours. He dictated special messages to his children, at a time when he felt almost too weak to converse with them, but he was afterwards able to see them. The servants he also desired to see; and after exhorting each of them to turn to Christ and give their hearts to Him, he thanked them for their kind care and attention of him. Towards the last he seemed to be freer from acute pain, but became gradually so weak that he could not speak much. He passed away on the 16th, we doubt not, to be forever with the Lord".

Edward left an estate valued at around £50,000. Anne continued farming on The Howe Estate and at Hill Farm. She also purchased Wash Farm, Hedingham Road, which was later farmed by her grandson, Francis (Frank) Vaizey. A farm bailiff was employed to manage Hill Farm in the 1880s, after a succession of bailiff's had over seen the general running of The Howe Estate. The bailiff also arranged the allocation of the allotments situated on the estate, which included those located on the opposite side of the road to Howe Cottages. The remains of the entrance gate to the allotments is just about visible today.

During the early 1890s one of Halstead football teams, the Excelsiors, had Anne Hornor's consent to play its home games on a field, next to these allotments. (Broadfield). It was common practice for local teams to seek a farmer's permission to host matches on ground which lay fallow during the winter months.

When the Excelsior Football Club was formed in 1894, it was rated as the second most important Halstead club; the Town Club being in top position. The first players to join the Excelsiors were chiefly members of Halstead Reserves who played during the 1893-1894 season with three or four players from the town's First Eleven who decided to join them. The club was really started in connection with the Parsonage Street Bible Class.

At a meeting held in August 1894 George Tyler was elected President of the club and Mr L Slaughter, the Vice President. W Wells was Captain and T Steed, Vice Captain, and the committee were: R Bowles, W E Raven, J Lawrence, H Butcher, W Smith, A Osborne, and Edward Constable was the Secretary.

In 1894 George Tyler rented a field from the Howe Estate for £5 per annum and kindly allowed the Excelsiors free use of the meadow.

The Excelsior team colours were chocolate brown and yellow. They apparently had a very successful first season, and won ten matches, lost three and drew four. However their performance the following year 1895-1896 was not so good!

Two reports taken from a Halstead newspaper. 12th November 1896: *The Excelsiors played Earls Colne 2nd on Saturday at The Howe. The fixture was for last week, but was postponed by Colne who were unable to raise a team on account of the league match at that place.* 19th November 1896: *Halstead Excelsior v. Colne Reserves (football). Colne sent over a good team but final result was Halstead Excelsior 1 Colne Reserves 0.*

The Excelsior football team 1899
Courtesy of The Halstead Gazette

The above photograph shows members of the old Excelsior football team and was submitted to The Halstead Gazette by Mrs. G. Peach, daughter of the late Edward Constable.

Top row, left to right: Reuben Bowles, George Last, Bill Smith, Edward Constable, Alf Bragg, Freddy Fairbanks, Charlie Hatfield.
Bottom row, left to right: Arthur Osborne, Bill Steed, Harry Wells, Tom Steed, Alf Osborne, Jim Lawrence.

Even as a widow, Anne continued to take an active interest in Halstead life. She supported a wide and varied selection of societies, some more unusual than others, and once she hosted an evening at The Howe for the Indian Female Normal School Instruction Society for the Reverend J E Lillie, formerly a District Judge in India. When Anne eventually became too elderly to attend events, she would send donations, gifts and produce which were grown at The Howe including fruit, vegetables, flowers and evergreens. Evergreens were usually sent to the Workhouse at Christmas time so they could be used by the inhabitants to make floral decorations.

The 1911 census return showed Anne, living at home in The Howe with her daughter, Florence. Beatrice Montgomery, a nurse was in attendance. There was also a cook, Ellen Garrity; a parlour maid, Lily Emma Branch; two housemaids, Eleanor Meadowes and Edith Eliza Weston; a kitchen maid, Grace Ada Goddard and a ladies maid, Eliza Norman.

Anne Hornor died 26th April 1914 at the age of 93 years having been a widow for forty six years. Like her late husband Edward, she, too, was much admired by the townsfolk and a large number of people gathered on Market Hill to pay their last respects as the cortege passed by. Remembered affectionately as a 'grand old lady', Anne was buried beside her husband in the Society of Friends burial ground.

Anne left an estate worth £42,048. Included in her will were legacies for four of her most valued members of staff: Henry Dring, gardener £25; Fred Alston, gardener £20; Edward Smith, bailiff £20 and George Sturmer her former coachman £20.

Florence, who had lived with her mother at The Howe moved to Red House, Colchester Road, and Samuel Augustine Courtauld became the new owner of The Howe and its estate.

Some of the Farm Bailiffs employed at The Howe:
Information taken from census returns, Kelly's Directories and various newspaper reports:

Years	Name	Notes
1841 - 1853	Thomas Norman	(until 1845 employed by Edward May and Charles Walter)
1853	Abraham Byford	
1886	Henry Beddall	(died 1901)
1895	George Stevens	
1899	Charles Parsons	
1902	James Thirkettle	(died 1917)
1902 -1914	Edward Smith	

NB:
It is perhaps a rather sad and sobering thought that most of the companies and buildings that the Hornor's either aided financially or had built, no longer exist or have been demolished. Therefore little is left for us to remember Edward Hornor by. This most generous benefactor and gentleman, may only have lived in Halstead for twenty three years, yet in that short time he did much to help the residents of the town. Edward's immediate family and descendants continued to take a great interest in Halstead and its inhabitants for many years.

Benjamin Hornor and his family

Generation No 1
1. Benjamin Hornor (1) was born in 1771 and died in 1836. He married Alice Birkbeck born in 1774 and died in 1850.

Children of Benjamin Hornor and Alice Birkbeck:
	i	Sarah Jane Hornor	b.1808 d.1827
2.	ii	Edward Hornor	b.1811 d.1868
	iii	Charles Birkbeck Hornor	b.1817 d.1858

Generation No 2
2. Edward Hornor (2) was born in 1811 and died in 1868. He married Anne Moline who was born in 1821 and died in 1914.

Children of Edward Hornor and Anne Moline:
	i	Francis Birkbeck Hornor	b.1843 d.1860	
	ii	Lewis Hornor	b.1845 d.1904	He married Catherine Burroughs Parks in 1888.
3.	iii	Alice Hornor	b.1846 d.1939	
4.	iv	Allan Moline Hornor	b.1848 d.1911	He married Caroline MacNair in 1873.
	v	Charles Ernest Hornor	b.1849 d.1896	
5.	vi.	Edith Anne Hornor	b.1851 d.1925	She married Senator General Joseph Roswell Hawley in 1887.
	vii.	Florence Hornor	b.1853 d.1931	
	viii	Beatrice Hornor	b.1857 d.1949	She married Thomas Aspley Rickman in 1902.

Generation No 3
3. Alice Hornor (3) was born in 1846 and died in 1939. She married John Robert Vaizey who was born in 1839 and died in 1900.

Children of John Robert Vaizey and Alice Hornor:
i	Robert Edward Vaizey	b.1868 d.1955	He married Eleanor Caesar in 1897.
ii	Francis Arthur Vaizey	b.1870 d.1955	
iii	John Leonard Vaizey	b.1871 d.1896	
iv	Alice Lilian Vaizey	b.1874 d.1905	She married Henry Wade in 1901.

4. Allan Moline Hornor (3) was born in 1848 and died in 1911. He married Caroline Christian MacNair in 1873.

Children of Allan Hornor and Caroline MacNair:
i	Ethel Caroline Hornor	b.1874 d.1951	She married Ambrose Hawke in 1914.
ii	George Edward Hornor	b.1876 d.1939	He married Dora Spiers.
iii	Maud Mary Hornor	b.1879 d.1879	

5. Edith Ann Hornor (3) was born in 1851 and died in 1925. She married Senator General Joseph Roswell Hawley who was born in 1826 and died in 1905.

Children of Joseph Hawley and Edith Hornor:
i	Alice Marian Hawley	b.1888 d.1987	She married Louis Coudert in 1919.
ii	Edith Josephine Roswell Hawley	b.1890 d.1970	

Edward Hornor with three of his children
Reproduced by courtesy of Essex Record Office

Children of Edward and Anne Hornor
(Please note the children are numbered 1-8).

1. Francis Birkbeck Hornor (1843-1860)
Francis Hornor (known as Frank) was born 2nd July 1843 at Iver, Buckinghamshire, the eldest son of Edward and Anne. He was probably not the most healthy of children and spent a fair amount of his time at home where he learned to play chess. He was a remarkable player, with an exceedingly good memory. Not only could he play chess well, but he could sit down without a board, memorise the moves which were called out to him and still win the game! Sadly he died of tubercular consumption at the comparatively early age of seventeen years on 16th October 1860 at 7 Albion Street, Paddington, London.

2. Lewis Hornor (1845-1904)
Lewis Hornor was Edward and Anne's second son, born 5th March 1845 in Rome, Italy. During the 1850s and 1860s he lived at The Howe until he moved to London, where he was employed as an East India broker. In 1871 both Lewis and his brother, Charles Ernest, were lodgers at a house in Gloucester Road, Marylebone. Lewis was a good shot and liked to go big game hunting. On one expedition to India, a lion seized his friend and travelling companion. Undaunted, Lewis tracked the lion into the jungle and calmly shot it, thereby saving his friend's life. (Unfortunately his friend later succumbed to a fever and died). Lewis also pursued more recreational interests and was an extremely skilled billiards player. He was a member of the River Colne Angling Preservation Society, which was formed in 1878 and was elected onto the committee in 1887. In the early 1880s Lewis, who had a kindly disposition, followed in his father's footsteps and became a Justice of the Peace for the South Division of the Hinckford Hundred, sitting on the Halstead Bench.

Lewis married Catherine Parks formerly Burroughs, who was born 9th September 1839. Catherine was the daughter of Reverend Henry Burroughs and Sarah Burroughs formerly Tilden of Boston, Massachusetts. She was a widow, previously married to Luther Parks who died in 1886 in Paris. Catherine and Luther had a daughter, Sarah Tilden Parks born in 1861, whose married name was Sarah Tisseau, although she was also known as Countess Zboinska.

Lewis and Catherine were married at St. Barnabas Church, Kensington, Middlesex, on 16th October 1888. The assistant curate of St. Andrews Church, Halstead, Reverend John Brereton Andrewes, MA., travelled to London to perform the ceremony. After their marriage Lewis and Catherine divided their time between a property in Pau, Basses Pyrenees, France, The Howe, and the Constitutional Club, Northumberland Street, London. Lewis enjoyed a game of golf, and won several tournaments at Pau and elsewhere on the Continent. A fair amount of his time must have been spent at The Howe as he took his role as a Justice of the Peace very seriously, and frequently attended the Halstead Petty Sessions, a position he held until his untimely death. While travelling from Pau to England Lewis caught a chill and was taken ill while he was staying at the Constitutional Club in London with Catherine. Sadly he did not recover and died suddenly from pneumonia on the 22nd March 1904. Lewis was interred in Halstead Cemetery. Catherine continued to divide her time between Boston, Massachusetts and Pau after Lewis's death, and died on the 2nd October 1921 at 9 Rue d'Orleans, Pau.

Left amongst Catherine's many possessions following her death was a large silver bowl presented to Lewis by the Homburg Golf club and a silver cigarette case marked 'Pau Golf Club'. Also another silver cigarette case with the Hornor Coat of Arms and initials L.H.

3. Alice Hornor (1846-1939)

Alice Hornor was Edward and Anne's eldest daughter born 10th September 1846. She had a wonderful memory and as she grew older could remember many childhood events. One of particular interest dated back to 1851 when she recalled travelling to Hyde Park, London, to visit the Great Exhibition. Quite an expedition travelling from Halstead in those days!

Alice lived at The Howe until she married John Robert Vaizey (1839-1900) on the 9th November 1865 at St. Andrew's Church, when she was nineteen years old. As a young bride she took on the duties as mistress of Attwoods, a large house which was built in 1814 by her father in law, John Vaizey.

Attwoods was to be Alice's home for many years and where her four children were born:
Robert Edward Vaizey   1868-1955
Francis Arthur (Frank) Vaizey   1870-1955
John Leonard Vaizey   1871-1896
Alice Lilian Vaizey   1874-1905

Attwoods, Halstead

Alice took a keen and active interest in local and district affairs, although educational issues were her particular forte. She saw from an early age how The Howe School, built by her father, had benefited the poor children, and that it was important to have a good education. Alice was a member of the local sub committee of the Essex Education Committee and one of the first governors of the Halstead Girls Grammar School. She was a manager at the British School, which was later known as the Council School. Alice also served on the Board of Guardians for many years with her sister Florence, and two sons Robert and Frank, attending the last meeting before it disbanded in 1930.

Alice possessed a genuine warm and caring personality. She was on the local Care of Children Committee and the Halstead and District Nursing Association. She was actively involved with the Courtauld Homes of Rest and its occupants. At least once a year she treated them to a trip out with afternoon tea at her home. She also made Christmas gifts for the residents which were always delivered personally.

Alice was not without her own share of personal sorrow, losing her youngest son John, in a rail accident in 1896. Her husband, John died four years later in 1900 and her only daughter Alice died in 1905. After her husband's death she moved from Attwoods to Bentalls Farm, Sudbury Road, Halstead, in 1901, where she lived with her son Frank for twenty two years, before they both moved to 'Lyndhurst', a house in Sudbury Road, during October 1923.

Alice Vaizey formerly Hornor 1846-1939 *John Robert Vaizey 1839-1900*
Courtesy of the Halstead and Colne Valley Gazette

When Alice died at Lyndhurst on the 28th September 1939, Halstead lost a highly respected and loved resident, regarded by many as 'the last of the old Victorian contemporaries'. Her funeral took place at St Andrew's Church, where she was a regular worshipper. It was followed by interment at Halstead Cemetery.

Many tributes were made following her death, but perhaps the one that best summed up Alice was made by Canon Thomas Higham Curling:- *"To Alice Vaizey, Halstead was home in the truest sense of the word, she loved the place, and she loved the people who lived in it."*

Alice's husband - John Robert Vaizey (1839-1900)
John Robert Vaizey was born in 1839 at Kennington, South London, the son of John and Ann Vaizey formerly Bousfield. Following a university education John bought a large estate in Halstead which entitled him to become Lord of the Manor of Stansted Abells, known locally as the Manor of Halstead. John was very much involved with local and country life, and as well as being High Sheriff of Essex, he was also a Deputy Lieutenant, a Justice of the Peace and Chairman of the Halstead Bench of Magistrates.

He sat on the Halstead Board of Guardians and was chairman of the Halstead Rural Parish Council and a Rural District Councillor. John too, supported the local schools and helped to promote a better education for children. He was a kind, generous, Christian gentleman, who was always ready to help those who needed a guiding hand.

John was one of the first large landowners in the area to invest capital in the Colne Valley and Halstead Railway with his father in law, Edward Hornor and later, became a director. He contributed very handsomely to the building fund of the Congregational Chapel in Parsonage Street and laid the foundation stone on 29th August 1865. Although later in life, he became a Church of England supporter and worshipped at Holy Trinity Church where he was a Church Warden.

John died on the 1st November 1900 at Attwoods aged 60 years. His funeral service took place at Holy Trinity Church and he was interred at Halstead Cemetery.

The Board of Guardians outside the Union Offices, Colchester Road, Halstead

A photograph taken to mark the last meeting held by the Board of Guardians in March 1930
Back row, left to right: F Bishop, S Philp, G Newton, Reverend T Curling
Centre row, standing: D Unwin, A Mann, T Bell, J Jackson, E Doubleday, J Porkess, Reverend B Cann, A Metson, L Delf, T Goodchild, E Parker, Canon Lampen, B May, A Gardiner, J Kirkwood, E Knight
Seated: J Nott, H Hills, Mrs A Vaizey, Miss F Hornor, R Vaizey, T Whitlock, S Long, A Blomfield, F Vaizey.

John Robert and Alice Vaizey's children:
Robert Edward Vaizey (1868-1955)
Robert Edward Vaizey who was born in 1868, was John and Alice's eldest son. He was educated at Harrow and Trinity College, Cambridge and married Eleanor Caesar in 1897. Robert and Eleanor lived at Tilbury Hall, in Tilbury Juxta Clare, Essex before they moved to Attwoods in 1919 where they lived for the rest of their lives.

Robert was a well known, respected gentleman who gave much of his time to public service. He served on many local government committees and was a Justice of the Peace who sat on the Hedingham Bench. He was a school governor and an active member of Holy Trinity Church. At the outbreak of the Second World War Robert was appointed chairman of the Halstead District Advisory Committee, which was set up by the War Agricultural Committee.

Robert was always a keen participant at local shoots and held many shooting parties at Attwoods during the winter months. In the summer he enjoyed a game of tennis. Robert died at Attwoods in 1955.

Tilbury Hall

John Francis (Frank) Vaizey (1870-1955)
John Francis Vaizey, known as Frank, was born in 1870, and like his brother was educated at Harrow and Trinity College. He became a farmer and lived at Attwoods until 1901, before he moved to Bentalls Farm. Also in 1901 Frank was Captain of the 2nd Voluntary Battalion Essex Regiment, a position he held until 1903.

As a Justice of the Peace, Frank was a very active member of the Halstead Court serving from at least 1903 until 1946. He was a man with deep religious convictions who cared for the welfare of the town's inhabitants. Frank was a Church Warden for over thirty eight years, a licensed lay reader, and secretary and treasurer of Halstead Rural Deanery. As a Sunday School teacher for fifty four years, he often took the children to The Howe for Sunday School treats when his Grandmother and Aunts lived at the house. Frank died at Lyndhurst in 1955, nine months before his brother Robert's death.

Two long serving maids worked for Alice and Frank Vaizey. Rhoda Plumb who was born in 1893 and Edith Tyler born in 1894. As young girls they both worked at Courtaulds Mill, before going into service together. They worked firstly for Alice and later for Frank and were highly valued members of their households. Neither lady married and when they retired in 1950 they moved to the Courtauld Homes of Rest. Both of them were avid knitters and produced an array of garments for many satisfied customers during their retirement. Rhoda died in 1970 and Edith continued to live alone until ill health forced her to move to Blackthorns Care Home in Halstead. Edith died in 1990. Plaques in their memory were placed in the garden at the Homes of Rest in 1991, each a memorial to two much loved ladies.

Robert Edward Vaizey 1868-1955   *Francis Arthur Vaizey 1870-1955*

John Leonard Vaizey (1871-1896)
John Leonard Vaizey, known as Leonard, was born in 1871. He lived at Attwoods with his parents and at the beginning of the 1890s he was a solicitor's pupil. Perhaps he decided that a career in the law was not for him, as in 1896 Leonard was employed as an assistant superintendent in the Locomotive Department of the Norwich District Railway at Thorpe Station. Sadly tragedy struck on the 26th August while Leonard was examining a truck with the foreman. He was knocked down and seriously injured by some trucks which were being shunted down the line. John and Alice dashed to Marks Tey and travelled by train to Norwich and were with Leonard when he died from his injuries later that day. An inquest was held, the Coroner reporting that no one was to blame for the accident as Leonard was virtually standing in a blind spot, and the driver would not have seen him. However he strongly advised that many more stringent safety measures were put in place to avoid such an accident occurring again.

Leonard's funeral took place at Holy Trinity Church and the whole town seemed to be in mourning for this extremely likeable young man, who was highly thought of by all who knew him. He was interred at Halstead Cemetery.

Alice Lilian Vaizey (1874-1905)
Alice Lilian Vaizey was John and Alice's only daughter, who was born 1874. Alice, like her mother, was a very kind, popular young lady with lots of admirable qualities. She was instrumental in forming the local branch of the Children's League of Pity, (now known as the NSPCC - National Society for the Prevention of Cruelty to Children), and spent many hours visiting and comforting the sick and poor people in Halstead. Alice often accompanied her mother when she visited the Workhouse inhabitants, and on one occasion, the day before her wedding in 1901 they took two wedding cakes with them. These were shared among their 'old friends' over a cup of tea as a pre-wedding celebration. The next day Alice married Henry Oswald Wade of Manningham, Bradford, Yorkshire, at Holy Trinity Church, Halstead. It was a quiet wedding as the family were still in mourning following the death of her father the previous year.

Alice and Henry lived at Wilmer Lodge, Heaton, Bradford and had three children:
John Leonard Wade	1902-1963
Alice Margaret Wade	1903-1984
Oswald Tetley Wade	1904-1995

Alice sadly died from tubercular consumption at Wilmer Lodge on 7th April 1905 aged 30 years, just four years after her marriage.

In 1911 Alice and Henry's children lived with two spinster Aunts, Sarah and Mary Wade at the Wade family home in Bradford. Henry Wade, was a solicitor, and a Colonel in the West Yorkshire Regiment (1914-1920). His second wife was Eileen Rawson Ackroyd, who he married in 1916. Henry and Eileen attended his mother in law, Alice's funeral at Halstead in 1939.

John Leonard Wade, Henry and Alice's eldest son, a Notary, married Marjorie Helen Owthwaite (1910-1991) in 1932 in the Keighley District, Yorkshire.

Alice Margaret Wade married William Wilkinson in 1932, in the St. Neots District; William became a Church of England Canon in Barnsley, Yorkshire.

Oswald Tetley Wade qualified as a doctor and married Gertrude Mary Garrad (1912-2005), in 1937, in the Settle District. Towards the end of his career Oswald had a practice and family house at Bingham, Nottinghamshire.

4. Allan Moline Hornor (1848-1911)
Allan Moline Hornor was born on the 10th January 1848, and spent his childhood at The Howe before he attended the University of London during the 1860s and lived in Tottenham, London. Allan was a big, powerfully built man, and a good cricketer who played for his University. He married Caroline Christian MacNair (1850-1887), known as Carrie, who was born in India, on June 4th 1873 at the St. John's Wood English Presbyterian Church, Marylebone, and they lived in Ealing before they moved to Hampstead where Allan worked as a tea merchant's clerk until he retired. They had three children:-

Ethel Caroline Hornor   1874-1951
George Edward Hornor   1876-1939
Maud Mary Hornor   1879-1879

Caroline died early 1887 aged 37 years, while the children were still at school. Allan continued to live in Hampstead, moving house twice before he settled in Fairfax Road with his daughter Ethel until his death on 19th October 1911.

Allan and Caroline Hornor's Children:
Ethel Caroline Hornor (1874-1951)
Ethel Caroline Hornor was born in 1874. She married Ambrose Lansdale Hawke (1883-1931) in 1914 in the Hendon District, when Ambrose was Assistant Secretary to the Benevolent Society. In 1916 he enlisted in the 45th TRB and saw action in France. He was discharged six months later in 1917 and, according to King's Regulations was, *"No longer physically fit for service"*. Ambrose died in 1931 in Worthing aged 46 years. Ethel died at Worthing in 1951. The Treasury Solicitor appealed for seven years for her next of kin to contact him to inherit her meagre estate.

George Edward Hornor (1876-1939)
George Edward Hornor was born in 1876 and remained at home during his younger years. He followed in his father's footsteps and became a tea merchant's clerk, before he worked as a poultry farmer for James Spiers at Corbetts Hill Farm, Leighton Buzzard, some time before 1911. George lodged with the Spiers family and their daughter, Dora Lily Jane (1886-1958), who he later married. George and Dora lived in Leighton Buzzard for most of their lives, eventually moving from 'The Osiers' to 'Oakland' Herne Bay, Kent. George remained in contact with his Halstead relatives and attended his Aunt's and Uncle's funerals. George died on 27th April 1939 aged 63 years and Dora died 25th May 1958.

5. Charles Ernest Hornor (1849-1896)
Charles Ernest Hornor, the fourth son of Edward and Anne was born 28th December 1849. He lived at The Howe until he was old enough to move to London. A Mechanical Engineer by profession, he lived at a house in Finborough Road, Chelsea for many years. In 1896, Charles, who never married, was taken ill at his lodgings with a throat infection. As his condition worsened, an eminent London Surgeon performed a tracheotomy and, when Charles was well enough to travel, he was sent by ambulance to The Howe to recover. Unfortunately after his arrival complications arose and Charles died on 24th April 1896. His funeral took place at St. Andrew's Church and he was interred in Halstead cemetery.

6. Edith Anne Hornor (1851-1925)
Edith Hornor, the second daughter of Edward and Anne was born 3rd December 1851. She spent her childhood days at The Howe, but became by far the most adventurous and well travelled of the Hornor children.

Edith trained as a nurse at Addenbrooke's Hospital, Cambridge, the Radcliffe Hospital, Oxford, and the Charing Cross Hospital in London, and graduated around 1875. In 1879 as 'Sister Edith Hornor', she travelled to Natal, South Africa, with six nurses who were all members of the Stafford House South Africa Aid Society. On arrival at their destination the other nurses were dispatched to various hospitals within South Africa, but Edith remained in Durban where she carried out her nursing duties. Edith was awarded both the South African Campaign Medal, without date clasp, which was issued on the 15th July 1884, and the Royal Red Cross, one of the first nurses after Florence Nightingale to receive this honour.

By 1887 Edith worked as the Assistant Head Nurse at the Brockley Hospital, Philadelphia, United States of America. She married Senator General Joseph Roswell Hawley on 15th November 1887 at St. Clements Protestant Episcopal Church, Philadelphia, becoming his second wife, after the death of his first wife Harriett. Later, when they visited England, a large wedding breakfast was held at The Howe to celebrate their marriage, with the American Ambassador to the United Kingdom, Edward John Phelps attending. He was a friend of the Hawley family.

Edith and Joseph had two daughters:-
Alice Marian Hawley   1888-1987
Edith Josephine Roswell Hawley 1890-1970

Before Joseph died in 1905 he requested that Edith live for at least six months of the year in America. It would appear that she divided her time between Europe and America with several visits to England to visit her mother and sisters. Edith died 6th February 1925 after being taken ill on board a ship travelling from America to Italy, where she had intended to take a holiday. She was buried at sea.

Edith's husband - Joseph Roswell Hawley (1826-1905)
Joseph was born 31st October 1826 at Stewartsville, Richmond County, North Carolina. He studied law and was admitted to the Bar in 1850. Joseph was the editor of the Hartford Evening Press, later the Hartford Courant before he enlisted in 1865. During the Civil War he was a Captain in the Union Army and brevetted Major General before he mustered out in 1866. Joseph had a long career in American politics. He was Governor of Connecticut and later became a Republican Congressman serving intermittently until retiring in 1905. He was appointed a Brigadier General in the United States Army on the 'retired list', shortly before he died on 17th March 1905. He was interred at Cedar Hill Cemetery, Hartford, Connecticut.

Edith Anne Hawley nee Hornor   *Joseph Roswell Hawley*

Edith and Joseph Hawley's Children:
Alice Marian Hawley (1888-1987)
Alice Hawley, known as Marian, was the eldest daughter of Joseph and Edith who was born 1st December 1889, Washington, District of Columbia. Marian married widower Louis Leonce Coudert (1865-1928) following the death of his first wife, Adelaide (Addie) formerly Lockwood, who had died in 1919. Louis worked for many years for the American Bank Note Company and travelled extensively around the world. After their marriage Marian accompanied her husband on one or two business trips. They had a son Joseph Hawley Coudert (1923-2007) who married Ann Morse Bravo. From a young age Marian had visited her grandmother in England frequently and continued to visit her Aunts after she was widowed. Marian died at home in Hartford 15th June 1987 aged 99 years.

Alice Marian Coudert nee Hawley *Louis Leonce Coudert*
Copies of Passport Photographs circa 1920

Edith Josephine Roswell Hawley (1890-1970)
Edith Hawley, the second daughter of Joseph and Edith was born 31st October 1890, also in Washington. In 1917 she joined the American Red Cross and was posted to France helping with 'war relief work' before returning to Hartford. Edith, who was employed as a librarian, was fond of travelling and spent a considerable amount of time touring around Europe; France, Italy and Switzerland being her favourite destinations. Edith also visited her English relatives, crossing the Atlantic Ocean many more times than any other member of the family. When Edith was not abroad, she spent her time in Hartford where she died 27th October 1970 having never married.

7. Florence Hornor (1853-1931)
Florence Hornor, the third daughter of Edward and Anne, was born 24th October 1853 and spent most of her life at The Howe. Florence had a kind disposition and, as she did not marry, dedicated her life to helping others, especially those who lived in the Halstead area. She was generous with her time, and as a young woman helped out at The Howe School. Florence always carried out her duties in an efficient and quiet manner.

A Quaker from birth, Florence was a member of the Society of Friends until some time during her youth when she decided to become a member of the Church of England. She worshipped at St. Andrew's Church and soon became involved with church affairs. During her lifetime she was a member of the Parochial Church Council and held Mother's Meetings at her home, with Violet Morton, the wife of Gerard Sinclair Morton, a local solicitor. Florence enjoyed flower arranging and assisted with the arrangements which decorated the Church; her flowers were usually placed beside the altar. She was also a manager of the Church of England Elementary School for many years.

Florence worked very hard for the Halstead Board of Guardians being elected in 1874 as one of its original members serving on the Board continuously until it was dissolved. She regularly visited the inhabitants of the Workhouse in Halstead and for a long time was a member of its House Committee. When the Workhouse closed during the First World War, and its inhabitants were transferred to Kedington, near Haverhill, Suffolk, Florence would visit them.

Florence Hornor 1853 - 1931
Courtesy of the Halstead and Colne Valley Gazette

Florence actively supported the local branch of the National Society for the Prevention of Cruelty to Children, an organisation which appealed to her sense of justice for those children who, by no fault of their own, were less fortunate than others. She was involved with the District Nursing Association and the work of the Cottage Hospital. As Florence lived at The Howe and spent much of her life supporting local causes, she was always on hand to assist with the organisation of the many Garden Parties, Church and Sunday School outings and treats that took place there.

After her mother's death in 1914, Florence moved to Red House, Colchester Road where she lived until she died on the 24th November 1931 aged 74 years. At her request Florence was cremated at Ipswich before a well attended funeral service that took place at St Andrew's Church.

8. Beatrice Hornor (1857-1949)

Beatrice Hornor was the fourth daughter and last child to be born to Edward and Anne. She spent much of her time at The Howe, where she kept her mother company, especially as she was only nine years old when her father died. Beatrice lived a comparatively sheltered life although as a young woman she assisted her sister Florence at The Howe School.

Beatrice was a very kind hearted girl willing to help others whenever she could. She liked to work with those less fortunate than herself and when the inhabitants of the Workhouse took part in the Brabazon work scheme, she was most supportive. The scheme was designed to relieve the hours of monotony experienced by residents in an institution by encouraging them to partake in some kind of occupational therapy. Encouraged by Beatrice, the residents made fancy goods which were sold periodically at 'work sales' and any profit made was spent on making life more comfortable for the residents. Beatrice was a good entertainer and very musical. She and her friends, sang and played musical instruments at these sales which enlivened proceedings enormously.

Beatrice was involved with quite a few local societies and helped to raise money for various causes. In 1891 she took part in a promenade concert held in Halstead, and the following year had a lead role in a farce, staged by the Girls Club, called 'A Rough Diamond'. She performed songs at the Total Abstinence Society's annual fete and assisted Mr Cook in Great Maplestead when he gave a concert with members of his Glee Club. Beatrice raised money for the East Essex Poultry Fund and the Parish Nurse Fund too. She was also very knowledgeable when it came to plants and flowers and would judge exhibits at local flower, fruit and vegetable shows, which were held in neighbouring villages, a task that she and Florence both enjoyed.

At the age of 44 years, Beatrice married Thomas Apsley Rickman, a surveyor and Justice of the Peace, at St. Andrew's Church on the 3rd July 1902.

A report in the Essex Newsman stated: "*A crowded congregation was present to witness the ceremony. Flags were hung in the vicinity of the Church. The new flag given by Harriet Amy Portway, waved from the Church tower and large concourses of people stood in the street. The service was choral, a full choir being in attendance. The officiating clergy were the Reverend Edwin Oakley, Vicar of Halstead, and the Reverend C Sharp. The bride was given away by her brother, Lewis Hornor JP and Ernest E Gladstone, a friend of the bridegroom acted as best man. The bride looked extremely well in a flimsy white lace dress over white silk and a white hat. She wore a pearl brooch, the gift of the bridegroom, and a pearl pendant, the gift of the bridegroom's sister. She carried an exquisite bouquet of lilies of the valley and white roses. Her maids were Miss (Alice) Hawley and Miss Edith Hawley, nieces. They wore rose powdered muslin dresses and white straw hats, trimmed with white satin ribbon and pink roses. They also wore newly minted gold coins in the form of pendants on gold chains, a present from the bridegroom. The honeymoon will be spent in Wales and Ireland after which Mr and Mrs Rickman will take up their residence at Addlestone. The presents which were numerous and costly included a handsome silver mounted hair brush and silver mounted tortoise shell dressing comb and clothes brush from the Halstead Choral Society of which the bride has been the efficient Hon. Secretary; a silver bowl on ebony stand from the Addlestone Cricket Club; a silver egg stand from the servants of the bridegroom's family and a silver toast and butter rack from the servants at The Howe. Merry peals were rung on the Church bells*".

Thomas already owned his house in Addlestone where he and Beatrice lived for the rest of their lives. Thomas died 22nd November 1945 and Beatrice died 12th December 1949 aged 92 years.

The Howe – 1910

The entrance to the walled garden at The Howe – 1956
Courtesy of David van Asch

Chapter Nine
Fetes and Garden Parties held at The Howe during the Hornor years

The Hornor family allowed different organisations and societies to hold fetes and garden parties in The Howe grounds. Many of these events were reported in the Halstead newspapers and were evidently the highlight of most children and adults social calendar! Processions would start out from the Market Hill, often accompanied by a brass band as everyone made their way to The Howe, either on foot, or in one of the wagons provided by the local gentry.

The Halstead Temperance Society held their annual fete in the grounds for many years with various bands entertaining their members, including the Earls Colne Brass Band and the 12th Essex Regiment Brass Band. Tea would be served in The Grove, an area of meadow land situated to the right hand side of the main drive. This land was also sometimes referred to as the Plantation. The number of those who attended the fetes could vary from three hundred people to a thousand, no doubt dependent on the weather. The day was usually brought to a conclusion with an open air Church service. In 1861 the Reverend William Clements of North Street Baptist Church conducted a service which attracted well over a thousand people.

Sunday Schools held their annual treat at The Howe, particularly the High Street Congregational Sunday School, the North Street Baptist Sunday School and the New Congregational Church Sunday School. Often this involved tea for some two to three hundred children, which would be taken in three or more sittings so that those who could not attend until the evening were catered for. Games were played, hymns were sung and at dusk fire balloons were released into the darkening sky.

The North Street Sunday School outing at The Howe - 1914
Courtesy of Doreen Potts

Members of the local branches of the Mother's Union which included St Andrew's Church, Halstead, Pebmarsh, White Colne, Wickham St Paul and Helions Bumpstead, to name but a few, would meet from time to time at The Howe and enjoy a walk in the grounds before their meeting commenced.

One of the most prestigious garden party schemes was 'The Halstead Summer Garden Parties Organisation', which was formed in 1890. Held once a week during the summer months, large country houses in the Halstead area would open their grounds for public enjoyment. The garden parties started at 5pm and closed around 9pm and there was an admission charge, either at the gate or by season ticket. The ladies put on their best dresses, the bands played a good selection of music and there would be dancing on the lawn.

*An advertisement for a Halstead Summer Garden Party
held at The Howe on the 27th May 1896
Courtesy of Halstead and Colne Valley Gazette*

Houses which participated in the Halstead Summer Garden Party scheme for 1896 included:

Ashford Lodge	Mrs Elizabeth Tayler
The Cedars	John Gilling
The Croft	Charles Portway
Cut Hedge	George Courtauld
Dynes Hall	Charles Sperling
Gosfield Place	Reverend Basil Beridge
Greenstead Hall	Robert Allen
The Howe	Mrs Anne Hornor
Nether Priors	Frank Harris
Sloe House	Frederick Burt

Frederick Burt wrote a letter to the editor of the Halstead and Colne Valley Gazette after his garden party which was printed 10th September 1896.

*"Sloe House
Halstead
Sir,
Will you permit me through your columns to inform those interested in Halstead Town Garden Parties, that, although there were upwards of two thousand people there during the evening of Wednesday 2nd September at the illuminated fete, no damage of any kind occurred and I am pleased to add that I noticed particularly the quiet and orderly conduct of all present.
Yours
F Burt"*

Even over one hundred and fifteen years ago, people must have worried about opening their gardens to the public!

Fetes were arranged to raise funds for a wide range of local clubs and associations, which included Halstead Football Club, the Local Volunteer Fire Brigade and the Halstead Town Band. Two popular bands, which performed at these events, were the Town Band and 'E Company Essex Volunteer Battalion Brass Band', whose Commanding Captain, was Frank Vaizey. Anne Hornor also permitted her grand daughter, Alice Vaizey to use The Howe grounds to raise monies for The Children's League of Pity, a cause which Alice worked for tirelessly.

Halstead Town Band circa 1900

The conductor, Tim Healey is seated in the middle of the centre row wearing a top hat. Other men known to have been members of the band around this time and who may feature on the photograph are: Wally Gibbs, 'Curly' Spurgeon, Albert Lawrence, 'Hathy' Beadle, Fred 'Dido' Hunt, Herbert Harrington, George Taylor, Bill Suckling and Uncas Hunt. William John Corder is seated far right in the centre row.

Although the Temperance Society held fetes at The Howe, in 1909 it hosted a Temperance Demonstration which was held in connection with the North Essex District Division of Son's of Temperance Benefit Society. Approximately ninety seven members in the district division assembled at the Railway Station Yard, having travelled to Halstead by train, brake and bicycle. The banner of the local Lodge was proudly held aloft and the demonstrators marched to The Howe. After the rally and speeches were over, a splendid tea was provided by Frank Rayner of Head Street. The band played, while the marchers enjoyed the swings and donkey rides. The youngsters apparently had great fun romping in the newly mown hay. Evidently a case of mixing business with pleasure! In the evening, members of the public who were over sixteen years old, paid 3d to be admitted into The Howe gardens and hot houses. Once again the band played and dancing was permitted on the lawn.

The Howe early 1900s

The Howe Estate was used for other events too, for example, in February 1893, The Attwoods Foot Beagles 'met' at The Howe. According to a newspaper report *"The first two hares to be flushed out by the pack hid in The Howe grounds and shrubberies. Later in the morning the hounds found a fox in the middle of a wheat field, which belonged to Fitz John's Farm. The fox was cunning and soon disappeared into it's lair! A third hare was chased over Wash Farm, past the Union Workhouse through Star Stile and Ashford Lodge as it made for Maplestead Grounds. It then headed for Birchleys Farm and ran parallel with the Wickham to Pebmarsh Road. The hare tired and the hounds gathered speed until it was caught between Pebmarsh Mill and the Church. The chase took an hour and a quarter and covered a distance of five to six miles"*. As the pursuers were on foot it was not surprising to learn that only five members of the hunting party finished the chase, which included one 'unnamed' lady!

It is obvious that when a venue was required to hold an event, the kind hearted Hornor family would always offer the use of Howe Grounds. This would have involved plenty of extra work, especially for the gardeners who prepared the grounds for public inspection and enjoyment.

Chapter Ten
The Hill Farm, Ridgewell, Essex

The Hill Farm, a timber framed Manor House, situated in Ridgewell, was known by several names over the centuries. It has been referred to as Pannells Farm, Ridgewell Hill Farm, The Hill or Hill Farm. The present farm house was built in the 16th century; a date of 1589 and initials "I M P" are visible on a carved and moulded bressumer. *(A Bressumer is a beam, either of wood or iron, spanning a wide opening and generally supporting a wall above)*. In his book written in the 1760s, Morant, an Essex Historian, called the Manor 'Pannells le Hill', and said that the Pan(n)ell family lived there from 1385-1613.

In 1843 Charles Gilbin of Swaffham Bulbeck, bought Ridgewell Hill Farm and Green Farm for £5,750, having paid a deposit of £111 19s 0d to secure the purchase.

Hill Farm was purchased by Edward Hornor on the 21st December 1852, and inherited by his widow, Anne in 1868. It consisted of 245 acres of arable and pasture land. The soil was mostly loam, clay and gravel. The main crops grown were wheat, barley, and beans. Ten to fifteen men and four boys were usually employed to work on the farm.

The Hill Farm

In June 1865 Edward Hornor applied for an Award or Deed of Enfranchisement on copyhold property which belonged to Hill Farm, and was held in the Manor of Little Yeldham. The Lord of the Manor was James Spalding Gardiner of Borley, Essex.

A quote from the application: *"All those pieces or parcels of Meadow Ground in Little Yeldham, in the said County of Essex, containing together by estimation five acres, with the appurtanences, lying near the meadow formerly of Sir Josiah Child, Knight, commonly called Tilbury Meadows, and abutting upon the lands heretofore of Josiah Clark, Esquire, called Long Meadow towards the west, and the lands formerly of the said Sir Josiah Child called Common Field towards the east, with the appurtenances, and previously to this Enfranchisement held of the said Manor of Little Yeldham, by Copy of Court Roll, and the annual quit rent of eight shillings and four pence. To which said pieces or parcel of land, and hereditaments the said Edward Hornor was admitted tenant, to him and his heirs out of Court before the Steward of the said Manor, on the twenty first day of December one thousand eight hundred and fifty two, on the absolute surrender of John Sudbury".*

The Copyhold Commissioners granted an Award of Enfranchisement to Edward Hornor on the 30th October 1865.

In 1869 Anne Hornor and John Robert Vaizey of Tilbury Hall, whose lands adjoined one another, 'tidied' up their estates by exchanging some land.

Anne exchanged: Number 111 'Little Pigley' in Tilbury Juxta Clare, and 7a, 8a, 9a, 10a and 11a 'Common Mead' in Little Yeldham totalling 4 acres 2 rods and 37 perches; for Number 143 'Round Meadow' 144a 'Part of Grove' in Tilbury Juxta Clare and 260 'Part of Round Meadow' in Ridgewell totalling 4 acres and 16 perches which belonged to John Vaizey.

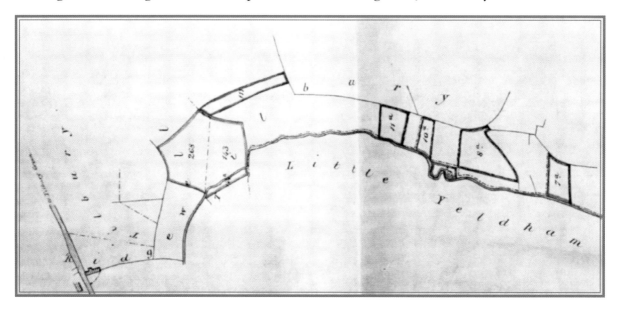

Extract from a plan showing the lands exchanged by Anne Hornor of Hill Farm and John Robert Vaizey of Tilbury Hall in February 1869.

According to Kelly's Directories from 1850 to 1906, and Census Returns from 1861 to 1901, various tenant farmers and farm bailiff's lived at Hill Farm. Some farmers stayed for little more than a year, whilst others like the Norden family were tenants for about twenty five years. By 1885 Anne Hornor had employed a farm bailiff to supervise the running of the farm.

Hill Farm and its estate made the Hornors one of the largest landowners in Ridgewell. Anne was an elderly lady when she decided to sell the farm and land at auction in 1905. The auctioneers were Messrs Balls of Castle Hedingham and the sale took place at the Mart Token Yard in London on 17th July 1905. The entire estate consisted of the large farm house, 243 acres of deep staple, arable and pasture land, and four newly erected labourers cottages. These cottages were built by the Hornors at Tilbury Green. At the time of the sale the cottages were rented by:- John Underwood and Robert Collar, who each paid £4 15s 0d rent per annum and Joseph Ashby and Robert Greenwood who each paid 5 guineas per annum.

There were five lots for sale:
1. Freehold pasture land
2. The Freehold Deep Staple Arable Field
3. Arable Land
4. Freehold Agricultural Estate (The Hill Farm)
5. Cottages.

If any of the lots 1-3 were not sold off separately, they were to be included with the farm house in lot 4.

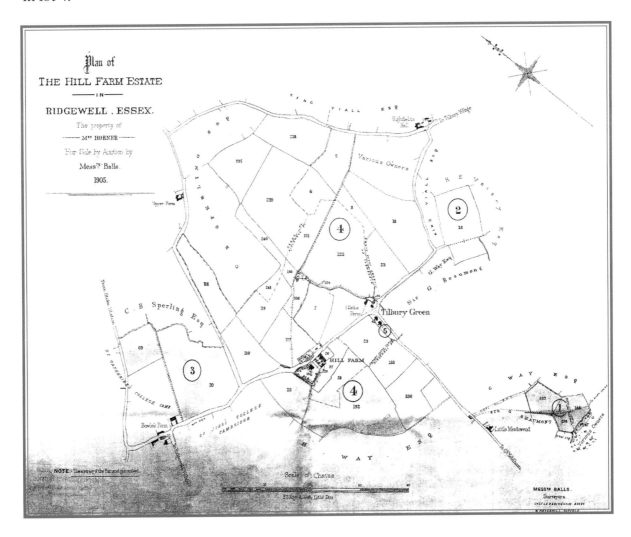

Plan of The Hill Farm Estate, in Ridgewell, Essex
The property of Mrs Hornor, for sale by Messrs Balls 1905
Reproduced by courtesy of Essex Record Office

Field number on plan	Name of Field	Parish of Ridgewell			Parish of Tilbury			Parish of Ashen		
		A	R	P	A	R	P	A	R	P
128	Orchard and Stackyard	0	2	31						
130	House, garden & pt Homestead	1	2	19						
26 131)	Part Homestead & Stackyard				0	2	4			
27)	Home Pasture	0	0	13	2	2	35			
115 28)	Dovehouse Field	6	3	25						
132) 29)	Hill Field	16	3	33	4	3	24			
133)	Zaggs Field	4	3	15	5	2	26			
230	Mill Hill Field	7	2	13						
127	Mud Pasture	7	2	33						
116	Long Field	8	2	19						
118 119)	Long Ley	9	0	25						
241)	Wood Field	7	2	28				1	3	21
126	Boilers Pasture	2	1	12						
7 120)	Boilers				5	2	35			
240)	Long Pasture	1	0	2				3	0	25
235 239)	Ashen Hays Field							9	3	34
121) 6)	Tithe Free Field	4	3	9	4	2	32	18	2	27
238)	Gardiners Field							9	3	24
5)	Tilbury Field				6	0	37			
18 8)	Upper Daniels				15	0	37			
122)	Ridgewell Field	17	2	0	2	2	35			
124	Private Road	0	0	32						
22	Lower Daniels				6	3	5			
23	Cartway to Ridgewell Field				0	0	5			
		97	2	29	55	0	35	43	2	11

Summary of Acreage

	A	R	P
In Ridgewell	97	0	29
In Tilbury	55	0	35
In Ashen	43	2	11
Total	196	1	35

Field names which correspond with numbers on the plan of Hill Farm Estate for sale in 1905
Extacts taken from the sale catalogue:
Lot 1.
Two valuable enclosures of freehold pasture land known as 'Round Meadows' and small plantation in the parishes of Ridgewell and Tilbury. Having a running stream at side of same, thus rendering them valuable for grazing purposes.

Lot 2.
The freehold deep staple arable field known as 'The Leys' in the parish of Tilbury.

Lot 3.
Arable land known as 'Thompson's Field' and 'Turbot's Meadow' in the parish of Ridgewell.

The Hill Farm – 1905
Reproduced by courtesy of Essex Record Office

Lot 4.
Freehold Agricultural Estate known as 'The Hill Farm' in the parishes of Ridgewell, Tilbury and Ashen. An old fashioned farm house built after the Tudor style of brick, stone dash and tile construction.

It consists of:
Entrance hall with old oak beams
Front sitting room with oak beams
End sitting room
Large kitchen or hall
Pantry, scullery and dairy

Eight bedrooms, passage and large attics
At the back of the house is a brick and slated washhouse with bake oven, coal house, two fowl houses, timber and thatched shed
Pump and well of water
At the side of the house is the garden and adjoining this a well stocked orchard. These are bounded on three sides by a moat.

The Hill Farm and farm buildings, taken from Home Meadows – 1905
Reproduced by courtesy of Essex Record Office

The catalogue details also described The Hill Farm as follows:
"Thus forming Rustic and Rural Surroundings of Natural beauty and capable of forming a really pretty Country Home for any person desiring such, about 50 miles from London with good roads therefrom for motoring". Today's estate agent jargon would probably state: 'Large country house within easy reach of London, in need of some modernisation - viewing at earliest opportunity essential"!

The farm buildings comprise of:
Brick and pantiled open cattle shed, pigs courts and meal house
Brick and pantiled open cattle shed, weatherboard and pantiled erection of 4 pig courts and open horse shed
Timber and thatched cowshed for 5 cows, and calves pen
Weatherboard and pantiled erection of root house, loose box and coal shed, small timber and thatched pantiled shed
Timber and pantiled double 5 bayed horse shed with mangers
Timber and thatched double barn, two slated lean-to granaries, slated lean-to cart lodge and pantiled lean-to cart lodge
Timber and thatched cart horse stable for 8 horses with chaff house and loose box
Brick, weatherboard and tiled erection of nag stable, chaise house and 2 sheds with granary over, brick and tiled fowl houses, 5 cattle yards

On the opposite side of the road, timber and thatched cart lodge, timber and pantiled 3-bayed cart lodge and corrugated fowl house
Capital pond of water for cattle.

Lot 5.
Four substantial and nearly new brick and slated cottages in the parish of Tilbury. Well situate with good gardens and two bake houses in rear. The cottages have all the same accommodation: Three upstairs and three downstairs rooms.
There is a well of water to which all tenants have a right of use.

It would appear that the estate remained unsold after the Auction and was therefore sold privately at a later date because, in 1906 Mr Strutt was the new owner of The Hill Farm, Ridgewell.

The Hill farm - Tenant farmers
John Underwood was the tenant farmer at Hill Farm from 1851 to about 1855 before the arrival of the Norden family who lived at the farm by 1859.

George Norden the elder was born c1784 at Sudbury, Suffolk. Before he moved to Hill Farm, Ridgewell, George was the farmer at Hill Farm in Assington. With his wife Susanna, who was born at Ashen, George had eight children between 1831 and 1844; Sarah Charlotte, George, Thomas, Mary Ann, Lucy, William, Emily and Bartholomew. By 1859 George and his family were at Hill Farm, Ridgewell, and, during the 1860s, George employed approximately ten men and boys to help with the work on the farm. After he died in 1867, aged 83 years of age, Susanna, who was twenty years younger than her late husband, ran the farm. She was helped by three of her sons, George, Thomas and William, and fifteen men and four boys. Susanna died in 1872 aged 67 years of age. Lucy, George and Susanna's daughter, had died in 1859 aged 21 years.

George Norden the younger was the eldest son and probable heir to the farm. However by 1880, he had retired from farming and moved to The Strand, London. He had also married Henrietta formerly Franks, a naturalised British Subject, who was born in Gothenburg, Sweden. They remained in London and later moved to Greenwich where George died in 1905 and Henrietta died in 1909.

William Norden, George and Susanna's third son, ran the farm following the death of his mother and George the younger's departure to London. He lived at the farm with his two unmarried sisters, Charlotte and Mary Ann, and employed several labourers to assist with the farm work. By 1891 William had also retired from farming and moved to Mill Road, Ridgewell, where he lived alone. After William left Hill Farm it was occupied by farm bailiffs for a number of years.

The Hill Farm - Farm Bailiffs
Henry Beddall was born in 1841, the son of Henry and Harriett Beddall. In 1861 he lived at Daw Street Farm, Braintree, with his parents and siblings and was employed as a farm worker. In 1871 he had moved to Hob Trees Farm, Arkesden, Saffron Walden, but by 1881 he was back at Daw Street Farm, which he ran for his elderly widowed father. In 1885 he was employed as the farm steward at Hill Farm and his two sisters Harriett and Caroline lived with him. Around 1895 Henry moved to Tilbury Hall, where he was employed as farm bailiff to Robert Edward Vaizey, Anne Hornor's grandson. Henry died in 1901.

Ernest Barrett took over as farm bailiff in 1895 when Henry Bedall departed and remained until 1901.

William Frost was born at Borley, Essex, and in 1856 he married Emily Thompson. In 1861 he was employed as a farm labourer at Leys Farm, Foxearth. William and Emily had at least four children. Martha, Stephen, Ann and William, born between 1860 and 1876. William became a farm bailiff and moved frequently from farm to farm. In 1871 he was employed in Thorpe Morieux, Suffolk, and in 1881 he was at Folly Farm also in Thorpe Morieux. In 1891 he lived at Shardloes Farm, Gosfield, before he worked for Anne Hornor at Hill Farm in 1901 where he remained until the farm was sold and he retired. By 1911 William was a widower and he lived at Rookwoods Cottage, Sible Hedingham with his housekeeper.

Tenants at the Cottages at Tilbury Green in 1905
When Anne Hornor decided to sell Hill Farm in 1905, she included the newly built cottages at Tilbury Green. They were rented to the farm workers who were local families and appeared to be born at either Ridgewell or Tilbury.

Robert Underwood was born about 1833. He married Ellen Bush, born in 1836, the daughter of George and Elizabeth Bush, who worked as a straw plaiter during the early years of their marriage. They had at least eight children between 1854 and 1873; Susannah, James 1856-1873, Ann, Isaac, John, Eleanor, Emma and James John.

Joseph Ashby was the son of Henry and Elizabeth Ashby who married Mary Humphry in 1859, the daughter of Charles and Ann Humphry. Mary was also a straw plaiter. They had nine daughters born between 1860 and 1878; Martha, Emily, Mary Ann, Rachel, Emma, Elizabeth, Anna, Rosanna and Lilly. By 1901 Joseph and Mary's daughters had left home and their grandson Stanley Ashby, aged 7 years, lived with them. In 1911 Eli Underwood, another grandson also lodged with them, along with Stanley. Mary died in 1912 aged 74 years followed by Joseph in 1914 aged 77 years.

Robert Collar was born in 1851, the son of Thomas and Maria Collar. He married Emma Bush who was born in 1854, who was also a daughter of George and Elizabeth Bush. Robert worked as a farm labourer and looked after the horses on the farm, while Emma was a straw plaiter. They had five children Thomas George, Walter, Anna Maria, Emily and Polly, born between 1872 and 1881. Robert died in 1924 aged 72 years.

John Underwood was born in 1865, the son of Robert and Ellen Underwood. He married Rachel Ashby who was born in 1866, the daughter of his neighbours Joseph and Mary Ashby. John worked as a farm labourer and they had four children:- James born in 1890, Eli 1893, George 1898 and Minnie in 1900. When Rachel and Minnie died in 1907, John and his son George left the area and moved to Heston, Brentford, Middlesex where they found work on a farm. Eli did not leave with his father and moved in with his grandparents, Joseph and Mary Ashby.

Four families whose lives appeared to be intricately related to one another by marriage.

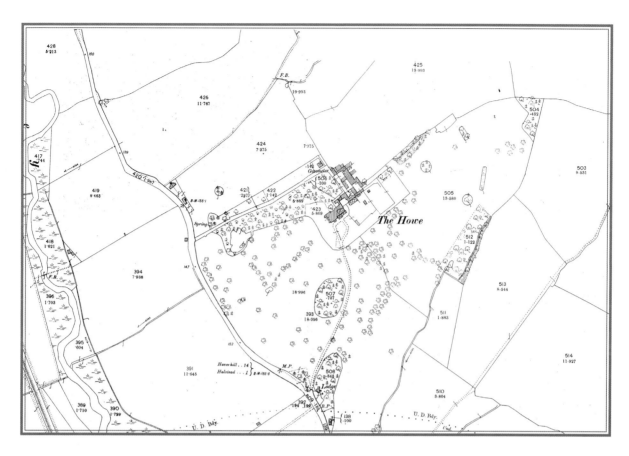
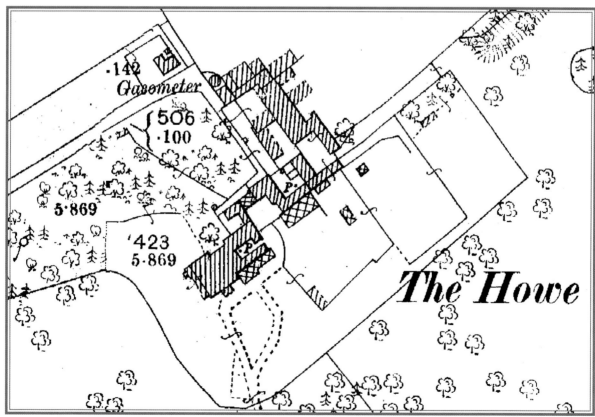

Extracts from the 1897 Ordnance Survey Map Second Edition showing The Howe and farm buildings, lodge and cottages

Samuel Augustine Courtauld
8th February 1865 – 20th January 1953

Chapter Eleven
The Courtauld Family

Samuel Augustine Courtauld 1865-1953
Samuel and Augustine are Christian names that have been used by the Courtauld family through the generations. Therefore to avoid any confusion with other members of the family of the same name, I shall refer to Samuel Augustine Courtauld (1865-1953) who lived at The Howe as SAC. He was a great benefactor to Bocking, Halstead and nearby villages, and, as practically every building endowed by SAC bears his initials on the exterior, it seems appropriate.

SAC was born 8th February 1865 at Bocking, Essex. He was the eldest son of George Courtauld (1830-1920) and his second wife Susanna Courtauld formerly Savill (1838-1879). Shortly after his birth the family moved to Cut Hedge, Gosfield where SAC spent his childhood before he was educated at Charterhouse, a public school in Surrey.

His mother died when he was fourteen years old, and his elder step sister Katherine Mina Courtauld took over the role of looking after the family.

Cut Hedge, Gosfield
The house where SAC lived with his parents, George and Susanna Courtauld.

SAC joined the family business when it was known as Samuel Courtauld and Company in 1884 and would ride to work daily on his pony from Cut Hedge to Halstead. In 1894 he was made a Director of Samuel Courtauld and Company Limited, a position he held for fifty six years. (In 1913 the company became known as Courtaulds Limited). His working life was devoted to Courtaulds where he saw the business extend its textile operation from making vast amounts of black silk mourning 'crape' or 'crepe', following the death of Queen Victoria, to the manufacture of rayon, which was to make him a very wealthy man. As an employer he was well respected as he cared for his work force and their welfare.

In 1896 SAC became a Justice of the Peace, sitting for the South Hinckford Division. Petty Sessions were held every alternate week at the Police Station, Fairfield Road, Braintree, and in Halstead. At this time SAC lived at 'Little Bradfords' in Bocking, a house he continued to reside at for several years before he moved to The Howe.

Little Bradfords, Bocking
Braintree District Museum, ©Braintree District Museum Trust Limited.

On the 22nd October 1903 Samuel Augustine Courtauld married Edith Anne Lister (1876-1951) of 'Great Walton', Eastry, Kent at Eastry Parish Church. After their marriage they returned to 'Little Bradfords' where their three children were born:
1. Augustine Courtauld   1904-1959
2. Edith Elizabeth Courtauld   1906-1992
3. Walter Pierre Courtauld   1910-1989

When 'Little Bradfords' became too small for their growing family SAC looked at several larger properties before he bought the more modest sized Howe in 1914, and promptly extended the property. Two of the first things SAC arranged on his arrival at The Howe were a) the construction of a 'dug out' in the parkland close to the house, which fortunately never had to be used during an air raid, and b) a gateway was placed in the South boundary wall of the estate, opposite the entrance to Box Mill Lane, and a tarmac footpath was laid across the field situated on the far side of the footbridge, which spanned the River Colne, at the end of Box Mill Lane. This path led into Halstead and was made so that SAC could walk back and forth to the factory without getting his boots muddy. (The gateway is still in use today, although minus the gate). SAC rarely drove a car, as his early experiences behind the wheel are probably best forgotten! He preferred to walk everywhere whenever possible although he did own various motor vehicles and employed chauffeurs to drive them.

In 1916 SAC was appointed High Sheriff of Essex and became a Deputy Lieutenant for the county in 1937. For thirty five years he was also a member of the Joint Standing Committee which administered the Police Force and was its Chairman for twenty one years.

When you think of the name 'Courtauld' and its association with Halstead, many things are brought to mind; Courtaulds Factory, The Courtauld Homes of Rest, The Cottage Hospital and the Courtauld built houses. All these buildings have a connection with SAC, who liked to invest his money in bricks and mortar, although he never built himself a new house and was content to live at The Howe.

Cottages situated near the entrance to Wash Farm, North Street /Hedingham Road.

These cottages, once known as the Crown Public House, were demolished around 1926 by Samuel Courtauld, and replaced by houses built in the 'Courtauld Tudor Style'. The entrance to Wash Farm is just before the cottages, on the left hand side.

A number of old cottages along North Street which SAC considered both an eyesore and wretched accommodation for their occupants were replaced by houses built in what has become known as the 'Courtauld Tudor Style' - an arts and crafts, garden suburb style. The new houses were built in the back gardens of the old cottages and, when completed, the inhabitants of the cottages moved into them. The old dwellings were demolished, leaving the tenants with front gardens. A total of forty five houses were built in North Street, Box Mill Lane, Mill Chase, Mallows Field and Colchester Road between 1920 and 1940. These houses were named after local manors, families, Jane Austen novels, Fanny Burney and characters from her novel 'Evelina'. 'Prunum' in Beridge Road, was the last dwelling to be built by him in 1940.

On the left hand side of the photograph are some of the cottages in North Street, which were demolished by Samuel Courtauld. The wall on the right hand side stood in front of the Union Workhouse. The tenement beyond the workhouse was removed and replaced by Courtauld Tudor style houses in the 1920s.

These cottages at The Wash were also demolished by Samuel Courtauld circa 1920s. The Howe School built in 1861 by Edward Hornor is just visible through the trees in the background.

Abel Cottages, at the Corner of Hedingham Road and Box Mill Lane circa early 1930s. The entrance to Wash Farm is on the right hand side of the road.

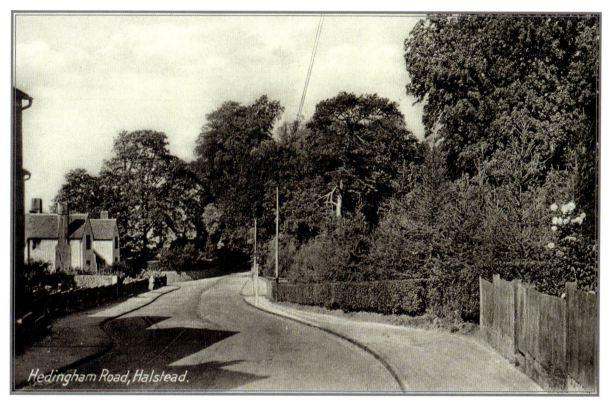

Abel Cottages circa 1950. The fencing on the right hand side borders the garden of St Martin Cottages, built in 1925.

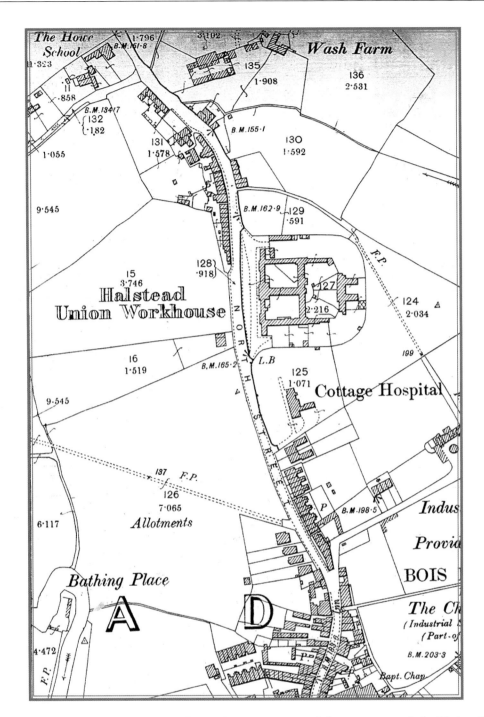

A section of the 1897 Ordnance Survey Map showing many of the cottages and the Union Workhouse which were demolished by Samuel Courtauld.

In 1916 the 'inmates' from the Workhouse, Hedingham Road which was built in 1838 to provide shelter for the destitute poor of Halstead and surrounding area, were transferred to the Risbridge Union Workhouse at Kedington, Suffolk. The building was then used briefly during the First World War to house German Prisoners of War, before it was purchased by SAC who demolished it when he built a crescent of twenty single storey rest homes, primarily for Courtauld employees to occupy during their retirement years. The homes, which were designed by Edward William Coldwell of Coldwell, Coldwell and Courtauld were ready for occupation in 1924. (Major John Sewell Courtauld MC MP, (1880-1942) a partner in the above firm, was a first cousin of SAC). As the Workhouse had been used by the Halstead Board of Guardians to hold their meetings, SAC had new premises built in Colchester Road for them to use which were known as the Union Offices.

The Courtauld Homes of Rest.

Congratulations! Fred and Polly Meadows, celebrate their Golden Wedding Anniversary with family and friends in 1950. Far left: Gerald and Dora Brown, their son in law and daughter. Their newly married grandson Alwyne Brown and his wife Miriam (formerly Coe) are seated on the ground at the front. The photograph is taken outside the Courtauld Homes of Rest.

SAC was very involved with the Halstead Cottage Hospital which was endowed by his father George Courtauld. In 1928 he provided money for a new operating theatre, sterilising and anaesthetics rooms to be built. The building was opened by SAC in 1929 and the hospital continued to flourish with him as its President from 1920 to 1948. He continued to help financially to ensure that its equipment was modern and up to date. In 1934 when the hospital celebrated its Golden Jubilee, SAC was the only person at the Annual General Meeting who had attended its opening in 1884. He had, therefore, supported the hospital for fifty years. In 1936/7 he provided an additional private ward, and in 1938, a new mortuary chapel and fully equipped autopsy room. During the Second World War, the Ministry of Health required the hospital to use an independent water supply, so arrangements were made with SAC for water to be obtained from springs and ram on The Howe Estate. The water was conveyed to the hospital in a water cart and into a tank which was placed on the hospital allotments.

SAC had a strong association with other medical institutions as he was President of the Essex County Hospital for forty four years, and Vice President and a Member of the Board of the Middlesex Hospital. For sixteen years he was Chairman of the Council of the Medical School. He assisted medical research by endowing the Institute of Bio Chemistry and financing special wards for Clinical Research. In 1936 The University of London conferred on him the honorary degree of 'Doctor of Laws'. SAC was without doubt a wonderful benefactor to the field of Medicine.

In 1924 the Essex Agricultural Society Show was held on the fields which ran along the side of Hedingham Road to Doe's Corner, beside the River Colne. To make the site more accessible the cottages at Doe's Corner were demolished, and the road was widened. On the opposite side of the road, on the site of the former golf links, car parking was available for one thousand vehicles.

SAC was a shy, reserved gentleman with a strong sense of humour. He and his wife Edith preferred to live quietly and did not entertain lavishly. They had little interest in London society despite owning a large house, known as 'Noel House', at Palace Green, Kensington, where they often stayed. SAC was much happier in the country, sitting by the fireside in his study at The Howe with a cigar and a good book. When in London SAC visited the Courtauld offices on London Wall, walking there and back from Noel House, whenever possible.

In 1926 the Duke of York, later King George VI, visited Bocking and Halstead to inspect the Courtauld factories. It was an informal visit arranged by the Industrial Welfare Society of which he was President. SAC along with James Addison, a fellow director at Courtaulds, travelled to Chelmsford Station in SAC's Rolls Royce where they met the Duke of York. They visited the Bocking factory in the morning before joining Edith Courtauld for lunch at The Howe. During the afternoon the Duke of York, now accompanied by Edith, visited the Courtauld Homes of Rest before he made a tour of the Halstead factory. He was then driven back to Witham Station where he caught the train to Liverpool Street Station. The day was hailed a great success.

SAC was a highly educated gentleman. He was Chairman of the Board of Governors of Felsted School for twenty six years, during which time he endowed scholarships and, in 1938, he built the new Science Laboratories and Art School. A fellow of the Huguenot Society, SAC enjoyed literary works and spent many hours reading. He loved his books and the library at The Howe contained several thousand volumes, all of which he could name. He could be found engrossed in 'Horace' written in Latin one evening and happily ensconced in a Jane Austen novel the next evening. He read books by P G Wodehouse and enjoyed the works of Walter Scott. SAC published An Anthology of English Metrical Translations of Horace which was reprinted twice. He was interested too in The Royal Literary Fund, which assisted writers who had fallen on hard times.

The Duke of York with SAC touring Courtauld's factory in 1926

During the Second World War when SAC was seventy five years old, he became a Welfare Officer. One of his tasks involved visiting the soldiers who manned the search lights. As these posts were often situated in very lonely positions, travelling to them could not have been easy for him. However SAC enjoyed chatting to the men and always made sure they were as comfortable as possible.

For relaxation SAC sat for hours beside a pond in The Howe grounds fishing for perch. He was a good shot and, although he did not care for 'grand shoots', he travelled to Scotland for the grouse shooting in his later years.

During his lifetime SAC owned carriages and several carriage horses, harnesses and stable equipment which were used in his early days at The Howe. He had at least two cars and often employed two chauffeurs at the same time, as it was quite common to see both SAC and his wife, Edith out and about in separate vehicles.

SAC was always ready to help local organisations, especially those who tried to raise funds using their own initiative. He gave financial aid to the local Town Football Club when they acquired their new ground so they could buy much needed equipment. He allowed the local Horticultural Society and other clubs, organisations and societies to use the immaculately kept Howe grounds to host functions.

In 1951 after his wife Edith died, SAC sold the lease on the family home in Palace Green and spent the rest of his days at The Howe, with a few faithful members of staff.

Samuel Augustine Courtauld died on the 20th January 1953 at The Howe. The funeral service, which was very well attended, was held at St Catherine's Church, Gosfield and he was interred in the graveyard.

On his gravestone is carved one of his favourite lines from 'Horace'.
'Integer vitae scelerisque purus', translated, it reads: 'He was an upright man of unstained heart'.

Before Evening Service on the following Sunday, the bell ringers of St Mary's Church, Bocking rang a quarter peal of Bob Major with clappers half muffled. Campanologists included in this tribute were the daughter*, brother* and sister* of Ernest Snowden, who was employed on The Howe Estate for thirty eight years. The conductor was Ronald Suckling, whose grandmother had taught SAC to weave when he first joined Courtaulds in 1884.

The bell ringers who took part were:
Treble	Miss Hilda M Snowden	*daughter
2	Claude Snowden	*brother
3	Mrs Jarvis	
4	Harold Moore	
5	Mrs H Moore	
6	Cecil Barker	
7	Ronald Suckling (conductor)	
Tenor	Miss Hilda M Snowden	*sister

Houses built by SAC:

<u>Halstead</u>
1921	'Pair of cottages')	
1934	'Jocks House')	Fitz John's Farm
1922	1 - 4 Box Mill Lane Cottages	Box Mill Lane
1920	'Abel Cottages'	Hedingham Road
1924	'Clare Cottages'	Hedingham Road
1925	'St. Martins Cottages'	Hedingham Road
1926	'Bousser Cottages'	Hedingham Road
1926	'Tryon Cottages'	Hedingham Road
1927	'Pride'	Hedingham Road
1927	'Prejudice'	Hedingham Road
1928	'Mansfield Park'	Hedingham Road
1928	'Persuasion'	Hedingham Road
1929	'Sense'	Hedingham Road
1929	'Sensibility'	Hedingham Road
1927	'Fanny Burney'	Colchester Road
1928	'Branchton'	Colchester Road

Architects drawing of a pair of Courtauld Tudor Style houses built in the 1920s

Courtauld Tudor Style houses in Hedingham Road

| 1928 | 'Mirvan' | Colchester Road |
| 1935 | 'Duval' | Colchester Road |

| 1928 | 'Evelina' | Mallows Field |
| 1929 | '1 - 3 Orville Cottages' | Mallows Field |

| 1928 | 'Northanger Abbey' | Mill Chase |

| 1940 | 'Prunum' | Beridge Road |

Blackmore End
1925	Village Hall and Caretakers house
1930	Pair of Cottages
1939	1-3 Bronte Cottages

Bocking
| 1926 | Village Hall | Church Street |

Sible Hedingham
| 1934 | 'Sparrow's Farm House' | Halstead Road |

All the buildings were built in the 'Courtauld' style, and the majority of them in the 'Courtauld Tudor Style'.

The Howe and other farms inherited by SAC's son, Augustine Courtauld:

The Howe	48.204 acres
Wash Farm	111.192 acres
Fitz John's Farm	134.723 acres
Hepworth Hall and Wallace's Farm	239.947 acres
Slough, Brook Street, Sparrows, Foxborough Hills and Boaleys Farms	390.380 acres
Woodlands and plantations	187.002 acres
Total	1111.448 acres

Land and Properties also owned by SAC and inherited by Augustine were in Blackmore End, Gosfield, Sible Hedingham and Wethersfield and comprised of:

Summers Hall, Waver, Shinborough and Beazley End Farms	Wethersfield
Bakers and Reading Farms	Wethersfield
The Hyde Farm	Wethersfield
Leylands or Lower Wrights and New Barn Farms	Wethersfield
Hawkwoods Farm	Gosfield and Wethersfield
Woodlands, Plantations and Cottages	Gosfield, Sible Hedingham and Wethersfield
School Green Farm or Stammers Farm Green and Clevelands Farm	Wethersfield
Valley Farm	Wethersfield
Village Hall and Playing Fields	Wethersfield
Pattens Farm	Wethersfield
11 Cottages	Blackmore End
The total acreage for the above:	1542.734 acres

Samuel Augustine Courtauld and his family
(Three generations only)

Generation No 1

1. Samuel Augustine Courtauld's father was George Courtauld (1) who was born 1830 and died 1920, and his mother was Susanna Elizabeth Savill who was born 1838 and died in 1879. They had ten children of which the eldest was:-
2.   i   Samuel Augustine Courtauld (2)   b.1865 d.1953.

Generation No 2

2. **Samuel Augustine Courtauld (2)** was born 1865 and died in 1953. He married Edith Anne Lister (known as Edian) born 1876 and died 1951. Married 1903.

Children of Samuel Courtauld and Edith Lister:
3.	i	Augustine Courtauld (3)	b.1904 d.1959.
4	ii	Edith Elizabeth Courtauld	b.1906 d.1992.
5.	iii	Walter Pierre Courtauld	b.1910 d.1989.

Generation No 3

3. Augustine Courtauld (3) *Samuel Augustine (2), George (1)* was born 1904 and died 1959. He married Mollie Montgomerie born 1907 died 2009. Married 1932.

Children of Augustine Courtauld and Mollie Montgomerie
	i	Perina Courtauld	b.1932 married 1) Christopher Jeremy King Fordham in 1956. 2) Robin Neville, Lord Braybrooke in 1998.
	ii	Augustine Christopher Caradoc Courtauld	b.1934 married Elizabeth Molland in 1978.
	iii	Julien Courtauld	b.1938 married 1) Theresa Caroline Mott Ratcliffe in 1964. 2) Patricia Worboys (Paddy) in 1974.
	iv	Stephen Napier Courtauld	b.1940.
	v	William Montgomerie Courtauld	b.1943 d.2010 married Caroline Patricia Buckley in 1966.
	vi	Susanna Ruth Courtauld	b.1950 married Peter Hamilton in 1983.

4. Edith Elizabeth Courtauld (3) *Samuel Augustine (2), George (1)* was born 1906 and died 1992. She married Ralph Herbert Rayner born 1897 died 1977. Married 1931.

Children of Edith Courtauld and Ralph Rayner:
	i	Fleur Revere Rayner	b.1932 married John Herbert Walbeoffe Wilson in 1953.
	ii	Ranulf Courtauld Rayner	b.1935 married 1) Diana Margaret Gort in 1962. 2) Annette Binney in 1970.
	iii	Nicholas Courtauld Rayner	b.1938 married 1) Marina Patriavca in 1968. 2) Laetitia Reynolds in 1987.
	iv	Andrew Piers Courtauld Rayner	b.1942 married Mary Mackenzie in 1970.

5. Walter Pierre Courtauld (3) *Samuel Augustine (2), George (1)* was born 1910 and died 1989. He married 1) Faith Dorothy Caldwell Cook in 1940, 2) Sylvia Davis in 1966.

Children of Walter Courtauld and Faith Cook:
	i	Simon Pierre Courtauld	b.1940 married Philippa Burrell in 1967.
	ii	Sarah Louise Courtauld	b.1943 married James Michie in 1964.
	iii	Richard Savill Courtauld	b.1946 married Anthea Priestley in 1969.
	iv	Julia Elizabeth Courtauld	b.1949 married David Hare in 1969.

Children of Walter Courtauld and Sylvia Davis:
	v	Martha Jane Courtauld	b.1967 married Robert MacGuffog in 1993.
	vi	Jonathan Louis Courtauld	b.1970.

Samuel Augustine Courtauld's wife:
Edith Anne Courtauld formerly Lister (1876 - 1951) - *(Referred to as EAC)*

Edith Anne Lister, known as Edian, was born in 1876 at 'Great Walton', Eastry, Kent. She was the daughter of Walter Venning Lister and Lucy Lister formerly Reid.

Walter Venning Lister was born in 1840 at Hampstead, the son of Isaac Solly Lister and Anne Lister formerly Venning. Lucy Reid was born in 1851 and was the daughter of James Reid a doctor, who later qualified as a surgeon, and was a Fellow of the Royal College of Surgeons, and his wife Ellen. James and Ellen lived at Canterbury where Lucy spent her childhood at home, before attending a private boarding school in Brighton, Sussex. Shortly before her marriage in 1871 the family lived at 13 Bridge Street, Canterbury.

'Great Walton', Eastry, Kent
The family home of Walter and Lucy Lister

Walter and Lucy lived at 'Great Walton' where they raised their family. Edian, (EAC) their eldest child and only daughter was followed by four sons, Henry born in 1878, Walter 1879, James 1886 and Arthur in 1891. Walter Venning Lister was a brewer and a Justice of the Peace who died at sea in 1908. Lucy continued to live at Eastry for a short time after Walter's death but had moved to 1 Shorncliffe Road, Folkestone by 1911. She lived in Folkestone for many years and died at Haywards Heath in 1942 in her 91st year.

Local newspaper Obituary:
"Lister – In loving memory of our mother Lucy Lister who passed peacefully away January 19th 1942; and our father Walter Venning Lister who died at sea January 23rd 1908 - Edian, Hal, Ken, Jim".
('Family names' for Edith, and her brothers, Henry, Walter, James and Arthur).

EAC was a kind, quiet, home loving lady, who after her marriage to SAC became very interested in the welfare of the girls who worked at the Courtauld factory and in the Girl Guide Movement. She was one of the founder members of the Halstead troop and became a Commissioner. The Brownies originally known as 'Rosebuds', along with the Girl Guides, would often hold events at The Howe which were arranged by EAC. As a trustee at the Courtauld Homes of Rest, EAC regularly visited the residents who always made her very welcome and looked forward to seeing her.

One of EAC's most cherished gifts to the town was the Memorial Cross which stands in St Andrew's Church Yard. It was given by EAC as a thank you offering for the safe return of her four brothers from the First World War and to honour the memory of the 145 Halstead people who lost their lives. (144 men and Nurse Minnie Yerbury).

Engraved on the Memorial Cross are the badges of the Royal Air Force and three Regiments namely, The Auckland Mounted Rifles New Zealand, Royal Garrison Artillery and Royal Fusiliers, in which EAC's four brothers served.

One of those commemorated on the Memorial Cross with a Howe connection is:
Charles Edwin Rayner who was killed in action in 1917. He was the son of Charles Henry and Fanny Rayner who lived at The Lodge on The Howe Estate. *(For further details see Chapter Nineteen page 173).*

The Service of Dedication led by the Right Reverend
The Lord Bishop of Colchester DD

The Memorial Cross, Halstead, given by Edith Anne Courtauld which was dedicated on 8th May 1920

The main inscription states:
To the honoured memory of 145 Halstead people who gave their lives in the Great War 1914 - 1919.

The inscription referring to Edith Courtauld's brothers, written in Latin, transcribed into English, states: *E A Courtauld, their sister caused this Cross to be erected in grateful memory of her four brothers who fought in the war, each of whom returned in safety when peace was accomplished.*

> ✝
>
> ## Parish Church of St. Andrew,
> ### HALSTEAD.
>
> Saturday, 8th May, 1920, at 3 p.m.
>
> ## Unveiling and Dedication
> ### of the
> ## Halstead Memorial Cross.
>
> **Unveiling of the Cross by**
> GENERAL THE LORD BYNG OF VIMY,
> G.C.B., K.C.M.G., M.V.O.,
>
> ✶ ✶ ✶ ✶ ✶ ✶
>
> **Dedication by**
> THE RIGHT REVEREND
> THE LORD BISHOP OF COLCHESTER. D.D.

The front cover of the Order of Service for the Unveiling and Dedication of The Memorial Cross, Halstead – Sunday 8th May 1920

Edith Anne Courtauld's Four Brothers:
Henry Reid Lister was born in 1878 and attended Grove House School, Guildford before he stayed with his uncle in London, where he was an articled clerk (law) in 1901. In 1911 he was a qualified Solicitor and lived in Folkestone with his mother. He enlisted in 1914 and served as a trooper with the Auckland Mounted Rifles. He was discharged in 1917 having been wounded. Henry died in 1958 and probate was granted to his widow Ivy Elizabeth Lister.

Walter Kendrick Lister was born in 1879 and educated at Farmers House School, Canterbury. In 1901 he lived with his parents and was a Brewers pupil. By 1911 he had moved to Ash near Canterbury. During the First World War he served with the Royal Garrison Artillery in France and reached the rank of Captain. He returned home and in 1921 married Edith Remelion Herbert, formerly Cooper, the widow of Robert Kentish Herbert, at St Peter's Church, Cranley Gardens, Kensington, London. Walter and Edith lived at Cyprus House, Ash, Kent after their marriage. Walter died in 1959 in the Folkestone area.

James Solly Lister was born in 1886 and in 1901 he was a cadet at the Nautical Training College, on HMS Worcester at Dartford. By 1911 he was a 'Mate' on board the vessel 'Catalina'. However he left his life at sea and joined the newly formed Royal Air Force during the First World War. He married Kathleen Florence Melville in 1923 at Klerksdrop, South Africa and appeared to have remained there until he died in 1948.

Arthur Venning Lister who was born in 1891, was the youngest son of Walter and Lucy. He was educated at St Lawrence's School in Bexhill, Sussex. In 1911 he was a student and lived with his mother, and brother Henry in Folkestone. During the First World War he was a Second Lieutenant in the 1st London Regiment (Royal Fusiliers) and later a Lieutenant in the 1/4 Wiltshire Regiment. By 1920 he had moved to Kettering in Northamptonshire and, in 1921, at St Peter's Church, Kensington, he married Mary Isobel Murray Cunningham formerly Allison, the widow of Captain Kenneth Cunningham who died in 1914. When Arthur died in 1972 he lived at Red Cottage, Long Bottom, Seer Green, Beaconsfield, Buckinghamshire.

EAC knew Malcolm Sargent (1895-1967), who was for many years conductor of the Halle Orchestra, the Liverpool Philharmonic Orchestra, and the BBC Symphony Orchestra. EAC enjoyed his concerts and they became good friends, with Malcolm Sargent visiting the Courtauld family at The Howe. Malcolm Sargent was knighted in 1947.

SAC had a cousin, also named Samuel Courtauld (1876-1947), who lived at Stanstead Hall in Halstead and also owned a London residence. In 1901, Samuel, who became the Chairman of Courtauld's Limited, married Elizabeth Kelsy (1875-1931). Elizabeth Courtauld along with Malcolm Sargent were the inaugurators of the Courtauld-Sargent Concerts held between 1929-1940, which continued to be successful for some years after Elizabeth's death in 1931. The object of these concerts was to encourage members of the public to take an interest in music and to help those who loved music, but who could not usually afford the high price of tickets, to subscribe regularly to concerts. Nearly all performances featured the London Symphony Orchestra. SAC and EAC supported the scheme.

EAC, who enjoyed music, kept a black baby-grand pianola in her sitting room at The Howe. As a treat she would allow her grandchildren to listen to Beethoven's Moonlight Sonata, or a Chopin etude on it when they visited her. The sound was produced from 'a paper roll' which was clipped into the pianola.

EAC loved her garden too, and was especially fond of carnations. She enjoyed her daily walks around the greenhouses, which were usually taken after tea. Situated close to the house EAC would carefully inspect the lemons, limes, citrons and oranges which grew in them.

Edith Anne Courtauld (EAC) died at The Howe on the 13th November 1951, her funeral and interment took place at St. Catherine's Church, Gosfield.

Samuel Augustine and Edith Anne Courtauld's Children:
1. Augustine Courtauld (1904-1959)
Augustine Courtauld, known as August, was the eldest son born 20th August 1904 at Little Bradfords, Bocking. August along with his siblings, was bought up by a succession of Governesses before being sent to St Christopher's School at Eastbourne and then to Charterhouse. When he left public school he studied Engineering and Geography at Trinity College, Cambridge and graduated in 1927 with a Bachelor of Arts degree.

August was an adventurer. His two passions were his boat and life as an explorer. In 1926 he joined an expedition to Greenland and a year later travelled to the Southern Sahara and the Mountains of Air. His most noted trip was a polar expedition between 1930 and 1931, when he joined the British Arctic Air Route Expedition whose remit was to check the weather conditions over the Greenland ice cap. Part of this mission involved establishing a station about 145 miles North West of the base camp, which was to be manned. August, with some colleagues, set off to relieve the men at this station, but due to the absolutely atrocious weather conditions the journey took far longer than was planned and it was obvious that their rations would not last if they all stayed at the station. August volunteered to stay alone on the ice cap, but, because the relief party had trouble locating him in the spring, he ended up spending five months there, far longer than had been anticipated. At times he was forced to live in total darkness, completely trapped in his 'snow house'. His immense bravery and courage earned him the Polar Medal which was presented by King George V in 1932.

August married Mollie Montgomerie (1907-2009) at Southwark Cathedral on 2nd January 1932. After their marriage they lived in London where their eldest children were born.

August and Mollie had six children:
Perina Courtauld	1932
Augustine Christopher Caradoc Courtauld	1934
Julien Courtauld	1938
Stephen Napier Courtauld	1940
William Montgomerie Courtauld	1943-2010
Susanna Ruth Courtauld	1950

August and Mollie also had a farmhouse near Tichfield, Sussex, before they moved to Spencer Grange known as 'Spencers', Great Yeldham, a large Georgian house built in 1750 by the grand daughter of the Duke of Marlborough.

August loved life at sea and owned a yawl (yacht) named 'Duet'. A boat which he and the family sailed in frequently around the British Coast and Overseas. Before the Second World War, August had joined an organisation which became known as the Special Operations Executive. Always prepared for action and excitement, August did not hesitate when he was requested by Naval Intelligence to sail Duet up the Norwegian Coast to gather information for them. During the war he joined the Royal Naval Volunteer Reserves and served as a Lieutenant, before he moved to Coastal Forces.

On his return to 'Spencers' August became involved with a number of organisations. He was a Deputy Lieutenant and later Sheriff of Essex. A Justice of the Peace and a County Councillor representing the Belchamp and Bumpstead Division. August represented Essex and sat on various hospital and educational committees, as well as supporting local organisations. He was President of Great Yeldham United Football Club and a member of the Yeldham Boys Club, to name just a few.

He was Honorary Secretary of the Royal Geographical Society and on the committee of the management of the Scott Polar Research Institute.

In 1952 August donated money for a new lifeboat to be stationed at Walton on the Naze in memory of his mother. She was launched by the Duchess of Kent, President of the Lifeboat Institution, and named 'Edian Courtauld'.

When his father, SAC died, August inherited The Howe Estate and wanting to keep the Estate employees in work, he turned part of it into a market garden. However, although they had plenty of produce to sell, they could not find suitable buyers and the venture failed. August and his family then considered selling 'Spencers' and living at The Howe, but despite putting 'Spencers' on the market with a large firm of London and Country Estate agents no-one showed any interest in the property. It was therefore with some reluctance that August decided to sell The Howe and a house which was labelled 'unsaleable' by estate agents was sold to Ralph van Asch.

In 1956 August built a house at Blackmore End, which was called 'Gino', named after his friend Gino Watkins, another Polar Explorer. He also established the Augustine Courtauld Trust. Its purpose was to assist Essex based charities to help disadvantaged people, especially youngsters, and to promote conservation in the country. It also supported Arctic and Antarctic Expeditions. Around this time too, August was diagnosed with Multiple Sclerosis and as the disease cruelly took hold, he wrote and dictated his autobiography, 'Man the Ropes'. August died on the 3rd March 1959 in London, and in accordance with his wishes he was buried at sea.

Augustine (August) Courtauld
1904 - 1959

1930's Mollie Courtauld nee Montgomerie
1907 - 2009

In April 1963 a service was held at St Catherine's Church, Gosfield, to 'Dedicate the Peal of Six Bells'. The original three bells were re-hung and three new bells were added. One of these, the second treble, was cast by John Taylor of Loughborough 1962 and inscribed, *"In Memory of Augustine Courtauld 1904-1959. Do good"*.

In 1974 August's brother, Walter Pierre Courtauld known as Peter, donated a lifeboat with the aid of the Mayor of Poole's Appeal, Dorset, in memory of his brother. She was named the 'Augustine Courtauld'.

Augustine Courtauld's Wife:
Mollie Courtauld (later Butler) formerly Montgomerie (1907-2009)
Mollie Mongomerie was born on 10th September 1907, the eldest daughter of Frank Douglas and Esme Montogomerie formerly Napier. Her father was a descendant of Lowland Scottish farmers and ran a chicken farm at Great Codham Hall, Shalford, which he rented from the Tabor family. Mollie spent her childhood at home and was taught by a governess before she attended an Academy at Wimbledon Common and a Finishing School in Switzerland. Mollie was very musical with a lovely singing voice. At one time she sang with the Philharmonic Choir. As young ladies, Mollie and Betty Courtauld, August's sister, were good friends, so Mollie grew up spending time with the family, which included August. After her marriage to August, Mollie spent much of her life at sea, before moving to Spencers in 1937. During the Second World War while August was away, she worked for the Women's Voluntary Service (WVS), the Soldiers, Sailors Airmen and Families Association (SSAFA), and the Voluntary Aid Detachment (VAD) at Moyns Park Hospital, Birdbrook. (Moyns Park being a large country mansion). Mollie also sat as a Justice of the Peace and was on the committee for the Welfare of the Physically Handicapped and the Victoria League in Essex.

Like SAC, Mollie enjoyed Jane Austen and P G Woodhouse novels. She lectured to the Royal Society of Literature on Marcel Proust (1871-1922), a novelist, essayist and critic of whose work she was particularly fond. With her musical interests, Mollie was also a member of the board of the London Mozart Players.

After August's death in 1959, Mollie married Richard Austen Butler, known as 'RAB' (1902-1982), who was a widower. His first wife, Sydney Elizabeth formerly Courtauld was August's cousin. RAB was a Conservative Member of Parliament and, at one time, Home Secretary, Foreign Secretary, Chancellor of the Exchequer and Master of Trinity College, Cambridge. Mollie died 18th February 2009 aged 101 years old and is interred in St Mary's Parish Church Graveyard, Saffron Walden.

2. Edith Elizabeth Courtauld (1906 - 1992)
Edith Elizabeth Courtauld, known as Betty, was Samuel and Edith's only daughter, who was born on the 10th October 1906 at Little Bradfords, Bocking. Betty spent her childhood at The Howe and Noel House in London. In her early twenties she was 'part of the London scene'. Young and glamorous, Betty attended the opera, ballet and balls, and was 'presented' by Countess Minto, at the first Court of the Season held in 1931 to King George V and Queen Mary.

At the beginning of 1931 Betty announced her engagement to Captain Ralph Herbert Rayner (1897-1977). Ralph, who had recently returned from Canada, was the son of the late Reverend George and Mrs Rayner of Holmfirth, Yorkshire.

Betty Courtauld
1906 - 1992

1931

Captain Ralph Rayner
1897 - 1977

Betty and Ralph were married on the 20th June 1931 at St Andrew's Church, Halstead. It was a grand occasion and vast crowds gathered to see the happy couple. There were banners, flags and streamers, and the Band of the Middlesex Regiment played a selection of music on the Market Hill. After the ceremony had taken place, a guard of honour formed by brother officers from the Royal Signals, Aldershot, greeted the bride and groom as they left the church, before they made their way back to The Howe for their Wedding Reception. They travelled in an old fashioned barouche, lent to them by Mrs Lowe of Gosfield Hall, which had once belonged to Betty's great, great uncle, Samuel Courtauld. It was drawn by six bay horses with postillion riders, with two other riders preceding the barouche, while two more riders formed a rear guard. The carriage halted at the Courtauld Homes of Rest and Ralph saluted the residents who had waited outside for them to pass by.

The Bride and Groom in the barouche travelling to The Howe

The Bridal Group at The Howe

Left to right: Sheila Rayner, Jeanne Courtauld, Penelope Freeman-Jackson, the Bridegroom and Bride, Mollie Montgomerie, Captain B D Willoughby, Betty Vaizey, Clemency Chamen.

Three hundred and fifty people attended the Reception, and were entertained during the afternoon by the band and an aerial display given by one of Betty's friends.

Ralph and Betty lived at Kiplin Hall, near Richmond, North Yorkshire, an old house built in 1625 by Lord Baltimore. Ralph retired from the army and, in 1933, he agreed to stand as Conservative Member of Parliament for Totnes and they searched for a property in that area. They purchased Ashcombe Estate and in 1934 they built 'Ashcombe Tower', an art deco style house, designed by Brian O'Rorke, (1901-1974) near Dawlish in Devon. It was situated on the spur of Little Holdan, above Dawlish Water. The tower, which was built as an observatory in 1833, and later used as a shooting box, was incorporated into the house and became the main staircase. While their house was being built they lived at The Moors in Bishops Teignton. The Rayners were generous hosts and Neville Chamberlain was one of the many guests to visit Ashcombe Towers.

Ralph and Betty had four children:
Fleur Revere Courtauld Rayner   b. 1932
Ranulf Courtauld Rayner   b. 1935
Nicholas Courtauld Rayner   b. 1938
Andrew Piers Courtauld Rayner   b. 1942

Ralph died in 1977 and his eldest son inherited the Ashcombe Estate. Betty moved into The Old Rectory at Ashcombe and died in 1992 aged 86 years.

Today Ashcombe Tower is still owned by the Rayner family, and Ranulf and his wife Annette live in the house. Their son, Ralph runs the estate, and Giles their younger son, with his father designs and makes world renowned water features.

Edith Elizabeth Courtauld's husband:
Brigadier Sir Ralph Herbert Rayner
Ralph Rayner was born on the 13th January 1897 and had a distinguished military career. He was commissioned into the Duke of Wellington's Regiment and served as a signals officer, before being seconded to the Royal Flying Corps and promoted to Captain in 1916. He served on the the Western Front and India, and was seconded into the Indian Army 1917 and served in the 3rd Afghan War. He transferred to the Royal Corps of Signals in 1920. From 1928 to 1930 he was Aide de Camp to the Governor General of Canada. He was promoted to Major in 1933 before he retired from the army. Ralph then entered politics and became the Conservative Member of Parliament for Totnes from 1935 to 1955. He rejoined the army during the Second World War and reached the rank of Brigadier. He was a Deputy Lieutenant of Devon in 1952, knighted in 1956, and High Sheriff of Devon in 1958.

Ralph died 17th July 1977.

Ashcombe Tower
The home of Sir Ralph and Lady Betty Rayner and their family

3. Walter Pierre Courtauld (1910-1989)
Walter Pierre Courtauld (Peter) was the third child of Samuel and Edith who was born on 1st March 1910 at Bocking. He, too, was educated at Charterhouse and joined the family business in 1928, working on the 'textile' side. Having progressed through the textile manufacturing departments, Peter was appointed to the Board of Courtaulds Limited in 1938, and was one of its youngest full time Directors. Although he remained a Director during the Second World War he was absent from the company for most of the time as he served in the Welsh Guards.

Peter married Faith Dorothy Caldwell Cook, 1913-2004, the only daughter of Arthur Caldwell Cook of Little Batsford, Gerrards Cross, Buckinghamshire, on the 13th January 1940 at Holy

Trinity Church, Consort Road, London. A war time wedding, the groom wore his army uniform. The reception took place at his parents house at Palace Green.

The Bride and Groom - 1940

Peter and Faith had four children:
Simon Pierre Courtauld	1940
Sarah Louise Courtauld	1943
Richard Savill Courtauld	1946
Julia Elizabeth Courtauld	1949

After the war Peter continued at Courtaulds Limited until he retired in 1965. He was a Non-Executive Director from 1959 to 1962 and the Deputy Chairman from 1962 to 1965.

During the mid 1950s Peter and Faith lived in London at St John's Wood, before they moved to a house near Petersfield, Hampshire, at the end of the 1950s. Peter and Faith were divorced and in 1966 Peter married Sylvia Davis. Their daughter Martha Jane was born in 1967, followed by a son Jonathan Louis Courtauld born 1970. Peter died in July 1989 having moved to Wadhurst, East Sussex.

Faith married again in 1971. Her second husband was James Scott Elliott.

'Cheeky chaps' enjoying themselves at a garden party!
John Steed (on the left) and Brian Benham 'posing' on the steps outside
The Howe drawing room windows
Courtesy of John Steed

From left to right: Peter Barker, ?, Brian Benham, John Steed
Courtesy of John Steed

Chapter Twelve
Staff employed by Samuel and Edith Courtauld

Over the years a large number of staff worked for the Courtauld family both at The Howe and Noel House. The more senior members of both households often travelled with the family between their two properties and resided in either Halstead or London when necessary. Some of the staff 'lived in', while others resided in Courtauld owned houses and cottages, or, with their families in the neighbouring area. *(A list of some of the 'live in' staff at both The Howe and Noel House taken from various Electoral Registers from c1920 to c1953, can be found in appendices IV and V. Some members of staff appear twice within the same year as they were registered at both properties. Please note that during the Second World War years Electoral Registers were not published).*

The household at The Howe would have included a butler, housekeeper, cook, maids, general domestic servants, and a footman, together with a coachman, later a chauffeur, a game keeper, numerous gardeners and estate workers. The following are just a few of the staff who worked for the Courtauld family and include chauffeurs, gardeners and butlers.

The Chauffeurs
Charles William Flood, who was the first chauffeur to be employed by SAC, worked for him while he was living at Little Bradfords in Bocking. Charles was born in 1870 at Great Yarmouth and married Ellen Utting in 1893. They had two children, Irene and Percy and, in 1901 the family lived in Haverhill, Suffolk, where Charles worked as a coachman. He joined SAC's household as a chauffeur and was employed to drive his primitive De Dion Bouton, a French manufactured car, in the days when few British Cars were invented! By 1911 Charles had left Bocking and worked as a 'motor driver' for a gentleman in Ipswich. His daughter Irene remained at Little Bradfords where she worked as a maid and later married James Newson in 1916 at Hammersmith, London.

Leonard Howard was the second chauffeur employed by SAC. He was born in 1888, the son of Herbert and Frances Howard. In 1901 Leonard, a schoolboy, lived with his family at Woodfield, Braintree. By 1911, at the age of twenty two years, Leonard was already employed as a chauffeur in SAC's household. His father, who worked in the boot making industry had moved to Maldon, leaving Leonard and his brother Percy in Braintree. The two brothers boarded with the Suckling family in Rayne Road.

Commenting on going out in the car circa 1911, Augustine Courtauld wrote in his book 'Man the Ropes', *"Our great treat was being taken out in the car, an open Argyll which clucked like a hen. Motoring was a bit of an adventure. There was always the hazard of getting the car up a hill in top: It wasn't done to change gear…………..If there was a fog, my father considered that the proper thing to do was to walk in front* (of the car) *while his man Howard, took the wheel"*.

In 1911 SAC employed a Parlour maid, Alice Humphry Diggons (1872-1941). While they worked together at Little Bradfords, Leonard and Alice apparently fell in love and married in 1914. They moved to Halstead when the Courtauld family acquired The Howe as Leonard continued his employment as SAC's chauffeur. Leonard and Alice were living at 25 Box Mill Lane when Alice died in 1941. Leonard married secondly, Jane Amy Woolgar in 1943 and they continued to live in the same house. As well as being SAC's chauffeur, Leonard was also his 'loader'. (The name given to someone who 'loads' the shotguns while out on a shoot). Leonard remained with SAC until he retired and died in 1951, shortly before SAC died in 1953, having given over forty years of faithful service.

Albert Saunders, his third chauffeur was born about 1889. In 1911 Albert lodged with Alfred Lee at Park Cottage, Gosfield, and worked for George Courtauld at Cut Hedge. Albert married Margaret Saward in 1914 and they lived in Gosfield. During the First World War Albert served in France and acted as Earl Haig's chauffeur. He was wounded and lost a leg, but, with the use of an artificial replacement, he continued to drive. Upon his recovery Albert returned as chauffeur to George Courtauld.

Albert remained at Cut Hedge until 1919 leaving shortly before George Courtauld died in 1920. SAC who had known Albert for many years offered him employment at The Howe and he became Edith Courtauld's personal chauffeur. One of his duties included driving the family between The Howe and Noel House, and taking them around London when they were in residence. This would have involved long periods away from home for Albert.

Albert and Margaret moved into one of the Howe Cottages on Wash Hill, where they lived until they moved to Box Mill Cottages in about 1923 shortly before Howe Cottages were demolished.

The Howe had its own electric light plant which provided the Courtauld family with their source of power and it was another of Albert's duties to make sure it ran properly. (The Howe was not connected to the National Grid until the end of the 1950s).

Albert died c1944 and Margaret lived at Abel Cottages for a number of years before she moved away from Halstead.

Nelson Peapell was one of the last chauffeurs to be employed by the Courtauld family. He was born in 1914 Nr Malmesbury in Wiltshire and married Agnes Scott in 1939 in the Newmarket District. While working for SAC, Nelson and Agnes lived in one of the Courtauld houses situated in Colchester Road. Nelson, too, would drive the family to London, and stayed in a mews house near to Noel House, which was provided by SAC for his chauffeurs. Nelson was not in SAC's employment for very many years before SAC died. However he was one of the pall bearers at SAC's funeral.

Gardeners
Numerous gardeners were required to work in The Howe gardens which were always immaculate. As well as the flowers, lawns, shrubs and vegetables there were huge glass houses filled with plants, ferns and various fruits, a very large 'walled in' garden, vines, a rhubarb house and an orchard to be maintained, along with woodland areas, meadows, ponds and a tennis court, as well as live stock to be cared for. At one time a large vegetable garden ran from the south side of the Bailiffs/Gardeners Cottage, along the length of Howe Chase. The soil was not very fertile and much patience and skill was needed to produce decent crops!

Frederick William Alston, known as Freddie, was born in 1869 at Cooks Yard, North Street, Halstead, the son of William (1839-1906) a French polisher, and Mary Anne Alston formerly Newton (c1840-1918). By 1881 the Alston family had moved to Boars Head Yard, North Street where they remained for at least twenty years. Freddie began his employment as a gardener's assistant and by 1901 he was employed as a domestic gardener. He probably worked at The Howe, as, eight years later, when Anne Hornor made her will, she left 'Fred Alston' a legacy.

In 1911 at the time of his marriage to Emily Rose Pamplin, Freddie lived with his widowed mother and two brothers, Herbert and Walter, at Belle Vue Cottages. Emily, was born in 1878 at Sible Hedingham, the daughter of Samuel and Maria Pamplin formerly Dyson. When Emily married Freddie, she was employed by Mrs Elizabeth Tayler of Ashford Lodge, as a cook.

Freddie and Emily moved into 'Howe Gardens' (Bailiffs Cottage/Gardeners Cottage) in 1921. Freddie was a colourful character who always wore celluloid collars on his shirts and a straw boater in the summer. He worked at The Howe as a gardener until 1954 when the estate was sold. Emily also worked for the Courtauld family when they required extra help in the house. After SAC's death, Freddie and Emily, who had served the family for forty years moved to the Courtauld Homes of Rest, where they remained until Freddie died in 1957 aged 88 years, and Emily died in 1962 aged 84 years.

Ebenezer Pamplin who was Emily's brother, was born in 1881 and in 1911 lived with his widowed mother at Cobbs Fenn, Sible Hedingham and worked as a stockman. In 1930 Ebenezer lived with the Alstons at Howe Gardens where he died in December, aged 49 years.

Victor George Cross, known as George, was born in 1890 at West Strickland, Dorset, the son of George (1858-1910), a horse carter, and Martha Ann Cross (c1859-1916) formerly House. A gardener for all of his working life, George started his gardening career in Viscount Portman's garden at Blandford, Dorset. He later moved to Poltimore Park, Exeter, Devon, where he worked as a journeyman gardener for Lord Poltimore. (This estate was sold in 1921, although the house remained within the family until 1944). By 1911 George was employed at The Gardens, Eastwell Park, Ashford, Kent, another stately house, and the home of Lady Northgate. He continued to learn his trade, and was a gardener journeyman with four other lads, under the watchful eye of John Weston, the head gardener. (Eastwell Park once served as a Royal Residence before it was demolished in 1926).

George married Elizabeth Ann Coombes in 1916 at Ashford and they had a daughter, Kathleen Dorothy, who was born in 1919. Later George was employed by the Christie family as a gardener, at Tapeley Park, Instow, Devon, a magnificent stately home. At Tapeley Park, he worked in the beautiful gardens which were created by Lady Rosamond Christie, including the Italian Garden, which is still much admired today. For five years before he moved to Halstead, George worked for The Duke of Devonshire at Chatsworth, Derbyshire, where as a foreman gardener he managed a team of fifty under gardeners.

From about 1926 George worked for SAC at The Howe, a position he held for twenty years. George lived with his family at Abel Cottages and, as head gardener, he was responsible for the upkeep of The Howe gardens and grounds, and for the welfare of the under gardeners who worked for him. When the Courtauld family were in residence at Noel House, it was his responsibility too, to see that fresh fruit and vegetables from the estate were sent up to London daily. In 1931 when Betty Courtauld married Captain Ralph Rayner, it was George and his team who had grown and produced all the magnificent flowers and foliage which decorated St. Andrew's Church and the house.

George, with his cheerful disposition was well known among the horticulturalists in Essex. He was good with plants and a successful exhibitor at local shows, and as a highly respected gardener he was frequently invited to judge exhibits at venues held around the County. He was a member of the Halstead Constitutional Club and served on the General and Entertainments Committee. George also enjoyed a game of snooker, and for ten years he was secretary of the Widdop Snooker Cup competition.

*Victor George Cross 1890-1946
Courtesy of Angela and David Kerrison*

When George suffered from ill health due to the effects from gas poisoning in the trenches during World War One, SAC ensured that he received the best treatment possible. Sadly George did not recover and died in a London Hospital in 1946 aged 56 years. Elizabeth moved to Head Street before she lived in one of the Coutauld Homes of Rest, from 1956 until 1971. She died in 1973 aged 86 years. Both George and Elizabeth are interred in Halstead Cemetery.

Kathleen Dorothy Cross (1919-2001) worked in the Design Office at Courtaulds before she married Kenneth James Kerrison (1915-1987) at Halstead in 1940. Kenneth and Kathleen's son David, worked as a weaver at Courtaulds for two years and, later on in his working life was employed as a handloom weaver at the Humphries Silk Weaving Company. The last piece of fabric David wove was the yellow 63inch Silk Damask which was used at Osborne House, Isle of Wight.

Ernest Arthur Snowden was born in 1900 at Boars Head Yard. He was the son of William, a brickmaker's labourer and Edith Ada Snowden, formerly Diss, who were both born in 1878. Ernest lived in Halstead with his siblings until he married Violet May Finch who was born in 1906, the daughter of John and Ellen Finch of Swan Street, Sible Hedingham. They had two daughters, Jean born in 1930 and Hilda in 1938. Ernest worked as a gardener at The Howe for thirty eight years and lived with his family at 'Northanger Abbey', Mill Chase. Following SAC's death, Ernest's daughter Hilda, brother Claude and sister Hilda were part of a team of bell ringers, who rang a tribute quarter peal in memory of SAC. Following his employment at The Howe, Ernest worked for a short time as a grave digger at Halstead Cemetery before he died in 1959 aged 58 years.

In The Howe Grounds
(a watercolour)
Courtesy of David and Angela Kerrison

Butlers
Charles Plumb was born in 1865 at Sible Hedingham. In 1891 he worked for George and Serena Courtauld as a footman at Cut Hedge, but by 1901 he had been promoted and was their butler. Charles married Ellen Knight in 1901 at Kingston upon Thames. Ellen was born 1873 at Hampton, Middlesex. After their marriage they lived at White Ash Green and their daughter, Mabel, was born in 1905. By 1911 Charles, Ellen and Mabel had moved into one of the cottages at Cut Hedge. After George Courtauld died Charles was employed by SAC as his butler. He worked at both The Howe and Noel House and travelled with the Courtauld family to London when they were in residence. Charles disliked London and much preferred working in the country. On one occasion while they were in London, thieves broke into Noel House, and drank the port. As SAC was a connoisseur they must have tasted some of the best port available. Charles was not amused! Charles lived at Abel Cottages until he retired to Colne Engaine, where he died in 1935.

One amusing anecdote involved Charles Plumb whilst he was employed by George Courtauld at Cut Hedge:- George Courtauld was driven daily to his three factories at Bocking, Braintree and Halstead. He travelled in a carriage which was driven by his coachman and spent time at each factory. While he was attending to matters at the Bocking factory his coachman would frequently nip across the road to the 'Black Boy' public house for a drink! On one occasion George Courtauld found he needed to return to Cut Hedge quickly as he had left his briefcase behind. Unable to find his coachman, he leapt onto the box and drove the carriage home himself. Charles Plumb heard the carriage arrive at the house and rushed to open the door to find the carriage empty. Without looking up at the coachman, Charles shouted out to him, "What have you done with the old b....r"? To which George Courtauld replied, "The old b....r is up here"! The following day the coachman was summoned by George Courtauld who told him, that the next time he wished to take a holiday, could he kindly have the courtesy of letting him know in advance! The incident did not appear to jeopardise Charles Plumb's employment with the family as he continued to work for George Courtauld and was left a legacy in his will.

Andrew Kiely who was a charming, dark haired Irishman with a 'theatrical' air, joined the Courtauld household at Noel House in 1945. When his duties took him to Halstead, Andrew did not 'live in' at The Howe, as he had lodgings in Colchester Road. Stephen Courtauld, SAC's grandson, can remember visiting his grandparents at The Howe when he was a boy and relates: *"At precisely one the gong was stentoriously rung by Kiely in a black tail coat and we trooped in silence into a long dining room. We were handed soup, main course and pudding with silent respect by a high-capped black uniformed maid and Kiely, who remained standing while we scoffed"*. Kiely remained at The Howe with SAC until 1953 and was one of the pall bearers at his funeral. (Andrew's life in service included working for King Peter of Yugoslavia, after the King sought exile in London and for Vic Oliver, the comedian).

Bernard Turkentine was born in 1929 at Colchester the son of Frank and Lily Ethel Turkentine formerly Root. With his parents and sister Elaine, the family moved back to Halstead at the beginning of the Second World War, when they feared that as a garrison town Colchester could be targeted by the Germans for bombing raids. They lived in a cottage in Hedingham Road for a while, but with the addition of another daughter, Sandra born in 1942, the family moved to Bousser Cottages. As one of the Courtauld built houses, the rent at this time was collected by Jack Salmon who worked for Stanley Moger, who had an office at Halstead. When Bernard was fourteen years old he applied for the position of a gardener at The Howe, however the vacancy had been filled and he was offered the position of under butler instead. Bernard accepted and he was soon taken to London to work at Noel House when the Courtauld family were in residence. It must have been both an exciting and daunting experience for the young man! When Bernard's mother and sisters visited him in London they stayed over night in Nelson Peapell's residence in Kensington. Unfortunately after about four and a half years, Bernard was forced to leave and enlist for compulsory National Service. When he returned to Halstead, Bernard entered the building trade. He married Evelyne Barthels in 1951 at Halstead and they had three daughters; Melanie born 1952, Elaine in 1954 and Lorraine in 1957. Bernard died in 2012.

Other Staff known to have been employed at The Howe included:
Harvey James Chudley was born in 1891, the son of Florence Chudley who lived with her mother Martha in Westminster, London. Florence had previously worked as a domestic servant for Lord and Lady Esme Angel Gordon at Little Paxton, Huntingdonshire. In 1911 Harvey worked as

a clerk for the Gaslight and Coke Company, when he joined the 23rd Battalion of the London Regiment Territorial Army, for a minimum of four years. He married Gertrude Wigzell in 1914 at Woolwich. Gertrude who was born in 1891 was the daughter of Moses and Elizabeth Wigzell.

Harvey and Gertrude had nine children, Harvey, Dorothy, Florence, Winifred, Irene, Leslie, Gladys, Douglas and Raymond, who were all born in London, between 1914 and 1930. Harvey and Gertrude were originally employed at Noel House although between 1945 and 1951, they travelled with SAC and EAC between London and Halstead. In 1951 they moved to Box Mill Cottages where they remained until Harvey died in 1959 aged 69 years. Gertrude died in 1967.

Sophia Ann Powter was born in 1869 the daughter of George and Emma Powter. George was an agricultural machinist and the family lived in the village of Shalford. In 1911 both Sophia and her elder sister Clara Jane were employed by the Courtauld's at Little Bradfords. Sophia was a housemaid and Clara a cook. Clara died in 1916, but Sophia remained with the family and moved to Halstead with them until she retired in 1937, after at least 26 years faithful service. She moved to Shepherds Compton, Berkshire where she died in 1938. Leonard Howard, chauffeur at The Howe was her Executor.

Beatrice Smith was born in Lewisham in 1903. She attend the Guard School as her father was with the Grenadier Guards South Africa Reserve. Beatrice was a lady's maid employed at Noel House in 1929, and, like most of the staff, travelled between London and Halstead with the Courtauld family. She married Henry Hill in Lewisham in 1931.

Jack Argent, nicknamed 'Tina', because of his surname, (Argent - Argen<u>tina</u>) lived in 'Pride', one of the houses opposite the Dog Inn in Hedingham Road. He worked for the Courtaulds as a chauffeur/handyman before he was employed at the Foundry.

Agnes Booth, was employed as a lady's maid by EAC towards the end of the Second World War and spent her time in both London and Halstead. She remained with the family until SAC died in 1953.

Henry/Harry Brown, was a head kitchen gardener who lived at Abel Cottages. He was renowned for having a lovely garden at his cottage..

Janet Drury, was employed as a daily help. **L. Lewis,** was a gardener who resided at Gosfield.

Mr and Mrs Thompson lived at Bousser Cottages, next door to the Turkentine family. When the Thompsons moved **Mr S.G. Rose** with his wife and small son were the next occupants. Both gentlemen were under gardeners at The Howe.

George Tibble, was a gardener.

Lily Turkentine, was employed as a daily help.

Also **Mrs Light** and **Mr W Shelley** - details of employment unknown.

All Aboard!

Members of the Baptist Church, outside The Manse in Hedingham Road hitching a lift to The Howe to attend a garden party when SAC was in residence. In the centre, standing, is Willie Hughes whose mother in law Mrs. Smith owned 'Smith's Bazaar' at the bottom of Halstead High Street.

Harold Ainsworth Peto

Harold Ainsworth Peto 1854-1933 was the eighth child of Sir Samuel Peto of Somerleyton Hall, Suffolk. He was educated at Harrow, and trained as an architect. In 1871 he went into partnership with Ernest George until it was dissolved in 1892 when Peto became disenchanted with London. He then began a career in garden design. Peto loved the Italian Renaissance period and travelled to Italy incorporating an Italian style into his gardens. He undertook a number of commissions, including one from Samuel Courtauld at The Howe. Influenced by the arts and craft movement Peto created a style that was sympathetic to the countryside around him. Before The Howe was sold to the developers most of the statues and stone used by Peto in the gardens was removed.

Chapter Thirteen
Noel House, Palace Green, London and Eastry, Frinton on Sea, Essex

Noel House

Samuel and Edith Courtauld spent a considerable amount of time travelling between The Howe and Noel House, their city residence, which was number 8 Palace Green, London W8. The house was designed by Horace Field and Charles Evelyn Simmons who were two architects with a practice in Westminster from 1906 to 1915. They were assisted by Amos Faulkner (1867-1940) who was also an architect. The house, a large, imposing red brick property was built in 1908 in one of the most opulent areas of London, which was then known as 'Millionaires Row'. The Courtauld family bought the house in around 1916, from Claude Goldsmid Joseph Montefiore (1858-1938), a prominent Jewish theologian and Reform leader.

Noel House, 8 Palace Green, London W8. 1971
Courtesy of City of London Corporation

A London property was required by SAC so that he could attend to his business commitments in the City of London where Courtauld's had company offices. A good many weeks of the year were spent at Noel House and a large number of staff worked and 'lived in', especially during the 1930s. In 1930, there were eleven staff listed on the electoral roll, plus the chauffeur who drove the Courtauld family between Noel House and The Howe. The butler also spent much of his time travelling between London or Halstead, and was busy running the two households. The house was used by all the family and, no doubt, they entertained many of London's aristocrat families when they were in residence, especially around the early 1930s when Betty was a debutante. Peter held his Wedding Reception at the house in 1940 when he married Faith Cook.

The Hall, Noel House, 8 Palace Green, London W8. 1971
Reproduced courtesy of City of London Corporation

Noel House was sold in 1951 following the death of Edith Courtauld, and for a time was the home of one of the Dutch Ambassadors.

Today Palace Green is described as a wide avenue, which runs from the southern end of Kensington Park Gardens to High Street, Kensington. It is lined with magnificent detached mansions, creating a mixture of Ambassadorial residences and family homes and is now known as 'Billionaires Row'! Noel House is divided into apartments.

Eastry

Eastry, Third Avenue, Frinton on Sea, was built on land that once formed part of a golf course, which was founded in 1895. The house was designed in 1906 by architects Harrington, Ley and Tompkins, who had offices in London and Romford as well as an Estate Office in Frinton. The house was built by Hawkins and Son for Miss Rose. When the house was first built it was named 'Wismar' before it was bought by Samuel Courtauld in about 1911 as a seaside holiday house for his family.

The house included a drawing room, dining room, bedroom, hall, kitchen, scullery, larder, W.C., coal house, tool shed and a verandah on the ground floor; Upstairs there were four bedrooms, a box room, bathroom, W.C., linen cupboard and a large balcony. Alterations were made to the house in 1913 when another bedroom was added. As the house was intended mostly for Edith Courtauld and the children's use, it was almost certainly EAC who changed its name to 'Eastry', after the village in Kent where she grew up.

Family holidays were evidently great fun and the family would set off in their car loaded with not only the usual holiday buckets and spades, but with all the family pets as well, which included the cat and 'Tort', the tortoise. Eastry was sold around 1933 when Miss Lee, the new owner, applied to make alterations to the house. It is perhaps interesting to note that in 1949 when grand houses were being converted into flats and retirements homes there was Council opposition to the application made by Miss Lee to change Eastry, by then a sixteen roomed mansion house, into four flats. However Council approval was eventually given to the application.

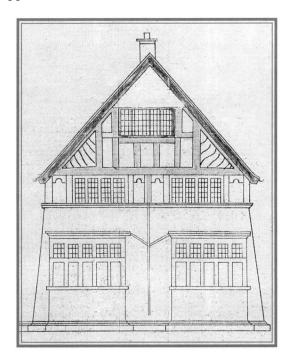

Plans of Eastry showing the front and back elevations
Reproduced by courtesy of Essex Record Office

In the Howe Grounds, looking towards Halstead
(a watercolour)
Courtesy of Angela and David Kerrison

Chapter Fourteen
The Howe – Auction of 1953

After the death of Samuel Courtauld in January 1953, his Executors instructed Balls and Balls, Castle Hedingham to sell by auction, pieces of antique and other furniture. The sale took place at The Howe on three consecutive days in October 1953. A large number of lots were for sale and included:

Turkey, Axminster, and Oriental carpets and rugs
Grandfather clocks
Book cases and writing desks
Queen Anne style dining chairs, Chippendale style chairs and Chesterfield settees
Sideboards and china cabinets
Decorative china, including, an exceptional Hedingham vase* (Bingham Pottery of Castle Hedingham)
Bronze and marble ornaments
China, glass and earthenware
Oil paintings, watercolours and engravings
Blunderbuss and antique duelling pistols
Library containing 1500 books
Large quantity of silver, including Georgian silver and silver plate
Bedroom suites
Numerous garden chairs and seats
Lead figure ornaments and sundial
Poultry houses etc.

Needless to say the auction attracted a vast number of people from far and wide, and bidding was very keen especially among the private sector.

Some of the principal prices realised were:

Oriental rugs	£20
Georgian mahogany grandfather clock	£36
Carved mahogany library table	£30
Marquetry inlaid rosewood writing table	£19
Chesterfield settee	£15
Carved oak dining room table	£80
Royal Crown Derby dessert set	£14
Dresden cups and saucers	£27
Oil painting by R. Nightingale - Hunting Scene	£21
Blunderbuss	£17
Pair of duelling pistols	£30
21 volumes of Hardy's works	£10
17 volumes Charles Dickens work	£40
Pair silver Corinthian column candlesticks	£19
George III engraved silver teapot	£31
Mahogany bow fronted bedroom suite	£165
Garden ornaments	£16 to £25 each
Portable poultry house	£12

*An exceptional Hedingham vase. This item was a Porsenna vase, which either remained unsold at the auction, or was withdrawn by Samuel Courtauld's executors before the sale, as it was later donated to Colchester Museum.

The Porsenna vase was a fine piece of Hedingham Pottery made by Edward Bingham (1829-1916), and it was one of his most ambitious pieces. It was pale blue with off white relief work depicting two scenes of ancient Roman history. One showed ordeal by fire, designed to portray Porsenna, the fortitude of the Roman character, and the other showed youthful hostages who were to be freed by order of Porsenna.

The Porsenna vase designed and made by Edward Bingham of Castle Hedingham and presented to the Colchester Museum November 1953.

Chapter Fifteen

The development of The Howe Estate during the mid 1950s including Howe Chase, Howe Drive and Ashlong Grove

In February 1954 before Ralph van Asch bought part of The Howe Estate from Samuel Courtauld's Executors, he submitted an outline planning application to the Halstead Urban District Council. He wanted to see how a request to develop part of The Howe Grounds for residential purposes would be received by the councillors. The General Purposes Committee welcomed the proposals, subject to all the proposed properties being connected to the main sewer and water supply, which could only be sited over a restricted area, and that the development layout was arranged so that any specimen trees would be preserved.

The following is a copy of the decision notice sent to Ralph van Asch by the former Halstead Urban District Council following his outline application.

"County Council of Essex (outline) Application, Town and County Planning Act 1947.
Town and Country Planning Development Order 1950.
Urban District of Halstead to Mr Ralph van Asch.

In pursuance of the powers exercised by them on behalf of The County Council of Essex as local planning authority this Council do hereby give notice of the decision on your outline application to GRANT PERMISSION for the following development:-

The erection of dwelling houses situate at The Howe, Halstead, Essex (Area coloured pink on Plan) in accordance with the plan(s) accompanying the application: subject to compliance with the following conditions:-

1.   *(1) As regards 'A' coloured pink on attached plan:*

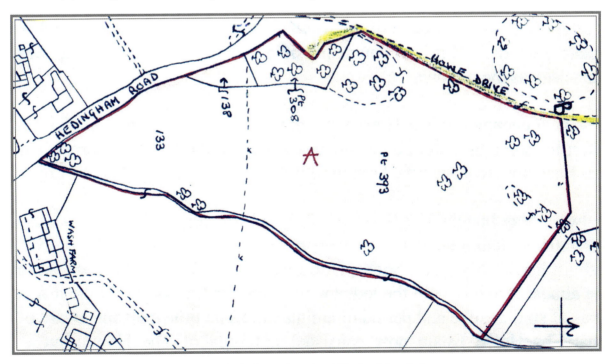

Attached plan, showing 'A' edged in pink

(1) The submission and approval of detailed plans and particulars showing the layout of the roads and siting and elevations of all intended buildings.

(2) The development shall be staged so that the development of the southern half of the land is substantially completed before development of land forming the northern half is concerned.

(3) 110' x 55' clear visibility splays shall be provided at the junction of the estate road with A.604.

(4) The new estate road shall enter the A.604 about the site of the existing drive and shall connect at right angles with the main road. For a distance of about 80 feet back from the main road the estate road shall be straight and at a point not nearer than this the existing drive shall be diverted into the new estate road and that part of the drive nearer the main road shall be closed.

(5) The layout shall be designed so as to conserve the wooded character of the site, no trees being felled without prior consultation with the local planning authority.

<u>General</u> *This permission shall not be valid unless the plans and particulars referred to in condition (1) above are submitted to the local planning authority within a period of three years from the date hereof.*

The reasons for the foregoing conditions are as follows:
(1) The particulars submitted are insufficient to enable detailed consideration of the application.

(2) So as to preserve as much land as possible in agricultural use.

(3) In order that vehicles emerging from the access shall have good visibility both up and down the main road.

(4) So as to restrict access to one point and design the access so as to secure maximum safety.

(5) So as to preserve the beauty of this approach into the town.

<u>General</u> *To prevent an accumulation of applications in respect of which no detailed plans have been submitted.*

<u>Note to applicant</u>
It is considered that any buildings erected on this estate should be of a high standard of design. This site is placed in a most attractive landscape and any new development should be planned so as to harmonise with its surroundings. In considering detailed plans the local planning authority will have regard to this.

DATED 28th day of April 1954.
Red House,   *(Signed) Ronald Long*
Halstead, Essex   *(Clerk of the Council)".*

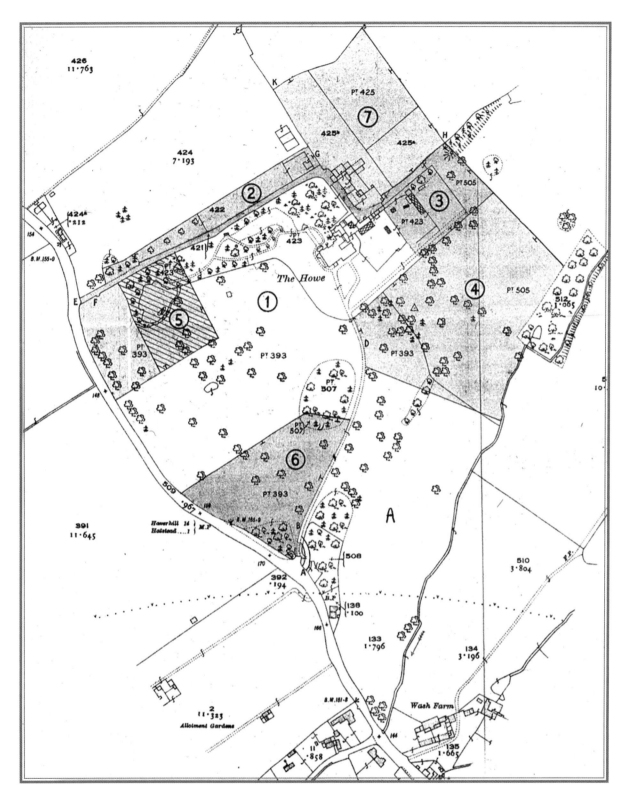

Plan of The Howe Estate

The plan of The Howe Estate taken from the sale catalogue of Messrs Balls & Balls in conjunction with Messrs Whatley Hill & Co. 1954, using a section of the 1923 Ordnance Survey map, third edition. Part of 'A' formed the remaining area of land bought by van Asch designated for 'The Howe Building Estate', later Ashlong Grove.

As van Asch's intentions met with general approval, he completed his purchase of 42.241 acres of The Howe Estate in May 1954, and in June took out a mortgage with Barclays Bank.

Enclosure numbers on Ordnance Survey map 1923 edition		Decimal	Acreage:
Part	425	4.500	estimated
	425a	.765	
	425b	1.204	
	423	5.910	
	421	.387	
	422 including cottage	1.108	
	423a	.252	
	393	19.184	
	507	.737	
Part	505	5.800	estimated
	508	.498	
	138	.100	
	133	1.796	
Total acres		42.241	

In early July 1954 van Asch was granted a building licence to carry out the work of building roads and drainage for a small private housing development in The Howe Grounds, commonly known as The Howe Building Estate. At this time van Asch also requested assistance in providing water mains to the Estate.

On the 24th November 1954 The Howe and part of its Estate totalling about 30 acres was offered for sale at public auction by van Asch. This took place at The Bull Hotel, Halstead and the auctioneers were Messrs Balls and Balls of Castle Hedingham, in conjunction with Messrs Whatley Hill and Company of London.

There were seven lots for sale:
Lot 1. The Howe
Lot 2. Detatched cottage and spinney
Lot 3. Building site with glass houses and gardens and driveway
Lot 4. Accommodation land
Lot 5. Building site
Lot 6. Accommodation land
Lot 7. Small farmery and area of farm land

Extracts taken from the sale catalogue.
Lot 1.
The Howe. The residence is situated close to the town of Halstead. It is reached by a gravelled drive through thickly timbered parkland and stands on high ground commanding extensive views over undulating well timbered country. It is well screened by the timbered park and plantations. The house is well built in brick, the greater part being stuccoed with slate roof.
The accommodation is as follows:
Main Hall
Lobby, cloakroom and separate WC
An electric lift to the first floor

Drawing room
Library
Study
Dining room
Staff sitting room
Back hall, kitchen and scullery
Housekeeper's room
Cheese store, dairy, and butler's pantry
Small sitting room and serving lobby
Extensive cellars with wine compartments
A wide oak staircase with massive balusters
16 bedrooms (one bedroom was formerly the day nursery, and one was formerly a school room)
4 bathrooms

Outside:
Lean-to boiler house
Range of brick, flint and slated buildings forming:
Knife house, store, WC, coal house, store house, power house, 2 store places
Lean-to building containing water storage tank.
Steel fire escape staircases to various parts of the residence

Out buildings comprise:
2 brick, flint Slate and iron Garages for 4 cars with hot pipes
Large partly covered-in wash down in front;
Brick, flint and slate stabling in 2 loose boxes and 2 stalls and harness room with loft over part
Brick and flint and slate range of fertilizer store, potato store, tool house with loft over and large lean-to potting shed
2 outside WC's
The delightful grounds are a special feature of the property.
There are lawns in front and to the side of the residence
Large sunken circular rose garden with flag stone paths, dwarf walls and a brick and tiled summer house
Extensive undulating garden with rustic summer house, gravel paths and shady walks beautifully decorated with ornamental and other trees
Choice rhododendrons, laurels, bamboo and other grasses
Berberis and other shrubs, magnolias and Judas trees
Rockeries with fountains
Large well maintained walled-in kitchen and flower garden with ornamental iron gates, and having choice fruit trees on the walls
Glass house
Together with well timbered parkland an area of about 11½ acres.

Lot 2.
Attractive country cottage with garden and plantations - approximately 1 acre
The cottage is built of brick with a slate roof and contains:
Sitting room
Living room with modern tiled stove and hearth
Scullery

3 bedrooms
Outside coal store and WC
Garden and plantations

Lot 3.
Building site.
Forming part of the gardens of the Estate with valuable greenhouses extending in all to about 2 acres
This lot stands in a fine position with charming views to the south over unspoilt country. It forms part of the garden to The Howe and is in excellent cultivation.
Lean to heated glass house 24ft x 8ft 9 ins
Span divided heated glass house 40ft x 15ft
Large lean to heated glass house about 74ft x 16ft with vines and fruit trees
Brick and slate potting shed with boiler
Brick and slate lean-to rhubarb house
Fruit store, fuel bunker, 2 large garden frames with lights
Large tennis court with thatched summer house
Extensive flower borders
Outline town planning permission obtained for no more than two private houses.

Lot 4.
Accommodation land.
6 and one third acres well timbered with mature and well grown oak, elm amd other trees.

Lot 5.
Building site.
With charming ornamental water garden with small lake fed by a spring
Park and woodland
Outline town planning consent for one house, approximately 2¾ acres

Lot 6.
Accommodation land.
2¾ acres of well timbered land

Lot 7.
Small farmery with an area of agricultural land over 3½ acres
Including squash court, which would convert into living accommodation if so desired
Brick, timber and slate cattle shed with mangers and cow house for 4 cows
Slated 3 bay open shed
Large brick, flint, timber, slate and asphalt building squash racket court
Incubator house
Straw store and large barn
Lean-to timber and slate piggeries
Brick, flint and slate building forming 2 loose boxes
Lean-to slated meal house
Brick and slate coal house
Timber and four bay open cart lodge

2 bay extensive timber and slate open shed with loft over
Large brick and slate poultry house
2 cattle yards
3 enclosures of rough pasture and arable land.

Unfortunately none of the lots were sold at auction and van Asch was left with a serious problem. The original plan to sell designated areas of land appeared to be no longer feasible and he decided to let prospective buyers have the freedom to negotiate and purchase their own parcels of land.

The formation of Howe Chase: On 8th July 1955 van Asch sold 12.927 acres of land at the rear of The Howe to Thomas William Richard Grant of Halstead. This comprised of enclosure numbers: 421, 422, 425a & b and parts of 423, 425 and 505, detailed on the 1923 Ordnance Survey map, third edition. *(See page 141)*, and access was via Howe Chase, (the back drive to The Howe).

This land was eventually divided into four plots, which were sold individually and four properties were built. Thomas Grant and his wife Elizabeth moved into the Bailiffs or Gardeners Cottage, known as Howe Cottage in 1955/56, where they remained for a short time. They started a business 'Howe Nursery Holding', probably to make use of the very large glass houses which were situated behind The Howe, however this venture was short lived. The Grants placed a prefabricated building on one of the plots of land and moved out of Howe Cottage. They lived in the 'prefab' while their house was built for them by Ernie Smith. Upon completion, the Grants moved into the house which was named 'Woodlands' in 1960.

Meanwhile, Ernie obtained a plot of land next to Woodlands and built a house for himself to live in which was named Naas. These two dwellings originally faced east and looked out towards Sudbury Road. The boundary line between The Howe and Grant's land ran from east to west, and crossed over a track which ran from The Howe's front drive, through part of the garden and passed the front of the newly erected houses. While The Howe was unoccupied, Thomas Grant and Ernie Smith used the track and Howe Drive, but this stopped when The Howe was sold in 1957. Howe Chase was extended and access to Grant's land was reinstated correctly. The two properties altered their dwellings accordingly; front doors facing westwards! Even today pieces of tarmac from the original track are unearthed in the vegetable garden at Woodlands. A third dwelling was built with its front elevation facing Howe Chase and occupied by 1966/67.

After the Grants left Howe Cottage it was occupied by Arthur, known as Mick, and Edith Osborne. Their son Ray ran a mobile grocery business and visited Ashlong Grove as well as some of the surrounding villages. They also ran a small holding and traces of its existence are visible today. When Howe Cottage was sold, a new house was built which was attached to the cottage and included in the new building.

In the garden of Woodlands, an old wooden shelter was located which once stood next to The Howe tennis court. It was used by the Courtauld family who sat in it while they enjoyed a cup of tea, brought to them, in later life, by the under butler, Bernard Turkentine. Lawns and a flower garden now cover the court. Also in the original back garden stood a very large water tank which served all four dwellings; this was transported c1975 to The Colne Valley Railway Preservation Society, Castle Hedingham, where it is believed part of its structure was used in the construction of its present tank.

The formation of Howe Drive: On 5th December 1955, the piece of land which practically incorporated the entire plot of lot 6 in the auction catalogue, was sold to Major Michael Portway. It consisted of 2.81 acres and was formed from enclosure numbers part 393 and part 505. Michael built a very interesting single storey dwelling. It was the first house that Ronald Mobbs, ARIBA, designed entirely by himself. It was constructed above ground of double lignacite concrete blocks, these being two walled with a cavity between, and had two flat roofs. One roof sloped west to east and one sloped south to north. They were both made from laminated board, covered in pitch with heavy gauge roofing felt bonded to it, and then covered with small stones. (*For full house details please see Appendix number VI*). The house was built by J S Norton, Builders of Halstead and because of its unique construction was featured in a 1960s issue of Ideal Home Magazine. Michael, a long standing family friend, also built a swimming pool in the grounds, which was constructed by hand, 40 tons of earth being moved over a two year period! Although a large area of his land was made into a garden, part of it towards the Hedingham Road remained as meadow land. Over the years this field was used by the Territorial Army, the Boy Scouts and the Girl Guides who held their summer camps on it. It was also let to a neighbour as grazing land for her horse, and it was used annually by the residents from Ashlong Grove for their bonfire and firework display to celebrate Guy Fawkes night, when they were no longer able to hold them in the 'Grove'.

Thelric House, Howe Drive, Halstead circa 1970s

Built by Michael and Mavis Portway, this house, which was never referred to as a bungalow, has undergone substantial alterations over the years.

My late father, Bertram Hogarth, spent many hours walking around The Howe Estate contemplating where he would like to build a house and the kind of house that would suit the site. Being a mechanical engineer and a very methodical gentleman, every conceivable area was studied carefully. I know this, because, as a young girl, I spent many weekends in The Howe grounds holding one end of a surveyor's tape measure, while my father held the other end taking numerous measurements. His evenings were then spent looking through a collection of books on house designs, such as the 'Planahome, Book of House Plans', or else he sat at his drawing board and created his own house designs. Two areas which were seriously considered by my parents as possible sites to build their house were:- Inside the walled garden, next to The Howe, and an area of land to the east of it. Eventually these were both dismissed as unsuitable when my late mother Mary, decided that they were situated too close to The Howe, especially as no one knew at that time, what would happen to the house.

Eventually in October 1955 after more deliberations, my parents decided to buy a piece of land on the east side of Howe Drive where horses and cattle roamed freely. I can remember gingerly climbing through the fence, once again at one end of a tape measure, while four pegs were knocked into the ground by my father; these indicated the four corners of the piece of land he wished to purchase. Ralph van Ash agreed to the sale at once and the deal was done, all very casual compared with today! Naturally though, all the legal formalities had to be completed before the land was conveyed to my father, but before this happened van Asch formed a company called Ashlong Properties Limited, of which he was the director and his wife was the company secretary. On the 18th February 1956 'the company' purchased 8.400 acres of land to the east of Howe Drive comprising of enclosure numbers 133, 138, 508 and part of 393, for £1000 from 'Ralph van Asch'. This included two building plots, one of which was my fathers, and also the area of land designated for The Howe Building Estate, together with the spinney and road leading into the development.

On the 22nd March 1956, part of Plot A was conveyed to my father, who was the first person to purchase land from Ashlong Properties Limited. With concrete posts and wire placed around the boundaries 'we' became the proud owners of part of a very large field! Messrs Baker and Burton, architects based in Colchester prepared the house plans, and planning permission was sought. This however was not granted until my father agreed to plant a row of conifers on his west boundary, to screen our house from the road. These fir trees were deemed necessary by the planning officer at Halstead Urban District Council, because he thought that our house design, and that of our neighbours would 'clash', and would therefore not be pleasing on the eye if they could both be seen at the same time! How things have changed!

Rustlings and garden   May 1966 My father, admiring his Azaleas

The front elevation of Rustlings, circa 1970s, has not altered since it was built 1956/57. The car parked on the drive is a Triumph Toledo.

The built in garage at Rustlings circa 1970s before its conversion to create another room.

The formation of Ashlong Grove: The proposed Howe Building Estate development was also under way and the road, which forms a 'T' shape with cul de sacs at either end, was partly built and the main services were under construction. The southern area of the estate was the first part to be developed, plot boundaries were established, and this is where the larger houses and bungalows are to be found, built to owner's specifications. It is interesting to note too, that the plot numbers do not correspond with the property numbers of today. When van Asch/Ashlong Properties Limited created the estate in the 1950s, numbers 1 and 2 were designated to the two plots/houses on the right hand side of the road as you enter Ashlong Grove. The spinney on the left hand side of the entrance was never intended for development, and part of it was sold in 1957 on the understanding that it would be preserved as a wooded area, as was the rest of the spinney when it was sold in the early 1960s.

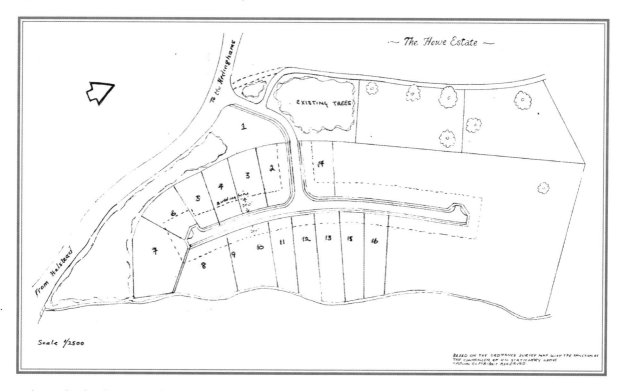

An early sketch c1956 showing the first building plots available for purchase on the Howe Building Estate/Ashlong Grove site, including the road, which was only partly constructed.

The first two plots to be sold on the Howe Building Estate were conveyed on the 22nd March 1956, followed by another plot on 23rd March. Plot No.13 was bought by Jack Rippingale and his house was one of the first on the estate to be built. The builder was the late Clarence Birch from Braintree, who was one of my husband's uncles. Other early purchasers were Rolfe Lacey, plot 10, who owned a perfume factory in Haverhill, and his manager Michael Rushbrook who bought two plots, 8 and 9. Margaret Bullivant, who was never without a dachshund by her side, built 'April House' on plot 4, this was also one of the earliest houses to be constructed. As a keen gardener, 'Bullie' as she was affectionately known by me, created a lovely garden at the same time as her house was being constructed. Permission was granted for both houses and bungalows to be built at the south end of Ashlong Grove and strict regulations were imposed by the planning officers, which is why the properties did not stray over the building line!

Fencing kept a number of cattle from roaming onto the building sites although, *'as the grass is always greener on the other side'*, the cows did manage to make a dash for freedom once or twice. On one occasion they completely demolished a large number of newly planted raspberry canes! A very red faced farmer rounded them up and, later that day, a tractor and trailer arrived with a large quantity of farmyard manure by way of an apology!

Ralph van Asch used a firm of Solicitors from Clare, Suffolk; Wayman and Long, and this led to the Howe Building Estate attaining the more prodigious name of 'Ashlong Grove'. 'The Grove' being the name which this area of land had been called for many years.

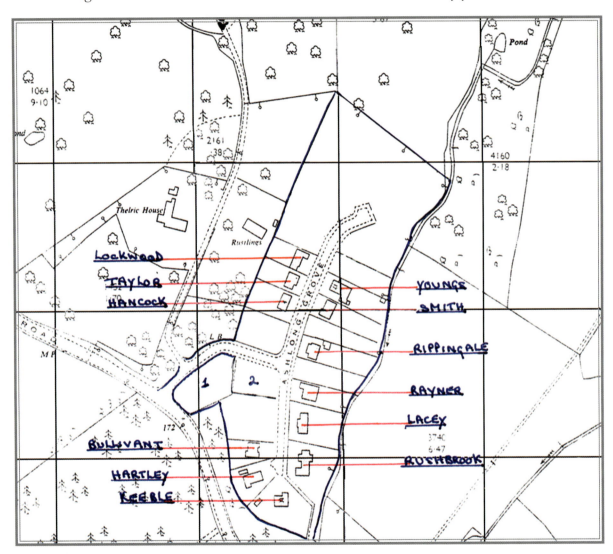

Partly developed area of Ashlong Grove sketched onto Ordnance survey map 1923 edition, showing the properties and their owners in 1959/60.

In 1958 the owners of the first houses to be built in Ashlong Grove appeared on the Electoral Register:

April House	Bullivant, Margaret
Rema	Lacey, Rolfe and Edna (The name 'Rema' was formed by using the first initial of the Lacey's Christian names; Rolfe, Edna, Michael and Anthony

Fagans	Rippingale, Jack and Joyce
In t' Veld	Rushbrook, Maurice and Kathleen

By 1959/60 eight more families had been added to the register, they were:

Glenfield	Lockwood, Cyril and Violet
Number 29 Ashlong Grove	Taylor, Frank and Joan Roslyn
Alney	Hancock, Sidney and Alma
Ainsdale	Hartley, Donald and Dilys, and Hartley, Elsie
Therons	Keeble, John and Lilian
Perdita	Rayner, Frank and Gem
Chantek	Smith, Eric and Beryl
Le Chene	Youngs, Philip and Eunice

Ralph van Asch by now had invested heavily in the development and, although he had sold the majority of the plots on the south side of Ashlong Grove, he needed to sell off the land at the north end. He offered the plots of land situated on both sides of the unmade road to a Hedingham builder, Stanley Wilding for £2000, but the offer was rejected by the builder due to ill health. (Not included in the offer was the plot which had already been purchased by Mr. B A Andrewes). Eventually the remaining land was sold to Duncan Cameron, builders and contractors who were based in Bocking. They finished putting in the services, and completed the tarmac road. They built most of the properties which stand at the north end of Ashlong Grove and had to follow strict regulations; only bungalows were permitted to be built, and these had to be individual in design. Most purchasers employed their own architects.

In about 1962 the properties in Ashlong Grove were renumbered, so the houses built on the original plots 1 and 2, became 30 and 31. The renumbering commenced with number 3, (today Grove House) when numbers 1 and 2 were incorrectly designated to the spinney area on the west side of Ashlong Grove, which was never to be developed.

By 1965/66 all 29 plots of land were built on and the properties occupied by the following people, as shown in the Halstead Directory for 1965/66.

Ashlong Grove

No. 3	Chaplin, C.F.		No. 18	Smith, E
No. 4	Hancock, S.W.		No. 19	Eagle, R.D.
No. 5	Taylor, F.		No. 20	Frankland, R.S.
No. 6	Whittle, C.		No. 21	Broughton, J.M.
No. 7	Bowen, D.		No. 22	Rayner, F.A.
No. 8	Wenn, R.D.		No. 23	Lofthouse, A.
No. 9	Pritchard, J.C.W.		No. 24	Mercer, N.S.
No. 10	Skilton, C.H.		No. 25	Keeble, J.
No. 11	Farrant, J.H.		No. 26	Langford, G.
No. 12	Croker, C.F.		No. 27	Hartley, D.M.
No. 13	Moore, B.O.		No. 28	Bullivant, M.I.
No. 14	Jones, C.M.		No. 29	Mitchell, W.G.
No. 15	Howard, G.F.		No. 30	Collett, B.F.
No. 16	Andrewes, B.A.		No. 31	Laidler, F.R.
No. 17	Youngs, P.I.			

By this time some of the original owners of the properties had moved. *(For more comprehensive lists please see Appendix VII).*

In 1962/3 the third house known as 'Rathearne' in Howe Drive was completed and occupied. It was 'a design' from The Planahome Book of House Plans, and was built by Vic Christie, who worked in the building trade. Christie and his wife did not stay long and eventually emigrated to Australia. By 1965 Hugh Ware and his family moved into the house which was renamed Sandy Lodge. This house has undergone substantial alterations in recent years.

An illustration from The Planahome Book of House Plans, published by 'planahome, publishers of technical information'. Rathearne, now renamed Sandy Lodge, was based on the design which was referred to as 'The Walton House'.

What became of The Howe?
Ralph van Asch found he could not sell the house because prospective buyers felt it was too large and that its modernisation programme would be too costly. Desperate to sell The Howe, van Asch decided to reduce its size and hopefully make it a more viable proposition. One day a loud explosion was heard and the wing which had been added by SAC was removed! A quick and unique way to create a smaller house.

In 1957, The Howe was sold to Lionel, (known as Dudley) and Ursula Darrell. Originally they intended living in the house temporarily until they found a farm to buy in the area. However following the birth of four children between 1957 and 1965, and the death of Dudley in 1992, The Howe is still the family home.

Chapter Sixteen
Ralph van Asch

Ralph Gerritt van Asch was born in 1907, the son of William and Matte van Asch and was bought up in Hawkes Bay, New Zealand as part of a well known family. His grandfather, Gerritt van Asch, who was born in Marken, Holland, emigrated to New Zealand in 1879 as an internationally famous teacher of the deaf. Gerritt was a pioneer in both Britain and New Zealand of the oral method of teaching deaf people the art of communicating known as lip reading. He founded the world's first State School for deaf children in Christchurch. Ralph's father, William, was also something of a pioneer, as he started farming in what was previously bush land in Hawkes Bay. He, too, made a name for himself not only by building a large state of the art house, largely in concrete, which was designed by the most celebrated New Zealand architect of the time, but also for his inventiveness and creativity. A gene he clearly passed on to Ralph.

Following the 1920s depression, which hit most families, Ralph van Asch left New Zealand and came to England in 1936. He was already engaged to Jula Davida Rennie who was born in 1913, the daughter of an Auckland family who were farmers and lawyers. Ralph and Jula were married at Cambridge in 1939 and had four children: Pattie 1941, Jennifer 1944, David 1945 and Mary born in 1948. Ralph and his family lived at Farmer's Farm, Stoke by Clare, Suffolk, before they moved to Copt Hall*, Little Wigborough, Essex in 1946. Ralph was a very forward thinking man and farmer, and he was one of the first men to own a caterpillar tractor. Ralph and the family made several trips to New Zealand and in 1950 with Jula and David they visited for 4 months sailing on SS Rangitiki.

Ralph van Asch 1907-1981
photograph: circa 1972
Courtesy of David van Asch

In 1952 the family moved to Greystones, Shrub End, Colchester and in 1954 Ralph purchased part of The Howe Estate. Seizing the opportunity he took a risk, as in the 1950s private developments, where individuals purchased land, designed and built their own houses was in its infancy. No wonder he did not inform his bank manager of his intention until after he had bought the site! Ralph had also planned to move his family into The Howe when he bought the estate, but it never happened and they remained at Greystones, although his children's two ponies spent time grazing in The Howe fields. Ralph, helped by his schoolboy son David, did much of the preparatory work on the Ashlong Grove site. He even bought a steam roller which was used in the construction of the road. Young David being allowed to drive it while his father roared with laughter as he 'steamed off' into the distance!

Ralph invented a log splitting tool which was very successful and he was well known for his explosives work. He specialized in removing unwanted trees and, on several occasions, explosions would be heard as he removed a tree stump somewhere on the estate. He apparently kept the explosives in a special bunker in Colchester.

Jula died in Colchester in 1978. Ralph returned to Hawkes Bay where he died in 1981.

With hindsight had Ralph van Asch speculated just a little too early in the property market? Probably the answer is yes, because not long after he had sold out to Duncan Cameron, Britain entered 'a property boom', and the price of land and houses soared.

* Copt Hall Marshes is now a National Trust site.

The Howe in 1956 before the right hand wing was demolished, with Ralph van Asch and his daughter Mary walking towards the house.
Courtesy of David van Asch

Chapter Seventeen
The Howe Estate – Howe Ground Cottages and occupants

Several cottages once stood on land known as How(e) Ground which was situated to the left hand side of Howe Chase. Originally they would have been tied cottages built to accommodate the farm labourers who worked on the estate.

These cottages were not all built at the same time although at least one tenement was there in 1750; this was the tenement nearest to Howe Chase, which is number 1070 on the 1838 Tithe Map. An extract from the Manor of Hepworth dated 1750 records; *"Leaseholder: Robertus Tweed Esq. A tenement near The How, late of John Reery, and now in the occupation of (stands empty), parcel of the Demense of this Manor - 1s"*. (rent). Also Land Tax records commencing 1782 frequently referred to owners and tenants at How(e) Ground. The properties changed hands frequently, and it was not unusual for the cottages to be sub-let.

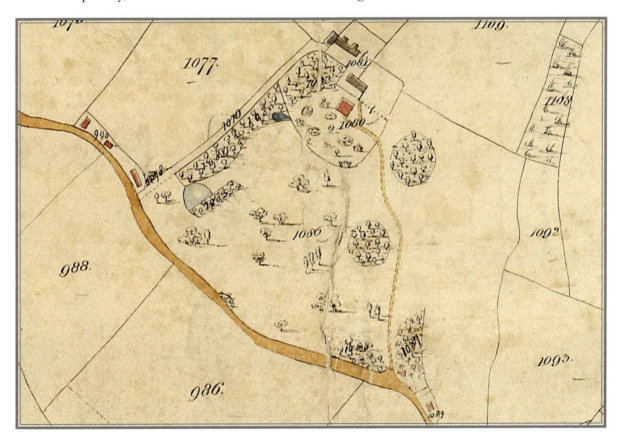

Extract taken from the Tithe Map -1838
showing The Howe and three buildings to the left hand side of Howe Chase

The 1874 Ordnance Survey map for Halstead shows that the tenement nearest to Howe Chase comprised of at least six cottages with gardens. However, following a number of poor harvests caused by inclement weather, arable farming was on the decline, and farmers struggled to make a living. At the beginning of the 1890s Anne Hornor decided to rent some of her land on the estate to tenants, therefore with fewer fields to farm, less agricultural labourers were required. Gradually the necessity to accommodate farm workers dwindled, and by 1897 the tenement had been demolished. Today the only visible signs left of these long demolished cottages are a well where the inhabitants would have drawn their water, and a few garden shrubs.

Two gentleman who leased land described as 'part of The Howe' and 'Near the Howe' were Charles Portway and Harry Harvey Portway. Although not the same field, it is perhaps rather a coincidence that some sixty five years later, their great grandson and grandson, Michael Portway, built a house on part of the estate.

The pair of cottages 'end on' to Hedingham Lane were constructed in brick with flint infill, which was very similar to the building materials used on Howe Lodge and the stable block. Therefore they were almost certainly built around 1826 by Edward May, and were occupied by workers on The Howe Estate. The Sturmer family occupied the cottage closest to Hedingham Lane for several decades, while Edward and Sarah Smith lived in the adjoining cottage from the early 1870s. Albert Blackwell moved into the cottage once occupied by the Sturmer family, and, when Sarah Smith moved out of the next door cottage in 1933, he converted the premises into one property. Albert later built a bungalow on Howe Ground, and these cottages were demolished.

Cottages at Howe Ground
Showing the cottage which was built 'end on' to Hedingham Road in the background, and the cottage with the verandah in the foreground.
Courtesy of Richard Blackwell

The cottage with the verandah is something of an enigma. Unfortunately due to the lack of documentation available there is nothing to establish its origin.

In the above photograph taken during the 1900s, the building appeared to be constructed of red brick with a plain tile roof, and had a verandah which ran along the front and both sides. Verandahs were introduced into this country from about 1850, when travellers visited India and were influenced by Indian Architecture. Lewis Hornor travelled to India during the 1870s. Could he have added a verandah to an existing property, or demolished a pair of old cottages and built another house to replace them?

As these cottages were not built on Copyhold land, their owners were not required to attend Manorial Courts to record ownership or tenants names. However, with the use of the Tithe Map, plus the 1874 and 1897 Ordnance Survey maps, census returns from 1841 to 1911 and electoral registers, it is possible to establish that a dwelling occupied the site from at least 1838 to 1932. This property was sometimes occupied as a single dwelling and at other times it was classed as a two family residence.

Following a succession of tenants over the years, William and Eliza Norman lived in the cottage from around 1891, followed by their daughter Mary, until the last occupants, the Basham family with three sons from Emma Basham's first marriage moved in. Members of the Basham/Clarry family lived in the cottage from 1923 to 1932. After Albert and Emma, and Reginald Clarry moved out of the dwelling it was demolished by Samuel Courtauld.

In 1925 when SAC was President of Halstead Golf Club, he presented them with a club house which was built on land behind the Howe Ground cottages. The nine hole golf links ran from approximately Howe Chase to Does Corner, however it was not really successful and it closed after the Second World War in 1948.

How(e) Ground Cottages - the occupants
All the people listed below lived in the cottages, and the majority of them were employed on The Howe Estate. Unfortunately once again, lack of documentation for the earlier years makes it difficult to state exactly who lived in a specific cottage.

Census Return 1827
The information supplied on the Census Return for How(e) Ground in 1827:-

Year	Name	Age	Occupation	
1827	Phillip Byford	-	sand carter	worked for Thomas Smoothy
	Phillip Byford (son)	25 yrs	sand carter	worked for Thomas Smoothy
	Thomas Drury	-	broom maker	self employed
	James Kemp	46 yrs	labourer	worked for Edward May
	Thomas Norman	24 yrs	labourer	worked for Edward May
	John Parker	52 yrs	labourer	worked for Edward May
	John Parker	46 yrs	labourer	worked for Mr. Sparrow
	Thomas Chapman	41 yrs	labourer	worked for Edward May
	James Evans	40 yrs	labourer	worked for Edward May

Land Tax Assessments for Halstead 1828, show that Edward May was the owner of cottages on How(e) Ground, which were occupied by John Parker, Thomas Wheeler and Thomas Norman.

Census Returns 1841-1911 for Howe Ground:
The following lists were compiled as the enumerator transcribed them. He should have worked from Howe Chase towards the cottages which stood 'end on' to the main road. However please remember that the enumerator may have deviated from his planned route! Also do not follow the lines across the page believing that as one family moved or left a cottage they were replaced by the next name. Sadly this was not always so.

	Name	No. of occupants		Name	No. of occupants
1841	Rebecca Wilson)		1851	William West	2
	Maria Roberts)			James Tyler	6
	Henry Roberts)				
	Sarah Smith)	4			
	William Sturmer	3		William Sturmer	5
	John Parker	4		John Parker	2
	Thomas Wheeler	3		William Norman	4
	Unoccupied			Thomas Wheeler	2
	Thomas Norman	5		Thomas Norman	5
	James Kemp	2		James Butcher	4

An extract taken from the 1958 'Abstract of the Title of Ashlong Properties Limited' referred to cottages; *"Formerly in the several occupations of James Kemp and John Parker, afterwards of Nicholas Marriott and Ann Wheeler (widow of Thomas Wheeler) and John Kemp respectively, and then of Thomas Norman and James Kemp their under tenants or assigns together with the houses, outhouses with the pieces or parcels of land to the said messuage and farm site lying and being in the Parish of Halstead".* (Howe Ground around the time of the above Census Returns).

1861	William West	2	1871	Henry Sturmer	4
	William Sturmer	5		Henry Constable	2
	William Norman	8		John Parker	2
	John Parker	2		William Norman	11
	James Laysell	4		George Sturmer	2
	John Chapman	3		George Rayment	5
	Edward Raven	5			
	George Monk	5			
	Thomas Wheeler	4			
1881	Susanna Sturmer	2	1891	William Norman	3
	Mary Gaymer	2		George Sturmer	2
	George Bullard	6		Edward Smith	3
	John Parker	1			
	Edward Smith	2			
	William Norman	5			
	William Goodman	4			
	George Sturmer	2			
1901	William Norman	4	1911	Eliza Norman (widow)	3
	George Sturmer	2		George Sturmer	2
	Edward Smith	2		Edward Smith	3

The Norman family commencing with William Norman who was baptised in 1771 had a long association with The Howe Estate. *(See Chapter 21 for full details relating to the Norman family).*

John Parker was born c1795 at Halstead. By 1825 he was married to Susan and they had a son James born 1826. The family lived at Howe Ground and John worked as an agricultural labourer for Edward May. A second son William, was born in 1835 and died in 1843, the same year that his mother Susan, also died. John and James continued to live in the cottage and by 1851 John worked as a highway's labourer before he returned to work on the land. James remained a farm labourer all his working life. On the 1881 census return John lived by himself in the cottage and died in 1889 aged 94 years.

Thomas Wheeler was born in 1775 and his wife Sarah was born in 1786. They had a son also named Thomas, born c1818 who worked with his father on the Howe Estate. In 1847 Thomas the younger, married Sarah Howard who was a silk weaver, and they moved to another cottage on Howe Ground.

Thomas the elder and his wife Sarah were classed as 'paupers' in 1851, and by 1861 both families had moved back into one cottage. Thomas the younger was head of the household as his father was registered as deaf, dumb and blind, probably the result of a stroke. Thomas the elder died in 1864 and his wife Sarah died in 1865.

After the death of his parents Thomas and Sarah moved to Braintree Road but by 1881 they had moved to Mount Hill. Sarah died in 1881 aged 54 years and Thomas died in 1884 aged 66 years.

The Sturmer Family

The Sturmer family had a long association with the Howe Estate as two generations worked at The Howe and lived in the cottages on Howe Ground.

William Sturmer was born in 1814 at Halstead, the son of Joseph and Elizabeth Sturmer. He married Susanna Norman in 1839 at St Andrew's Church, Halstead, who was the daughter of William and Martha Norman. Susanna was baptised in March 1811. William worked for Edward May and lived with his wife in one of the cottages. They had three sons, Henry born 1841, George 1845 and Walter in 1847. By 1851 William was employed by Edward Hornor as his coachman, a position he held until his death in 1880 at the age of 66 years. His widow Susanna, continued to live at Howe Ground with her grand daughter Ethel Susanna Sturmer, (Walter's daughter). Susanna and Ethel moved to Howe Cottages about 1891 and Susanna died in 1898. Both William and Susanna left wills; Estates worth £450 and £192 respectively.

William and Susanna Sturmer's children:

Henry Sturmer was born in 1841 and in 1861 worked as a plumber journeyman while he lived with his parents. After his marriage to Rebecca Dedman in 1866 he continued to live at Howe Ground until he moved to North Street and had two children, William born in 1868 and Henry Edward, known as Harry in 1870. Henry, a plumber, decorator and glazier by 1881 employed his son William as an apprentice plumber. At this time the family lived in North Street in a cottage which was owned by the Trustees of Aaron Morritt's Estate. Rebecca died in 1897 aged 60 years and Henry married for the second time, Barry Howlett in 1899. In 1891 they had moved to another cottage in North Street. Barry died in 1919 aged 67 years and Henry died in 1925 aged 84 years.

George Sturmer was born in 1845 and in 1869 married Mary Ann Noble, born in 1844, at Coggeshall. They moved into one of the cottages as George was employed as a groom and spent his entire working life at The Howe with the Hornor family. By 1881 George had been promoted and was a coachman, a position he held for a number of years, until he was older, and took on lighter duties as a gardener. Mary Ann died in 1903 and George continued to live in his cottage for a few more years with his niece Emma Noble to look after him. As a highly valued member of her staff, Anne Hornor left George a legacy in her will when she died in 1914. George moved out of the cottage in 1915, and lived at 21 Parsonage Street when he died in 1929 aged 84 years. Both George and Mary Ann are buried in Halstead Cemetery. They did not have any children.

George Sturmer together with his father William, served as coachmen at The Howe collectively for over fifty years.

Howe Ground Cottages in the snow

Walter Sturmer the youngest son, was the most adventurous. Born in 1847 he lived with his parents until the mid 1860s. He moved firstly to Chelmsford and worked as a whitesmith before he married Sarah Henrietta Barker who was born in 1852, at Halstead in 1872. They had one daughter Ethel Susanna, born in 1874 before Sarah died in 1875 aged 23 years. Following her mother's death, Ethel lived with her grandmother Susanna Sturmer in Halstead. Walter moved to Leicestershire and continued to work as a whitesmith. Eventually he worked as a locksmith and formed a business partnership with Frederick Hopcroft, who was an ironmonger. Following her Grandmother's death Ethel moved to Leicestershire and lodged with the Hives family at Barrow Upon Soar. She gave birth to a son in 1901, who she named William Frederick Sturmer. Walter was a lodger with Frederick and his wife Sarah until he moved to Syston (Leicestershire) at the beginning of the 1900s and worked again as a smith and fitter. In 1911 he lived in the High Street at Syston with Ethel and William. He died in Leicestershire in 1928 aged 80 years. Ethel died in Barrow upon Soar in 1942.

William Frederick Sturmer married Lydia Angrave in the Barrow Upon Soar District in 1925.

William West was born c1789 at Appleton, Yorkshire, and by 1841 he was a gardener living at

Fulton Ambro with his wife Mary. They moved to Halstead and William worked as a gardener for Edward Hornor, while Mary became Alice Hornor's (Edward's mother) most devoted and faithful maid. An accomplished gardener, William exhibited fruit, plants and vegetables at various Halstead and North Essex Floral Society Shows and won several prizes. After the death of Mary in 1865, William moved back to Yorkshire and lived with his son William and family at Skipton, where he died in 1871.

Rebecca Wilson born 1801 lived at How(e) Ground in 1841. She worked as a straw plaiter until she died in 1847.

James Tyler was born in 1813 at Great Maplestead and his wife Harriett was born c1814 at Gestingthorpe. In 1851, James, an agricultural labourer and Harriett lived in one of the Howe Ground cottages. However they had moved to Witham by 1861 where James worked as a groom and a gardener. He later became a brewer and in 1881 lived with his wife in Braintree.

Henry Roberts was born in 1815 and his wife Maria formerly Keddell was in born 1821; both were from Halstead. They married in 1839 and moved into a cottage at Howe Ground. Maria died in 1846 and Henry married secondly, Susannah Clarke Hartley in 1851 and they moved to Braintree. Henry and Susannah had two children, Emily and Alfred. They lived at Martins Yard in Braintree for several years and Henry was employed as a hand loom silk weaver all his working life. Susannah (Susan) died in 1878 aged 60 years and Henry died in 1893 aged 78 years.

Edward Raven was born in 1825 at Great Leighs, and married Charlotte Smith in 1844 in the Braintree District. Charlotte was born at Hampstead, London. Edward was a miller in Rayne where his two sons were born, Edward in 1845 and, Walter William in 1851 who died in 1868. The family moved to Howe Ground Cottages and by 1853, Edward had a Ransome's Steam Threshing Machine and five experienced machinists which he hired out to customers.

> **THRASHING BY STEAM.**
>
> ON HIRE, RANSOME'S complete STEAM THRASHING MACHINERY.
> Five steady experienced men accompany the machine; eight or ten more are required, according to the work. The proprietor having ordered another of Ransome's six-horse engines and machine, hopes soon to be able to meet the requirements of the district.
> Apply, by letter or otherwise, to F. Raven, Engineer, The Howe Farm, Halstead, or T. Norman, Ridgwell Hill, Essex.

An advertisement placed by Edward Raven
for the hire of his Steam Threshing Machinery
Courtesy of the Chelmsford Chronicle October 1853

Edward and Charlotte had two more children, Mercy Alice born in 1859 and Edith in 1863. Edward and his family moved to New Road, (later New Street), and his son Edward who was an engine driver, married Mary Ann Ewin in 1864 at Halstead. Edward and Mary travelled around England with the threshing machines as their children's births were registered in various districts. Frederick was born 1865 in the Haverhill District, Mary Ann 1867 at Charlton, Kent, Edith Rachel 1869 at Bow, London and Walter Edward 1874 at Halstead.

In 1881 Edith was a pupil teacher and Mercy was employed as a Board School mistress before she married John Spurgeon, a merchant tailor in 1883 at the New Congregational Church. Edward died in 1891 aged 66 years, and Charlotte, with Edith, John and Mercy Spurgeon and their two sons Herbert and Stanley, all lived at 'The Firs', Kings Road. The business prospered and became known as Edward Raven & Sons, Colne Valley Ironworks of Kings Road. In the 1902 Kelly's Trade Directory the firm was listed as an Agricultural Implement Manufacturer, with Edward Raven as an Agricultural Machine owner. Edward died in 1908 aged 63 years and his widow Mary Ann, and mother Charlotte, continued to live at The Firs until Charlotte died in 1915 aged 93 years. Mary Ann died in 1923 aged 84 years.

Edward's son Frederick who was apprenticed at the Tortoise Iron Works with Portway & Son emigrated to America towards the end of the 1800s. Walter Edward, his younger son, known as 'Wal', carried on with the family business. He married Bertha Sayward in 1899 and they had a daughter Rose Elsie born in 1902.

A 10 horse power Fowler Steam Traction Engine no. 1053, new in September 1868, used for ploughing. Owned by W E Raven -1912

Walter retired in 1918 and, perhaps with no son to carry on the business, sold the ironworks and traction engines. Bertha died in 1941 and Walter died in 1946.

James Layzell was born about 1832 at Halstead and in 1855 he married Eliza Taylor, a British subject who was born in Bombay, India. They lived at Howe Ground, and James worked as an agricultural labourer while Eliza was a silk weaver. By 1871 James and Eliza had moved with their family to Box Mill Lane and James was employed as a threshing machine engine driver. After he died in 1876 aged 44 years, Eliza continued to live in the cottage with most of her seven children. In 1901 she had moved with her son Ernest, a baker, to Trinity Street.

George Rayment was born in 1838 at Little Maplestead and in 1862 he married Ann Maria Argent and they moved to a cottage at Howe Ground. George was employed as an agricultural labourer until about 1869, when he and his family moved to Sible Hedingham where George was employed as a mechanic and agricultural engine driver. In 1891 George and Ann had moved to Cobbs Fenn, in the village, where they remained until Ann died in 1900 and George died in 1903.

Henry James Constable was born in 1851 at Halstead, the son of Abraham and Mary Ann Constable, who lived in one of the cottages at Does Corner. In 1870 he married Sarah Ann Newman, who was born in 1849 at Castle Hedingham and they lived in a cottage at Howe Ground for a few years. Henry worked as an agricultural labourer and Sarah was a silk weaver. They left Halstead in 1879 and moved to Hatfield Peverel before they later lived in the Orsett area of Essex. By 1911 they had nine children, all of whom survived.

Mary Gaymer was born in Earls Colne and in 1851 lived in Prospect Place, Halstead, with her husband Edward, a plumber, and their four children. Edward died in 1856 and by 1861 Mary had moved to New Street. In 1881 she lived at Howe Ground with her unmarried daughter Mary. Mary the elder, died in 1883 aged 82 years.

William Goodman was born at Rochford in 1857 and married Emily Johnson from Coggeshall in 1876. They had two children, Bertie born 1877 at Feering, and Fred born 1881 at Wakes Colne. William had followed in his father's footsteps and was a harness maker when he moved to Howe Ground in 1881. They did not stay long in Halstead as they were in Rochford when Bertie died in 1882 and in Kings Langley, Hertfordshire, when their third son Alfred was born in 1888. The family had returned to William's home town of Rochford by 1901. William ran a successful and profitable saddle and harness business and by 1911 the family lived at 'Emily Villas' Great Wakering, Essex. Emily died in 1922 and William married Annie Florence Matthams in 1923. William died at Rochford in 1931.

George Bullard was born at Stisted and his wife Ann was born at Great Maplestead. They were married in 1857 and lived in Great Maplestead where George worked as an agricultural labourer. By 1881 they had moved from Alder Hall, on the boundary of Great Maplestead with Sible Hedingham, to Howe Ground where they remained for a while, before they moved to Box Mill Lane. After Ann died in 1893 aged 58 years, George moved to Tidings Hill and lived with his son George, a harness maker, daughter in law Laura and grandson Reginald. By 1911 George was a patient in the Workhouse, North Street and died in 1915 aged 78 years.

Edward Smith was born in 1852 at Ridgewell, the son of Samuel and Susan Smith. He married Sarah Humphry in 1872, who was also born at Ridgewell in 1852, and they lived at Howe Ground. Edward was employed as a railway worker before he later worked as an agricultural labourer on Howe Farm. By 1891 Edward's niece Sarah Ann Barnard, who later married James Laver, also lived with them. Edward was promoted to farm bailiff around 1902, a position he held until the death of Anne Hornor in 1914.

Edward and Sarah had occupied their cottage at Howe Ground for many years and after Edward died in 1919 aged 67 years, Sarah remained in the cottage until 1934. She moved to Bousser Cottages, Hedingham Road for a few months, before she moved again to Northanger Abbey, Mill Chase, where she died in the early 1940s. Both these houses were the newly built Courtauld houses.

Bertram James Springett was born in 1884 at Chilton, Suffolk, the son of Harry and Jane Springett. By 1901 the family had moved to Swan Street, Sible Hedingham where Harry, Bertram and two other brothers, Sidney and Maurice were involved in the brickmaking industry. In 1906 Bertram married Ada Clark who was from the Great Waltham area of Essex and they lived at Great Maplestead for a short while before they moved to Blue Bridge where Bertram worked as a cowman on a farm. They had two daughters, Muriel Eva, who was born in 1907 at Maplestead and Myrtle, who was born in 1911 at Halstead.

The family had moved to Howe Ground before Bertram, who then worked as a milkman, was sent to France to fight in the First World War. He joined the Royal Field Artillery as a driver. Sadly he was wounded in 1918 and died from his injuries. He was buried at Wellington Cemetery, Rieux-En-Cambresis, Nord, and is commemorated on both the Halstead War Memorial and the Sible Hedingham War Memorial in St. Peter's Churchyard. He was also commemorated on a tablet which was in the old High Street Congregational Church; It read *"In hallowed remembrance of the men of this Church who fell in the Great War"*. When the church was demolished the tablet was moved to the Parsonage Street Congregational Church where it was positioned on the North wall of the Chancel. Ada and her daughters continued to live at Howe Ground until they moved to Box Mill Lane Cottages in 1923/4 where they remained for a few years. Muriel married William Webber in 1929.

Albert Basham
Albert Basham was born in 1877 at Halstead, the son of Emma Basham formerly Rayner. In 1881 Albert lived at Sooty Square with his mother and siblings. By 1901 Emma worked as a housekeeper, and with Albert had moved to 9 Manfield, into a house which was almost next door to her son George and his family. Emma died in 1909 aged 73 years.

According to the 1911 census return, Albert, a farm labourer, 'boarded' with Rosalina Clarry, a widow and, her eight children, at 2 Manfield. Baptised Rosalina Twinn in 1865 at Glemsford, Suffolk, Rosalina married Edward Clarry, an agricultural labourer from Cavendish in 1890. After Edward's death in 1910 Rosalina and their children moved to Manfield and, in June 1911 Albert and Rosalina were married. Albert and Rosalina lived in the cottage with the verandah at Howe Ground from 1923 to 1932, before they moved to 20 Hedingham Road. Rosalina died in 1941 aged 75 years.

Frederick, Reggie James and Bertie George Clarry
Frederick born in 1899, Reggie James in 1900, known as Reginald on official documents, and Bertie George Clarry born 1903 and known as George, were three of the sons born to Rosalina and her first husband Edward. The three young men continued to live with their mother Rosalina, and Albert Basham and moved with them to Howe Ground.

Frederick was the first to leave the cottage in 1925, when he married Florence Smith, who was born in 1900; Frederick died in 1968 aged 69 years. George moved out in 1929 and married Maud

Newman; he died in 1975 aged 71 years. Reginald, a bachelor, remained at Howe Ground with his mother and Albert and moved with them to Hedingham Road, where he lived for a number of years. Reginald died in 1970.

Arthur Jarman was born in Halstead in 1887. He married Laura Maria Winifred Hambly born in 1890, who was the daughter of Charles Henry and Ann Jessie Hambly of Millbrook, Cornwall, in 1919. They lived at Howe Ground from 1924/25 to 1929, where their son Russell Charles was born.

George Burder was born in 1882, the son of Henry and Harriett Burder of Forrey Green, Sible Hedingham. He married Sarah Ann Basham in 1903 and they had twin daughters Daisy Annie and Ruth Rose who were born at Sible Hedingham in 1907. In 1911 the family lived in Gosfield where George worked on a farm and looked after the horses. They moved to Howe Ground in 1925 and stayed for about four years before they left in 1929. Daisy married Ronald Lilley in 1925 and Ruth married Thomas Laver in 1928, who was the son of James Laver who lived at Howe Lodge.

Albert Harris Blackwell who was born in 1903 at Fordham, Essex, was the son of Harris, a labourer in an iron foundry, and Ellen Mary Backwell formerly Saunders. Albert married Phyllis Edith Kate Fuller in 1927 at St Andrew's Church, Halstead.

Phyllis who was born in 1905, was the daughter of George, (1866-1937) a butcher, and Edith Clara Fuller formerly Brazier, (1874-1953).

In 1911 Albert lived with his parents and siblings at Hemp Green, Fordham, and Phyllis lived with her parents and uncle William Brazier, in Colchester Road. Phyllis's sister Winifred Daisy was born in 1913 and by 1923, the Fuller family had moved to 24 Box Mill Lane, a cottage owned by Samuel Courtauld.

Following their marriage Albert and Phyllis moved into the 'end on' cottages at Howe Ground and lived in the cottage nearest to Hedingham Road, which had recently been vacated by George Sturmer. The pathway, which led to the old golf links, and the garden wall with the purpose built holes, that allowed their chickens to pass through freely to forage in the field beyond, formed the boundary to the property. (The wall remains intact today).

A small herd of Jersey cows were kept on The Howe Estate and Phyllis worked as a milk maid in the dairy, which was situated near the top end of Howe Chase, close to The Howe. When Sarah Smith moved out of the cottage next to the Blackwell family in 1931, Albert acquired it and converted the two cottages into one larger dwelling. Phyllis did not escape the worries that war inevitably brings as, during the Second World War, Albert, was sent out to India, where he worked as an auxiliary nurse in one of the hospitals. Albert returned safely, and continued to work as a bricklayer; he had the reputation of being one of the best bricklayers in Halstead.

Around 1960 Albert built a bungalow at Howe Ground near the site of the demolished cottage with the verandah, and after its completion the family lived in it. Phyllis died in 1977 and Albert in 1996. The bungalow remains in the Blackwell family.

Albert and Phyllis had six children: Alec 1927-1972, Derek 1931-2011, Neil 1937, Janet 1939, Donald 1943 and Richard born in 1950.

The Cottage with the verandah at Howe Ground –1915
by Joseph Jarrom Harvey
This watercolour is reproduced by courtesy of Derek Reid who owns the copyright.

Joseph Jarrom Harvey who was born in 1883, was the son of Joseph Jarrom Harvey, a surgeon and his wife Mary Ann. Joseph moved to Head Street, Halstead in 1901 having previously lived in Bethnal Green, London and was employed as an ironmonger's clerk, before he later worked as a draper's traveller. Joseph married Frances Florence Frye at St Andrew's Church in 1914. Frances was born at Halstead in 1876, the daughter of Alfred Thomas Frye, a draper, who owned a shop in the High Street, and his wife Fanny. Joseph who was musical and artistic played the piano and violin and, provided the musical accompaniment in cinemas showing silent films. He also painted local scenes in both oil and watercolour. Joseph and Frances had two children, Joseph Philemon (1915-1996) and Florence Josephine (1916-1984). Frances died in Islington, North London in 1930 and Joseph died in 1943 at Halstead.

Chapter Eighteen
The Howe Estate – Howe Cottages and occupants

From at least 1746 Howe Cottage, a copyhold dwelling, stood on the right hand side of the hill leaving Halstead, just before where the entrance to Ashlong Grove is situated today. The cottage was built on the boundary of Great Thrift Field and the road, which was known in the 1700s as Thrifts Hill, Hedingham Lane. By the 1880s this hill was called Wash Hill, and later it was incorporated into Hedingham Road. Behind the cottage was a pond, which the tenants had permission to use to supply them with water. In 1746 George Brook, surrendered the cottage to Benjamin Tunbridge, a victualler of Halstead. Anthony Moul lived in the cottage and was probably one of the first tenants, followed by Stephen Moul.

John Blatch Whaley acquired the cottage in 1763 from Benjamin Tunbridge, and it was included in The Howe Estate. When John died in 1788 the tenant was Samuel Sargeant. John left the property to his son and heir John Blatch Whaley the younger, who resided in Threadneedle Street in the City of London. John decided to sell the cottage and appointed John Crump, the tenant farmer at How(e) Farm, to act as his attorney and agent. John Crump bought the cottage himself and was admitted the tenant in 1789 and, when he died, it was inherited by his widow Mary Ann. She transferred the cottage to her late husband John's son, also named John, an inn keeper, in 1802.

In 1812 Rebecca Cutts formerly Nokes bought the cottage from John Crump and, John Moul was the tenant. Following the death of his mother Rebecca, who was a widow, James Nokes was required to prove he was her legal heir and son, and next of kin. In 1828 James appeared at the Manorial Court and established that he was entitled to inherit his mother's estate and was therefore admitted the new owner of Howe Cottage. James sold the cottage to Edward May in October 1828 for £100, although he remained at the property as Edward's tenant and, in 1829, paid him a rent of two pence per annum.

Howe Cottage was a single dwelling when Edward May purchased the property and almost certainly renovated, refurbished and divided it into two, making a pair of cottages. The 1831 Tithe Map of Halstead clearly shows two cottages on Thrifts Hill and in 1833 Samuel Garrod and James Nokes were the tenants.

In October 1844 when Edward May sold the copyhold cottages to Arthur Macnamara and Major William Gossett for £260, Samuel Garrod and George Clements occupied the dwelling. Messrs Macnamara and Gossett sold the property to Edward Hornor in December 1845 when he purchased The Howe Estate. After Edward's death, Anne Hornor applied for the cottages to be enfranchised to convert them from copyhold to freehold; this was granted by deed of enfranchisement in 1869. They remained her property until they were sold to Samuel Courtauld in 1914. The cottages were demolished by SAC around 1923 after the last tenants, Albert Saunders and Martha Norman had been rehoused in cottages in Box Mill Lane.

In her excellent book 'A Look Back At Halstead', Doreen Potts describes the Howe Cottages, which were built of lath and plaster, as having: *"One large living room each, fitted with a cooking range. The one on the left had a small scullery with copper, sink and water tap and two bedrooms. The other was the same but had the added luxury of a sitting room".*

Howe Cottages occupants:
(L. = Left hand side cottage - R. = Right hand side cottage, as viewed from the road).

R. Samuel Garrod and his wife Sarah were born in Halstead; Samuel in 1805 and Sarah in 1806. In 1841 they lived in the right hand side cottage where they remained for the rest of their lives. Samuel's brother Alexander born c1814, who was a blacksmith, also lived with them until around the end of the 1870s, when he moved to Trinity Square. Samuel was employed as a carpenter for all his working life and Sarah was a straw plaiter. Samuel died in 1886 and Sarah died in 1891. During their occupancy of Howe Cottages the Garrod's had plenty of different next door neighbours:-

L. James Pryer/Prior lived with his wife Ann and children Sarah, Maria, Rebecca and John in the left hand side cottage. In 1841 James was employed as a cordwainer; he was widowed and had left the cottage by 1851 when he moved to Parsonage Lane where he lived with Rebecca and continued to work as a shoe maker.

Howe Cottages
Howe School is visible in the background, which helps to place where the cottages once stood on Thrifts Hill, later Wash Hill.

L. William Parker and his wife Elizabeth were born about 1818/1819. In 1841 William, an agricultural labourer lived with his wife and their sons William and John in Hedingham Lane before they moved to Howe Cottages some time before 1851. By 1861 William, Elizabeth, John and, Emma, born in 1853 at Halstead, had moved to Shalford where William worked as a gardener. William, their son, lived in the next door cottage with his common law wife Emma Dyer. In 1871 William and Elizabeth moved to Bardfield Saling and by 1881 they had moved to Bradwell on Sea, where Elizabeth died in 1898 and William died in 1901.

L. Thomas Hustler Maidwell was born in 1829 at Halstead and his wife Mary Anne formerly Halls was born at Gosfield. In 1851 Thomas lived with his parents in the High Street before he married Mary Anne in 1853. Their daughter Emma Frances was born in 1854. From at least 1861 Thomas, a journeyman tailor, and Mary Anne, a tailoress, with Mary's sister Emma Halls lived at Howe Cottages. By 1871 they had moved to a dwelling in North Street and Thomas was employed as a bill poster and town crier. He died in 1877 aged 49 years of age. Mary Anne married Thomas Cadby in 1880 and was widowed again when he died in 1895, one year before her own death in 1896. Emma followed in her parents footsteps and was a tailoress and dressmaker for a number of years, before she became a shopkeeper in Head Street.

L. James Richer was born in 1826 at Little Maplestead. He married Elizabeth Sayells or Searles, from Gestingthorpe in 1848. Following their marriage they lived at Little Maplestead where James worked as an agricultural labourer. By 1871 James and Elizabeth had moved to Howe Cottages where they remained until 1879.

When Elizabeth married James she already had a daughter, Emma Sayells/Searles, (c1843-1906), who became known as Emma Richer. Emma married Alfred Cockerton, (c1837-1910) in 1862. Four of their children were born in Halstead between 1864 and 1872; Alice Selina, Harry Alfred, Caroline Elizabeth, and Willie James. Alfred, an agricultural worker lived with his family in one of the cottages at Does Corner, near Hepworth Hall before they moved to Ilford in Essex, where Emily Kate was born in 1877 and Ernest Charles in 1880.

In 1879 James and Elizabeth Richer left Howe Cottage and moved to Ilford, where they lived with Alfred and Emma Cockerton and five of their children. Both James and Alfred worked as farm labourers on a nearby farm. By 1891 James and Elizabeth had moved into their own farm cottage next door to Alfred and Emma. Elizabeth died in 1898 aged 75 years and James died in 1901 also aged 75 years.

L. William Freeman Partridge was born in 1858 and his wife Eliza formerly Osborne was born in 1859. They married in 1879 and moved into Howe Cottages as William worked as a general labourer on the Howe Estate. They had two sons; William Robert baptised 1881 and Alfred George in 1883. Eliza died in 1884 aged 25 years. William's second wife was Alice Cook who he married in 1890. They moved to Factory Lane for a short time, before they lived in Parsonage Street. At this time William was employed as a painter journeyman. William and Alice had six children; one daughter Minnie died in 1904. William and Eliza's son, William Robert worked as a gas works labourer before he died in 1911 aged 29 years. William died in 1926 and Alice died in 1929.

L. Henry Dring was born in 1856, the son of Jonathan Dring (c1814-1873) and his wife Hannah formerly Dunt (c1817-1885). They lived in Parsonage Lane and Jonathan worked as a gardener at The Howe for the Hornor family for many years before he died in 1873.

At the age of fifteen Henry was also employed at The Howe as a gardener and was still working there when he married Eliza Elizabeth Bunn in 1884. Eliza was born at Hensted in Norfolk in 1855. They moved into the cottage vacated by William Partridge where they remained until 1903/4 when they moved into 'the cottage near The Howe', which was referred to as 'North Lodge'. Henry and Eliza had three children, Florence Louisa born in 1885, Sidney Walter in 1887 and Ernest George born in 1888.

In 1911 Florence Dring, formerly a milliner, worked as a self employed dressmaker and married William Goodey in 1921. They lived at Wash Farm Cottages.

In 1913 Sidney, a basket weaver and maker, emigrated to Canada and sailed on the Steamship Celtic. He enlisted in the Canadian Infantry (Central Ontario Regiment) and fought in France during the First World War, where he attained the rank of Lance Corporal. He was killed in 1915 and is commemorated on the Menin Gate Memorial at Ypres and on the War Memorial in St Andrew's Churchyard, Halstead.

In 1916 Ernest an oven fitter at the Iron Foundry married Gladys Corder. (A distant relation to my husband, Adrian).

Henry and Eliza continued to live in their cottage, now known as 'the gardener's cottage', until Henry died in 1920 aged 64 years, having worked for Edward and Anne Hornor for several decades and then for Samuel Courtauld. Eliza was at Wash Farm Cottages with her daughter and son in law when she died in 1925 aged 69 years.

Howe Cottages in the snow

R. Susanna Sturmer the widow of William Sturmer had moved with her grand daughter Ethel from a cottage at Howe Ground to the right cottage in 1891 where they remained until Susanna's death in 1898. *(See chapter 17 about Howe Ground Cottages for more information about Susanna Sturmer).*

R. Documentation shows that in 1898 **Charles Paflin** left Howe Lodge and, lived at Howe Cottages for a few weeks before moving to a property in North Street. Charles was followed by **Henry Watkinson**, but his stay at Howe Cottages was short too.

R. Charlotte Ann Reeve was born in Castle Hedingham c1816. In 1851 Charlotte was a 'live in' servant at The Howe and by 1861 she was employed as the cook, a position which she held until she retired at the end of the 1870s. In 1881 Charlotte had moved back to Castle Hedingham and lived at Pye Corner, where she remained until after 1891. Circa 1900 she had returned to Halstead and moved into in the cottage next door to Henry Dring, where she remained until she died in 1904. Charlotte never married.

R. James Henry Laver was born in 1872 at Ridgewell and married Sarah Ann Barnard also from Ridgewell in 1897. Sarah Ann was the niece of Edward and Sarah Smith who lived at Howe Ground for many years. By 1901 James, a farm labourer, and Sarah had moved to 77 North Street with their twin daughters, Lily and Violet, who at the time of the census were twenty one days old. Sadly Lily died a few months later.

In 1904 the family moved into Howe Cottages and James was employed as a cowman on The Howe Estate. Violet had been joined by Thomas George born in 1903, Walter James 1906 and Jennie in 1910. The family remained in the cottage until around 1915. Following a break of about seven years, (coinciding with the First World War years), James and his family moved back on to The Howe Estate and into Howe Lodge in 1922 where they remained until 1926. In 1938 they lived at Bousser Cottages. James died in 1949 aged 77 years.

In 1928 both Thomas and Walter married local girls. Thomas married Ruth Rose Burder, the daughter of George and Sarah Burder who lived at Howe Ground and Walter married Gladys Marvin.

L. Frederick Ramsey was born in 1868 in Tooting, London, the son of John Ramsey, a domestic coachman and his wife Lucy. By 1891 Frederick worked as a groom, and in 1896 he married Lydia Cooper from Drinkstone, Suffolk. They moved to Lexden, near Colchester where Frederick was a coachman for Colonel Morgan Crofton, who was an Army Staff Officer.

Frederick, Lydia and their two sons, John and Fred left Lexden and moved to Howe Cottages when Frederick was employed as a coachman at The Howe. He worked for the Hornor family until Anne's death in 1914. In November 1914 Frederick was seeking new employment and placed the following advertisement in the Essex Newsman, situations vacant column; *"Coachman or any place of trust; can drive a motor car; 10 years excellent character; left through death; wife good laundress. Ramsey, Howe Cottage, Halstead".*

Right or Left hand side cottage.
William Butcher lived at Howe Cottages from about 1915 to 1919.

Albert Saunders 1919 - 1923 *(See Chauffeurs employed at The Howe, page 126 for further information).*

Martha Norman c1915 - 1923. Martha with her sister Sarah had previously lived at 26 Box Mill Lane, (Red Cow Cottage), with their family for many years before they moved into Howe Cottage.

Howe Lodge circa 1910
Does anyone recognise the youngsters in the photograph? (Or can you name the dog)!

Chapter Nineteen
The Howe Estate – Howe Lodge and occupants

Howe Lodge was almost certainly built around 1825, at about the same time as The Howe was erected or revamped by Edward May. It was very similar in style to The Howe stables and the end on cottages at Howe Ground as it was built in gault bricks with flint infill. Howe Lodge comprised of five rooms and was located at the bottom of the main drive leading to the mansion house. It stood where the entrance to Ashlong Grove is situated today. Over the years Howe Lodge was also referred to as Lodge Cottage, Howe Gate and Howe Lodge Gate.

The Lodge was originally built for the occupation of workers on The Howe Estate, although when it was not required by Howe employees it was available for rent to non estate workers. These tenants were expected to keep the drive swept and to open and close the Lodge gates when residents of The Howe or their guests wished to pass through them.

Howe Lodge circa 1910.

After Edward May, Howe Lodge was owned for at least six decades by the Hornor family before it was sold to Samuel Courtauld when he acquired The Howe Estate. During this time many families lived at the Lodge. The following list includes the majority of these tenants:-

Robert Plant was born c1811 and his wife Isabella was born c1816. Neither of them originated from Essex but they had moved to Halstead by 1841 and lived at the Lodge. Robert was employed by Edward May as a gardener at The Howe.

Samuel Emberson was born at Great Waltham and he married Elizabeth Brand in 1835, who was at born Great Bardfield. In 1851 they lived at the Lodge and Samuel was employed as a drover. By 1861 they had moved and, in 1881, they lived in North Street and Samuel was employed as a gardener He died five years later in 1886 and Elizabeth died in 1890.

Henry and Hannah Norman were the next tenants who lived at the Lodge following their marriage in 1861. They moved to Box Mill Lane in 1869. *(See Chapter 21 which relates to the Norman family).*

Elizabeth and Martha Monk; George, an agricultural labourer and his wife Susan lived with their three daughters in a cottage at Howe Ground. Following the death of Susan in 1866 and George in 1869, two of their daughters, Elizabeth, known as Betsy, born 1831 and Martha, born 1833 moved to Howe Lodge in 1871. Betsy worked as a crepe weaver and Martha was a seamstress. They left the Lodge before 1881 and moved to Manfield where Martha died in 1887 and Betsy died in 1905.

Alfred Bragg and his wife Eliza were born in 1839. They were both from Halstead and occupied Howe Lodge from at least 1881 until they moved to 17 Box Mill Lane in 1891. Alfred was employed as an agricultural labourer for most of his life.

Charles Paflin was born in 1867 at Sible Hedingham. In 1890 he married Alice Rayner born in 1868 at Halstead. They lived in North Street and Charles worked as a groom while Alice was employed as a silk crepe weaver. They had two children, Mabel born 1891, and Basil who was baptised in 1896 at St Andrew's Church. The family moved to Howe Lodge in the latter half of 1894 and Charles was employed as a stockman on The Howe Estate. The family moved again around 1898 to another property in North Street. When Charles died in 1906 aged 32 years he was employed as a domestic gardener. Mabel died in 1906 aged 15 years and Alice died in 1916(?). Basil married Annie Morden in 1927.

Charles Henry Rayner was born 7th April 1865 at Halstead, the son of William, a bricklayer, and Mary Ann formerly Ellis. Charles spent his childhood around the Mount Pleasant area of Halstead and, by the time he was 16 years old, he was a labourer at the paper mill. In 1891 he was employed as a bricklayer journeyman by Harcourt Runnacles, a Halstead builder, in the construction of Bawdsey Manor, near Woodbridge, Suffolk.

Charles Henry Rayner 1865-1941

Charles worked with George Last who was also a bricklayer and they both lodged with 'Happy' Dunn at The Street, Bawdsey. On 26th December 1891 Charles married Fanny Carter at Holy Trinity Church, Halstead. Fanny, born in 1865 in Gloucestershire, was the daughter of Edward Carter who worked as 'a carter' at Portishead Docks. After their marriage they returned to Bawdsey and their first child Charles Edwin Rayner was born in 1892. His birth was registered at Woodbridge. On returning to Halstead three more children were born: Dennis Henry in 1893, Gladys in 1895 and Mildred Gertrude in 1899. The family moved from Mount Pleasant to Howe Lodge in 1900 and Charles Henry continued to work as a bricklayer journeyman.

'Bunny Boys' circa 1901
Left to right: Charles Edwin Rayner, Dennis Henry Rayner, Stanley Symonds,(?) unknown
Courtesy of Marcel Rayner

The photograph of the 'Bunny Boys' was taken at the rear of Henry George (Harry) and Florence Hughes garden at Westbourne, Chapel Street. They ran the Baptist Church Sunday School and allowed the youngsters to use their garden for social activities. A 'Bunny Club' was formed there, where Charles and Dennis bred rabbits along with other lads which were sold to raise money for the Baptist Church in North Street. The church then donated these funds to aid the Missionaries in Africa who helped the needy.

Charles Edwin Rayner, born 1892, the eldest son of Charles and Fanny ran away from home and joined the army in 1910. He fought in the First World War and was killed in action on 25th October 1917 aged 25 years, after seven years service with the 4th (Queen's Own) Hussars and the 15th Battalion Royal Warwickshire Regiment. Charles is commemorated on the Tyne Cot Memorial in Belgium and on the War Memorial in St Andrew's Churchyard, Halstead.

Dennis Henry Rayner, born in 1893, was thirteen years old in 1907 when he was employed by Frank Vaizey at Bentalls Farm, Sudbury Road as a houseboy. As well as indoor duties, Dennis helped to look after the livestock and worked in the garden. He worked seven days a week, and, with his daily meals provided was paid half a crown a week (12½p). He also had the use of a bicycle while he remained in Frank Vaizey's employment.

Dennis Henry Rayner with his bicycle outside Tylneys Paddock, Sudbury Road
Courtesy of Marcel Rayner

Charles Henry Rayner, as an elderly gentleman tending his bee hives

In 1911 Dennis left Frank Vaizey's employment and worked as a chauffeur in London for Dr. Field before he emigrated to Canada and joined the Canadian Army.

Dennis Henry Rayner 1912 when he joined the Canadian Army
Courtesy of Marcel Rayner

In 1914 Dennis returned to England with the 18th Battalion Western Ontario Regiment (Canada) before they were sent to fight in France in 1915.

In 1919 after the First World War the Rayner family left Howe Lodge and moved to 105 Hedingham Road. The next occupant at the Lodge was Ada Durward.

In 1924 Dennis married Constance Alice Steed born in 1900, the daughter of Walter Steed a painter and decorator and Alice Jane formerly Bragg. They had two sons, Dennis Edwin Rayner born in 1924 and Marcel John Rayner born in 1931. Dennis lives in Germany and Marcel resides at the Courtauld Homes of Rest in Hedingham Road.

Gladys Rayner married Alfred John Woods in 1925 and Muriel married Ernest Dymond known as 'Dolphus' in 1931.

*Dennis Henry Rayner circa 1914, 18th Battalion Western Ontario Regiment. (Canada)
Courtesy of Marcel Rayner*

Charles Henry Rayner died in 1941 and Fanny, his wife died in 1949.

Ada Hilda Durward was born in 1897 at Richmond, Surrey. She was the eldest daughter of Robert, a potato merchant who was born in Aberdeen, and Ellen, who was born in Hollesley, Suffolk. By 1911, Ada had left Surrey and moved with her parents and four sisters to Woodbridge where her father was employed as a gamekeeper. In 1919 Ada moved into Howe Lodge when she worked for SAC as a stockwoman and dairymaid on The Howe Estate. In October 1920, Ada entered a milking competition held at an Agricultural Show in London and won third prize in the women's section. She remained at the Lodge until around 1922 and in 1927, married Geoffrey William Highmore, (1897-1983) at Paddington, London. Geoffrey was the son of George, a Church of England clergyman and Kathleen Highmore formerly Brodrick. Geoffrey was also a clergyman and was curate of St. Mary's Parish Church, Beverley from 1927 to 1932 before he became vicar of Newport Parish Church 1932 to 1937. Geoffrey and Ada had three children, Richard, David and Jennifer born between 1949 and 1958. The family lived at Stonegrave vicarage in Yorkshire where Geoffrey was the Rector of Stonegrave with Nunnington Parish Churches. Ada died in 1972 and Geoffrey died in 1983.

In 1950 Beatrice Durward, a younger sister of Ada's lived briefly at 25 Box Mill Lane, next door to Leonard Howard, (a chauffeur to SAC) and his second wife Jane Amy.

James Laver 1922 -1927 *(See Howe Cottages, Chapter 18 for further information).*

Eliza Coe was born in Little Maplestead. She moved to Halstead and was employed at Courtauld's Mill for many years. Eliza occupied Howe Lodge from 1927 until 1930 when she moved into a cottage in Hedingham Road where she remained for the rest of her life.

George William Sibley was born in 1878 at Stisted, the son of William and Isabella Sibley. In 1881 he lived with his parents and four older sisters at Red Brick Cottage, Stisted. As a youngster George worked as a gardener's boy and, in 1901, he was employed with seven other gardeners at Alton Towers, Staffordshire, under head gardener Edwin Gilman. The young men, who came from all areas of the United Kingdom, lived together in the 'Gardeners Cottage' under the watchful eye of the foreman, Philip Bovington. George married Charlotte Elizabeth Last (1864-1925) in the Chelmsford area in 1907 and their daughter, Florence, was born later that year. George worked as a gardener all his life and, in 1911 lived at Coggeshall with his wife and daughter before they moved to 26 Box Mill Lane around 1920, when George was employed at The Howe. Following her mother's death in 1925, Florence married Albert Dicker in 1926 and in 1931 George relocated to Howe Lodge. He was one of the last tenants before it was demolished. In 1935 he was re-housed at Duval, Colchester Road, in one of the newly built Courtauld houses and died in 1945.

Hedingham Road, with the entrance to Ashlong Grove on the left hand side, late 1960s

Howe Lodge – 1915

Howe Cottages

Howe Lodge and Howe Cottages in the snow

Chapter Twenty
The Howe Estate – Bailiffs Cottage, North Lodge, Howe Gardens, Gardeners Cottage or Howe Cottage

During the late nineteenth century the cottage which stood towards the end of Cart Park and Chase close to The Howe was referred to in various documents as:- Cottage near The Howe, Bailiffs Cottage, North Lodge, Howe Gardens and Howe Cottage. It was also known, at one time as the Gardeners Cottage. It was primarily built for the use of the farm bailiffs, stewards and stockmen as it was situated close to the dairy, farmyard and farm buildings. However from the beginning of 1903 it was occupied successively by two of the gardeners who were employed at The Howe.

Built of red brick, it was probably erected during the mid Victorian period, after the tax on bricks was abolished. A dwelling on this site appeared on the 1874 Ordnance survey map, although the first direct reference to the cottage on the census return's is not until the 1891, when the cottage is referred to as, "Cottage in How Ground", with one of the occupant's, Derwick Rodgers, listed as "a stockman". (The other cottages at Howe Ground are transcribed as in "Hedingham Road").

When The Howe Estate was sold in the 1950s the cottage was bought by Thomas Grant, who lived in it for a while. It was later occupied by Arthur Osborne and his family before it was eventually sold and incorporated into a newly erected house.

The Bailiffs Cottage
The red brick building, which today forms part of a larger house

Dewick Rodgers was born in 1853 at Hanthorpe, Lincolnshire. His mother, Mary, died in 1859 and with his seven brothers and sisters he lived with his widowed father who was a farmer. By 1891 Dewick had moved into the cottage and was employed as a stockman on the estate. Dewick was married to Sarah Elizabeth and had a son Leonard and step daughter Elizabeth Gardner, when he moved to Halstead. However his employment with the Hornor family did not last long as Dewick died two years later in 1893 in the Romford area aged 40 years.

James Thirkettle was born in 1850 at Moulton, Norfolk, the son of a farmer. He worked on his father's farm and married Emma Myhill in 1871. Following Emma's death at Norfolk in 1896, James moved to Halstead and was employed by Anne Hornor as her farm steward. James lived at the cottage until 1903 with a housekeeper, Margaret Smith, who was also born in Norfolk. In 1911 he was the landlord of the Game Keepers Arms at Great Bentley before he returned to Halstead where he died in 1917 aged 67 years.

Henry Dring, a gardener moved with his family from Howe Cottages into the cottage following the departure of James Thirkettle and remained there until he died in 1920. *(See Chapter 18 for further details about the Dring Family)*.

Frederick William Alston, Freddie and Emily Alston moved into the cottage in 1921. Freddie worked as a gardener and Emily helped out in The Howe when required. They remained at the cottage until 1953/4. *(See Chapter 12 for further details about Freddie and Emily Alston)*.

The north west and south west elevations of the Bailiffs Cottage

Chapter Twenty One
The Norman Family

Three Generations of the Norman Family worked on The Howe Estate and would have seen many changes over the years.

1. William Norman
William Norman and Martha Spurgeon, who were both born in 1771, were married at St Andrew's Church, Halstead in 1797. They had at least three sons and two daughters:

1A.	William Norman	1798-1843	
1B.	Thomas Norman	1803-1856	
1C.	James Norman	1806-1828	
	Susanna Norman	1811-1898	married William Sturmer *(Please see page 159 for further information)*
1D.	Sarah Norman	1815-1896	

William Norman was employed as an agricultural labourer at How(e) Farm from about the age of eight years and was well acquainted with the Start family. During his employment on the farm he would also have worked for John Crump and John Sparrow, the tenant farmers. Therefore, in 1838, it was hardly surprising that he was required to make a legal statement regarding Box Mill Meadow when its ownership was disputed, as the parties involved were very well known to him.

From at least 1827 William and Martha and their family lived in a cottage at The Wash, Hedingham Lane. When William died c1846 he had worked for over fifty years on the farm. Martha continued to live in the cottage with her daughter Sarah and grandson Henry and was recorded as a pauper when she died in 1860 aged 89 years.

William and Martha Norman's children and their families:
1A. William Norman, the eldest son was baptised in 1798 at St Andrew's Church and, with his wife Ann born in 1801, they lived in one of the cottages at Doe's Corner, Hedingham Lane. Like his father William, a farm labourer, he was also employed at How(e) Farm. William and Ann had two sons:

2a.	William Norman	1826-1907
2b.	Henry Norman	1831-1910

Ann died during the 1830s and William died in 1843 aged 45 years.

2a. William Norman born in 1826 was the eldest son of William and Ann. By 1841 he had left the cottage at Doe's Corner and lived with his grandparents William and Martha, his widowed father, Aunt Sarah and brother Henry in the cottage at The Wash. After the death of their father in 1843, William and Henry remained with their grandparents.

William married Eliza Cook at St Andrew's Church in 1847 and they moved into a cottage at Howe Ground. William worked as an agricultural labourer on the farm for both Edward May and Edward Hornor.

William and Eliza had eight children:

Frances Norman	1848-1871
Mary Norman	1850-1925
Jane Norman	1851-1871
William Norman	1853-1923
James Norman	1856- ?
Henry Norman	1859-1926
Edward Norman	1861-1906
Ellen Norman	1864- ?

Two of William and Eliza's daughters, Frances and Jane who were silk weavers, died in 1871 within two months of one another and are interred in St Andrew's Churchyard.

By 1901, William who was now an elderly gentleman, worked as a gardener at The Howe until he died in 1907 aged 83 years, having given fifty years of faithful service. After his death Eliza received a pension and continued to live in the cottage at Howe Ground with her two unmarried daughters Mary and Ellen. Eliza died in 1911 aged 83 years and Mary remained in the cottage until she died in 1925.

Howe Ground Cottages

William Norman, William and Eliza's eldest son was born in 1853. In 1876 William married Clara Richardson who already had a young son Leonard and they lived in Halstead. William worked at Courtauld's Mill, firstly as a factory mechanic and later as a silk weaver. He died in 1923 and Clara died in 1924. Leonard married Alice Ethel Kibble and later was the Grocery Manager for the Co-operative Society.

Henry Norman who was born in 1859 moved to Yorkshire as a young man, where he was employed as a groom and gardener. He married Sarah Alice Holt in 1880 and they remained in the Hemsworth area of Yorkshire for the rest of their lives. Henry evidently preferred an indoor job and was a painter and paper hanger until his death in 1926. They did not have any children.

Edward Norman who was born in 1861, emigrated to Canada. In 1882 he married Sarah Elizabeth Norman at Guelph, Ontario. Sarah was the daughter of John Norman, a publican, and his wife Sarah who lived at Halstead. Edward and Sarah had nine children, Edward, Henry, Adelaide, Percy, Sydney, Stanley, Florence, Lancelot and Basil, born between 1883 and 1904. The family lived at Widdifield in the Nipissing District of Ontario and Edward's occupations varied from butcher to farm labourer and, at the time of his death, a farmer. Edward died in March 1906, but his death was not registered until September 1906 when it was stated that; *"Death was due to Justifiable Homicide"*. A newspaper report of the inquest stated that Edward was a quiet well behaved man when sober, but decidedly quarrelsome when drunk. Arguments in the Norman household had been a matter of notoriety for some time, when one Saturday Edward returned home in a bad temper and quarrelled with Sarah. Soon other members of the family were involved and Charles turned on one of his younger sons. The terrified lad picked up an axe, struck his father in self defence and the blow killed him. Both Edward and Sarah who were Baptists were buried at St John's Anglican Cemetery, North Bay, Ontario.

2b. Henry Norman who was born in 1831 was the youngest son of William and Ann. He lived firstly at Doe's Corner and then at The Wash with his grandmother and was employed as a gardener at The Howe. Hannah Parr was born in 1832 at Castle Hedingham, the daughter of George and Mary Parr and worked for Ann Hornor as a 'live in' servant. Henry and Hannah were married in early 1861 and moved into Howe Lodge. Henry continued his employment on The Howe Estate while Hannah was busy raising a family.

Martha Norman	1861-1939
Charles Norman	1863-1952
Arthur Norman	1865-1930
Herbert Norman	1867-1922
Sarah Ann Norman	1870-1943
William Norman	1872-1944

By 1869 Henry and Hannah and their growing family had moved into one of the Howe Cottages on Thrifts Hill. However they had not stayed there long, because by 1871 they lived at the Red Cow, a cottage in Box Mill Lane, a former public house, which had been recently refurbished by Edward Hornor.

Henry and Hannah remained in the cottage for the rest of their lives. Hannah died in 1904 aged 72 years and Henry died in 1910 aged 78 years having spent all his working life at The Howe as a gardener.

Henry and Hannah Norman's children:
Martha Norman, who was born in 1861 was the oldest child, and as she never married, she

spent her time with her parents in the family home, taking in needlework to earn a living. With her younger sister Sarah, they moved into 23 Box Mill Lane, one of the cottages next door to the Red Cow where they remained until they moved into the Courtauld Homes of Rest in 1928. Martha died in 1939.

Charles Norman was born in 1863 and he married Harriett Ann Scrivener from the Chelmsford area in 1888. They moved to Lewisham, London, where Charles worked as a domestic gardener. By 1891 Charles and Harriett had moved to Bromley, Kent, where Charles was a sub postmaster and draper. By 1911 he had dispensed with the drapery business and sold stationery at the Post Office instead. They had four children, Charles Henry, Hannah Rose, Ernest Samuel and Alice Annie, born between 1888 and 1899. Charles died in 1952 aged 89 years.

Arthur Norman was born in 1865 and in 1881 when he was 15 years old he worked as a page for a solicitor in Epping. He married Sarah Hill in 1888 and they lived in Chiswick, before moving to Acton in Middlesex. Following Sarah's death in 1893 aged 32 years, Arthur married secondly Amy Colbran Reader in 1894 and he worked as a greengrocer's carman. He had a total of six children with both wives; Arthur Hill, Henry Charles, Amy Dorothy, Emily Colbran, Louisa Martha and William David, born between 1889 and 1901. Arthur died in 1930 aged 64 years.

Herbert Norman was born in 1867 and lived with his brother Arthur for a while when he worked as a drayman. He married Kate Lawes in 1891 and they lived in Chiswick where Herbert was employed as a brewer's carman. They had two sons Herbert William born 1892 and Harold Frederick in 1895. Herbert died in 1922 aged 54 years and Kate married secondly John Townsend in 1925.

Sarah Ann Norman, known as Annie, was born in 1870, and with her eldest sister remained in Halstead with her parents. She moved to the Courtauld Homes of Rest with her sister Martha and died in 1943 aged 73 years.

William Norman, known as Willie, was the youngest son who was born in 1872. Like his brothers, he left Halstead and, in 1891, lived with Arthur in Chiswick and worked as a grocer's assistant. He married Emma Rose in 1900 and they lived in Tottenham, Middlesex, where William was employed as a grocer's manager. In 1911 they were in the same premises at 747 High Street, Tottenham, but Willie was now the shopkeeper - grocer and an employer. They had two children Leslie William born 1906 and Phyllis Muriel born 1909. Willie died in 1944 aged 72 years.

1B. Thomas Norman was born in 1803 the youngest son of William and Martha Norman. He was baptized at St Andrew's Church, Halstead, where he also married Eliza Parr in 1824. Eliza who was born in Castle Hedingham, was the daughter of Charles Parr and his second wife Mary Parr, formerly Barron. The Barron family, like the Sewell and Start families were bay and say makers in Halstead. (Eliza was an aunt of Hannah Parr who married Henry Norman). After their marriage Thomas and Eliza moved to a cottage on Howe Ground and Thomas was employed by Edward May as a farm labourer. By 1841 Thomas had a much more responsible position on the farm, as he was the farm bailiff - a position he held for a number of years. His duties would have involved managing both The Howe and Ridgewell Hill farms. Thomas and Eliza had at least three daughters:

Mary Ann Norman	1827
Susannah Norman	1837
Jane Norman	1840

Thomas died in 1856 and Eliza moved to Hedingham Lane where, according to the 1861 census return, she lived with Susannah and her Grandson Edwin Albon Norman? *(An error appears on the census return as Eliza's Grandson was baptised Edmund)*, until she died in 1867. Both Thomas and Eliza are buried at Halstead Cemetery. A headstone survives although some of the inscription has eroded away over the years.

'In memory of Thomas Norman, many years bailiff at The Howe Farm in this parish, who died June 14th 1856 aged 53 years. Much respected and regretted by all who knew him…..(unreadable)…..25 years. Eliza wife of the above who died March 15th 1867 aged 62 years'.

Mary Ann Norman, Thomas and Eliza's daughter worked as a dressmaker and married Robert Balls a bricklayer in 1851. They lived in North Street. They had five children, Emily, Jane, Thomas, Elizabeth and Kate, born between 1854 and 1865. Robert died in 1876 aged 49 years.

Susannah Norman, known as Susanna or sometimes Susan, was a silk weaver. She had an illegitimate son Edmund Norman, born in London and baptised at St Andrew's Church in 1859. Following her mother's death in 1867 Susannah and Edmund left the cottage. In 1871 Susannah a nurse, resided in Trinity Street with George Cressall and his family. Edmund who was twelve years of age, was an errand boy, who lived with Robert Thompson, a boot maker, and his family in the High Street. As a nurse, Susannah's work took her away from Halstead and she lived 'in house' to care for her patients. From 1881 she worked mainly around the London area and in 1901 had retired to the Brentford District where she died in 1916(?), a spinster.

Jane Norman, who was born in 1840 was living with her parents in 1851. *(It is possible that Jane may have worked as a parlour maid in Mortlake, Richmond, Surrey, in 1861).*

1C. James Norman was born in 1856. On the 1871 census he is living with his parents and employed as an agricultural labourer. *(No further information).*

1D. Sarah Norman who was born in 1815 was William and Martha's youngest daughter. When her sister Susanna married William Sturmer in 1839, Sarah, and Jacob Evans were the two witnesses. In 1860 Sarah was a straw plaiter living at home with her mother and nephew Henry. Following Martha's death in 1860, Sarah married Joseph Evans in 1861 and they resided in Hedingham Lane. Joseph was a pork butcher and the son of Jacob Evans, a farmer. In 1869 Edward Hornor appointed Joseph as his agent when he purchased some property at The Wash on Edward's behalf. By 1871 Joseph was a pig dealer and continued with his pork business until he retired in 1891. Hedingham Lane was renamed and Joseph and Sarah's cottage was number 50 North Street. Joseph died in 1892 followed by Sarah in 1896.

The old five bar gate into Abbey Croft Field, Box Mill Lane

Box Mill Bridge, looking across Abbey Croft Field towards Hedingham Road
(Both photographs circa 1960s)

Chapter Twenty Two
Cottages in Box Mill Lane and the Old School House

Box Mill Lane is situated off Hedingham Road, almost opposite the entrance to Wash Farm. At the opposite end of the lane a watermill once straddled the River Colne and a windmill stood near the west bank.

The Mills and Cottages in Box Mill Lane
In 1735 the watermill, known as Box Mill, was occupied by Isaac Sewell. Built close to the mill were five tenements which, in 1753, belonged to 'the late' William Swan. As requested in Swan's will, these tenements were held in trust by William Sewell and John Start until Thomas Swan, William's son and heir, reached twenty one years of age. Isaac Sewell acquired these tenements in 1753/4 and leased them to John Hallebread, Francis Wells, William Brown, Joseph Harrington and John Bentall.

When Isaac made his will in 1775, he instructed his Executors to sell his Customary or Copyhold messuage, watermill and windmill (the windmill having recently been erected on land near to Box Mill) to his nephew Thomas Greenwood for £800. If Thomas declined the offer, the estate was to be sold and he would receive £100 only. Isaac died in August 1781 and in 1782 Thomas was admitted to the above properties. However, by 1789 he had advertised them for sale in the 'Chelmsford Chronicle'. According to Land Tax Returns, dated 1789, Thomas Greenwood, a miller, had sold the two mills to William Digby who was the new owner and occupier. By this time the Box Mill property consisted of a watermill and windmill, houses, outhouses, barns, stables, kilns, yards, gardens, orchards, lands, meadows, pastures, feedings and hereditaments. In 1791 William Digby also purchased a further copyhold area of land from Thomas Greenwood, which had previously belonged to the Box Mill Estate.

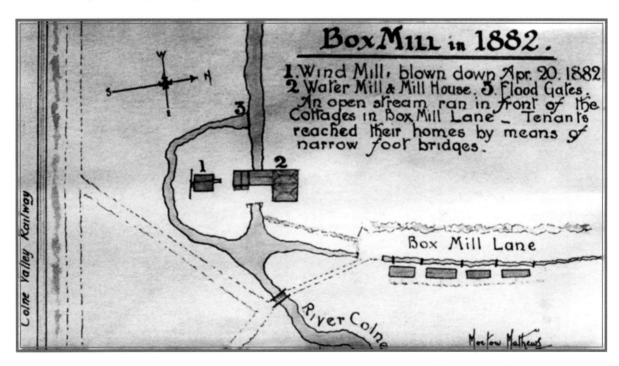

Sketch map of Box Mill in 1882 by Morton Mathews (1866-1953)

Although the sketch map overleaf is not an accurate map, particularly the compass points, it is representative of the layout. The river at Box Mill was approximately north to south and the watermill straddled the river approximately west to east. The Mill House was attached to the east side of the watermill and the windmill stood separately to the west.

Isaac Sewell did not leave all the Box Mill property to Thomas Greenwood, as Isaac's nephew, also named Isaac, inherited the five tenements which his uncle had acquired in 1753/4. As Isaac was a minor, his father John Sewell looked after the properties until he was twenty one years old. In December 1799 Isaac sold the five dwellings to William Digby.

Shortly after acquiring the tenements, William Digby sought permission from the Lord of the Manor of Abells to demolish the properties, after he had built a pair of cottages to replace them. The new dwellings were erected on the plot of land abutting onto his Box Mill property, which he had purchased from Thomas Greenwood in 1791. Permission was granted and, in June 1806 William returned to the Court to be admitted to the new cottages which he had recently completed. These two cottages were erected at the east end of Box Mill Lane near the Red Cow Public House. The old tenements were demolished and the land was converted into a garden for Box Mill.

Box Mill

Many families occupied these newly built cottages, including Jonas Sargeant and Thomas Sargeant in 1822. In 1824 William Digby left Box Mill and moved into the cottage vacated by Thomas Sargeant. After William's departure from the mill John Ruffle was admitted as the next tenant. William Digby died in 1827 and, in 1829, Edward May acquired the cottages from James Digby, the late William's son, for £159 3s 8d, when they were leased to John Slater and Edward Hostler.

Edward May also bought a Customary or Copyhold piece of arable land which was approximately one acre and one rod in size. Its south west boundary abutted on to the garden which belonged to Box Mill. The north east boundary adjoined the above cottages and gardens. To the north west was Broadfield, which was already in Edward's possession. The south east side of the land bordered Box Mill Lane. All these cottages and land were incorporated into The Howe Estate.

The Cottages built by William Digby were not numbered until around the 1870, when the left hand side cottage was known as 23 Box Mill Lane and the right hand side cottage as 24 Box Mill Lane. The following families also occupied these cottages. (Research ends at 1960).

No. 23 Box Mill Lane	No. 24 Box Mill Lane
Edward Hostler	John Slater
Mary Jeggo	
James Maxim	
George Kibble	
Alfred Reeve	
Frederick Legerton	Abram Drury
	Mark Goodey
John Goodey ---------occupied both cottages----------	John Goodey
Herbert Goodey ----- occupied both cottages---------	Herbert Goodey
Martha Norman	George Fuller
Stanley Fairbank	

In 1841, the left hand side cottage was occupied by Mary Jeggo, followed by James Maxim whose wife Sophia, worked as a housekeeper for the May family. The right hand side cottage was leased to John and Elizabeth Slater and their daughter Susan.

John Slater who was employed as a poulterer died in early 1844, the same year that Arthur Macnamara and William Gossett purchased the cottages and land from Edward May. In 1845 when Edward Hornor purchased the properties Elizabeth, known as Betsy and Susan remained the tenants, while the next door cottage was leased to George Kibble for a short time. Betsy worked as a laundress and, later, as a charwoman, while Susan was employed as a crepe worker. Susan died in 1864 and Betsy in 1866.

By 1851 George Kibble had vacated his cottage and it was occupied by Alfred Reeve, a master blacksmith, his wife Harriett and their children, Ann, Emily, Abraham and Alfred. Before 1861 the Reeve family had left the cottage and moved to Rosemary Lane and the Legerton family were in residence.

In 1851 Frederick Legerton, his wife Ann and daughter Julia Ann, with Frederick's brother Horace, lived at Legerton's Mill, Cut Maple in Sible Hedingham. The young men who were both in their twenties worked as millers and beer sellers. Their father Samuel lived next door at Hole Farm House with his wife and the rest of Frederick's siblings. Following Samuel's death in 1859 the family left Hole Farm and the Mill and, by 1861, Horace was married and lived in Swan Street, Sible Hedingham. Frederick, Ann, Julia and two more children Frederick Lewis and Alice Jane had moved to No. 23 Box Mill Lane.

Following Edward Hornor's death in 1868, the copyhold cottages were transferred to Anne and they were enfranchised in 1869. Also by 1871 the cottages were officially identified as Numbers 23 and 24 Box Mill Lane.

Following the death of Betsy Slater, No. 24 was occupied by Abram Drury a widower, who was a birch brush maker, and his three daughters, Ellen, Sophia and Maria. In 1874 Maria Drury married Mark Goodey who lived with his parents Alfred and Elizabeth at The Wash, Hedingham Road, and they took over the tenancy of Abram's cottage. Mark and Maria remained at the cottage until about 1891 when, with an ever increasing family, they had out grown No. 24 and moved to Parsonage Street.

When Mark left, his brother, John Goodey, a groom, moved into the cottage with his wife Ellen formerly Kemp and their three children. For the next four years the Legerton's were their neighbours. Frederick and Ann Legerton both died in 1895, after living in their cottage for about thirty four years. With the arrival of more children, the Goodey family took over the tenancy of No. 23 and therefore the family occupied both the cottages. By 1901 John, was coachman and groom to Anne Hornor. He also had eight children, Harold, who helped to milk the cows, Stanley, Daisy, Ada, Ethel, Maurice, Alfred and Eva. However by 1911 with the addition of four more children the Goodey family had moved to Braintree and John worked at the Silk Mill.

Numbers 23 and 24 Box Mill Lane
Courtesy of Doreen Potts

After John's departure No. 23 and No. 24 were once again let to a member of the Goodey family, John's nephew, Herbert Goodey. Herbert was the son of James, Mark and John's brother, and Matilda Goodey, who lived in one of the cottages at The Wash which was owned by the Hornor Family. Herbert, who was married to Annie formerly Earey, was employed as a millers carman and had four children, Herbert, Florence, Winifred, and Reginald. Herbert and Annie remained at the cottages until 1923. After the Goodey family had departed, Samuel Courtauld who had purchased the cottages to house past and current employees at The Howe returned them to two separate dwellings.

In 1923, No. 23 was occupied by Martha Norman and her sister Sarah Anne who had moved from the Red Cow to one of the Howe Cottages on Wash Hill. They returned to live in Box Mill Lane until 1928 when they moved into one of the Courtauld Homes of Rest.

Stanley Ernest Fairbank was born in 1890 in Halstead and married Annie Butcher in 1918. Annie died in 1924 aged 33 years and Stanley married Emily Rulton in 1927 and they moved into No. 23 when the cottage was vacated by Martha and Sarah Norman. They were still in residence in 1960.

Also in 1923, No. 24 was occupied by George and Edith Fuller and their two daughters, Phyllis and Winifred. Phyllis married Albert Blackwell in 1927 and they lived at Howe Ground. George died in 1937 and, three years later, Winifred married George Jarvis and they lived at the cottage with Edith who died in 1953. George and Winifred continued to live in the cottage and were still in residence in 1960.

Number 23 and number 24 Box Mill Lane Cottages were demolished around 1970.

The Entrance to Box Mill Lane
The School House is on the right hand side, hidden behind the trees

NB. The two cottages which stood at the far end of Box Mill Lane, on the right hand side, were built between 1841 and 1874, and were known as 'Box Mill Cottages'. Today, after substantial renovation work, they form a single dwelling. They are not to be confused with the cottages built by William Digby which became known as 'Box Mill Lane Cottages or 23 and 24 Box Mill Lane'

The Red Cow Inn/Cottage, later referred to as Numbers 25 and 26 Box Mill Lane
In 1834 Mary Draper (c1791-1859) attended the Manorial Court to be admitted to her late brother John Brown's property. This included the Red Cow, a public house which was situated at the Hedingham Road end of Box Mill Lane. Thomas Draper (1800-1855), a higgler and Mary's husband was the landlord. In 1841 their daughter, Sarah, lived with them but had left by 1851 when Thomas's niece, Sarah Ann Draper, was their lodger.

Thomas died in 1855 and in 1856 Mary rented the Red Cow with the dwelling house, stable, coach house, outbuildings, yard, gardens and orchards to Timothy Steward and Henry Stainforth Patterson of Norfolk. These two gentlemen were co partners in the firm of Steward and Patterson and Company, a brewery in Norwich. The lease was for fourteen years at £30 per annum. However, Mary had not sought permission from the Manorial Court to lease out the property which was only discovered after she died in 1859, when Isaac Drain was the inn keeper. In 1861 The Lord of the Manor, The Right Honourable William Richard Arthur, Earl of Mornington declared the lease invalid, and the Red Cow and hereditaments were forfeited and seized by the bailiff, George de Horne Vaizey, and returned to The Manor of Abells.

In 1862 Edward Hornor acquired the Red Cow which stood between the Box Mill Lane cottages and the newly built Howe School. As a member of the Temperance Society he quickly converted the public house into a residential property, although many of the original features remained. Edward also purchased *'a parcel of garden ground'*, formerly a gravel pit, which was five rods long and one rod wide. It's south west boundary fence abutted onto the garden of No. 24 Box Mill Cottages. This land was formerly owned by John Brown, before it passed to Thomas Draper.

In 1868 when the properties were transferred to Anne Hornor the dwelling house, (the Red Cow), was described as two customary or copyhold cottages with outhouses, outbuildings, yards, gardens, orchards and appurtenances. Thomas Norman and his family, and Samuel Disney were the occupants when Anne was granted a deed of enfranchisement in 1869 on both the cottages and the garden ground.

The Cottage on the left hand side was later known as No. 25 Box Mill Lane and the cottage on the right hand side cottage was No. 26.

Thomas Norman who was born in 1826 was the son of Christopher Norman a gardener and his wife Susanna. Thomas a factory labourer married Sarah Paine in 1849 and they lived at Tan Yard, Halstead. They had at least four children, Susannah, Thomas, Eliza and Christopher. The family moved into No. 25 Box Mill Lane in the mid 1860s. In 1871 Thomas was employed as a factory hand at the silk mill, and, Sarah and Eliza worked as laundresses. Sarah died in 1883 and Thomas continued to live at the cottage with his unmarried daughter Eliza, who was employed as a dressmaker. During early 1893 Eliza married William Chaplin, a gentlemen, some fifteen years older than herself, and they lived at Tidings Hill. Her father Thomas died later the same year.

Christopher Norman, Thomas and Susanna's son, was born in 1863 and lived at home with his parents until 1890 when he married Charlotte Allen, the daughter of John Allen, an agricultural labourer and his wife Hannah from Little Oakley. After they married Christopher who was employed as an upholsterer and Charlotte lived in North Street, not far from the entrance to Box Mill Lane. Following the death of Thomas and, Eliza's marriage, Christopher and Charlotte and their daughter Lenna Rose also born in 1893 moved into No. 25. They remained at the cottage for a number of years and were in residence at the time of the 1911 census.

Red Cow Cottages, 25 and 26 Box Mill Lane - 1965

Samuel Disney who lived in the right hand side cottage died in 1870. Henry and Hannah Norman and their family were the next occupants. Henry, who was a gardener at The Howe, had lived at Howe Lodge before he moved to one of the Howe Cottages prior to moving into No. 26 Box Mill Lane. Following the deaths of Hannah in 1904 and Henry in 1910 only their daughters Martha and Sarah were left at home. They remained in the cottage until about 1916 when they moved into one of the Howe Cottages on Wash Hill. (*For further details about Henry, Hannah and their family, see Chapter 21*).

Between 1911 and 1920 it is difficult to ascertain with 100% accuracy who resided in the cottages due to the lack of information recorded on the documentation.

Leonard Howard who was SAC's chauffeur and his wife Alice, moved from Braintree to Halstead when SAC bought The Howe, and lived at No. 25 from around 1915. Following the death of Alice in 1941 Leonard married secondly Jane Amy Woolgar in 1943 and she moved into the cottage. After Howard's death in 1951 Jane remained at the cottage until she died in 1958.

George and Alice Sibley and their daughter Florence moved from Coggeshall to Halstead and George worked as a gardener at The Howe for SAC. They lived at No. 26 from at least 1920 until they moved to Howe Lodge in 1931.

Following George's departure from No. 26 it appears that the two cottages, (Nos. 25 and 26) became a single dwelling and, for a number of years, it was occupied solely by the Howard's until Leonard's death in 1951. Following this date it was variously a single and a double dwelling.

The Howe School and School House
The Howe School with a master's house was built by Edward Hornor in 1861 and, was situated on the corner of Hedingham Road and Box Mill Lane, with access to the properties via a footpath off Box Mill Lane. Miss Louisa Kingsford who was the school mistress in 1862 was assisted by Florence and Beatrice Hornor when their help was required. Edward was also involved with the school children's religious education and held Sunday School meetings in the building.

In 1871, Emma Overall, who was born in 1848 at Ipswich, Suffolk, the daughter of James and Mary Overall lived and taught at the Howe School. Also resident at the house and listed as 'a boarder' was Sarah Jane True who was born in 1848 at Norwich, Norfolk, the daughter of Samuel and Sarah True. Sarah, like Emma, was a certificated school mistress although she taught at the British School in Halstead. By 1881 both girls had returned home. Emma lived with her widowed mother and sister Ellen, while Sarah worked as a governess.

In 1881, Margaret Paylen, a widow, lived at the house with her daughter Elizabeth Ann born in 1854, who was The Howe School mistress. Other residents included Margaret's daughter Frances aged 26 years, Mary Jane Gunton who was Margaret's 16 year old grand daughter and a pupil teacher, and Elizabeth Gill Farelly, a school mistress at the Girls British School. Elizabeth who was born in 1855 had trained in Liverpool as a pupil teacher in 1871. By 1891 the entire Paylen family with Elizabeth Farelly had moved to Newington, London. Elizabeth Ann and Elizabeth were both teachers at a Board School.

Although the actual Howe School closed in about 1881, Florence and Beatrice, with their friends help, held evening classes on the school premises. These classes allowed local girls, who did not have much freedom away from home, the opportunity to socialise with others who were in a similar situation. They learnt to entertain themselves by singing, drawing and taking up needlework.

By 1891, George Bean, an agricultural labourer born in 1836 at Acton, Suffolk, and his wife Eliza, a former charwoman, had moved from one of the cottages in Box Mill Lane, into the old school with their family, Frederick, Annie, Edmund, Ellen and Bertha, born between 1867 and 1879. George continued his work as an agricultural labourer, whilst Eliza ran a small laundry at the school house. As a laundress, Eliza employed both her daughters, Annie and Ellen, to work in the laundry. By the beginning of the 1900s George and Eliza had moved to Boyces, Tidings Hill.

In 1901, George Patrick, an agricultural farm labourer, born in 1861 at Great Maplestead, and his wife Sarah born at Groton, Suffolk, lived at the School House. They had five children who were born between 1881 and 1892. Ethel, Arthur, Mabel, Herbert, and Reggie. In 1901 both Sarah and her daughters were laundresses working at home and Arthur was a private in the Infantry Militia based at Colchester. By 1911 George was employed as a horseman and worked on a nearby farm, *(The Howe)?* while Sarah continued to run her laundry business; Their son Reggie, a schoolboy, lived with them. Ethel had married James Patrick in 1907 and Arthur, (nicknamed 'Tug') had married Isabella Spittles in 1909 at Halstead. They had two young daughters, Hilda and Violet, who were born in West Stanley, Durham. Arthur worked in an Iron Foundry and, at one time was the landlord of the Bricklayers Arms in Halstead. After Arthur was widowed he lived in the 'family' house with his sister Mabel who had never married.

Frederick Thomas Webb who lived at the School House from 1915 to 1949 was coachman to SAC. He was born in 1864 at Earls Colne, where he lived with his sister Beatrice and grandparents, John and Sarah Webb for most of his childhood. When he was seventeen years old he worked as a stable boy and groom. He married Amelia Bloys (1864-1925) in the Colchester District in 1887. They had four children born between 1889 and 1897, Beatrice Amelia, Jessie Lilian, Frederick John and Hilda Victoria who was born at Stisted.

As a young man Frederick was employed by Lord Hopetoun in Edinburgh and, at Holyrood Palace. He returned to England and in 1894 worked at Stisted Hall for James Noah Paxman (1832-1922). In 1904 when James Paxman was High Sheriff of Essex, Frederick acted as his official coachman. In 1907 Stisted Hall was bought by Cecil Sebag-Montefiore (1874-1923) and Frederick remained with the family until 1915. Whilst at Stisted Frederick was a member of the Church Choir for twenty years and he was Treasurer of the Village Institute.

As SAC was not particularly fond of 'the motor car' it is not surprising that he used a coach sometimes during his early years at The Howe, and therefore required a coachman to look after his horses and carriages. Frederick worked for SAC until he retired and continued to live at the Old School House until his death. He was a well known local character, a staunch Conservative and, as a member of the Constitutional Club he served on its committee for many years and was presented with a long service medal.

During the Second World War there was a road block opposite the Old School House which was manned by the Home Guard. Concrete blocks were placed on one half of the road, each with a storm light placed on the top, to make them visible at night time. The other half of the road was sufficient in width to allow vehicles to pass through in one direction at a time. There were iron girders nearby, which could have been placed vertically in holes in the road, in the event of a German invasion, to completely block the carriage way. No doubt Frederick was relieved when they were removed before the end of the war when the threat of invasion had passed. There was also an A.R.P. Warden's post in the Old School House and a large sign outside with the initial "W" on it, to indicate where the post was sited.

Frederick died on 21st May 1949. The funeral took place at St Andrew's Church where Augustine Courtauld read the lesson. All the local families Frederick had worked for, including Samuel and Edith Courtauld were represented in the congregation, which showed how highly he was regarded by everyone. Also present were staff or their families who had worked with Frederick at The Howe, and included Margaret Saunders, as well as Leonard and Amy Howard, who were his neighbours. Mary Ann Hart and Annie Evans were also residents at the Old School House when Frederick died.

Frederick and Amelia Webb's children: Frederick John married Zilla Pilgrim and Hilda married James Hall. Beatrice was unmarried. Jessie Lilian died in 1914 aged 24 years.

Eric and Dorothy Doggett and their two children, Nelson and Hilary occupied the house following the death of Thomas Webb, before they moved to the Worthy Vale area of Yorkshire.

Map References.
The School and School House appear on the 1874 Ordnance Survey map of Halstead as one property with the caption. "Boys and Girls School". From 1898 to 1922 inclusive, it was two separate properties and was numbered 27 and 28 Box Mill Lane. By 1954 it was once again one property, and numbered 28 Box Mill Lane.

A brief reference to other cottages in Box Mill Lane
A stream ran between The Howe Estate and Wash Farm which flowed across the Hedingham Road and, adjacent to Box Mill Lane, into the River Colne. To the left of the stream was a field known as Abbey Croft which was attached to Wash Farm. At one time it was owned by the Start family and John Crump was the tenant during the late 1700s before it was farmed by Thomas Smoothy from around 1809.

Several cottages were built on the edge of Abbey Croft which could only be reached by crossing the stream using planks of wood. No doubt some of the inhabitants took a ducking when they missed their footing after a good night out at the Red Cow public house! Over the decades the cottages had many owners and tenants, and although not part of The Howe Estate, several of the inhabitants worked at The Howe especially during the Hornor years.

Cottages in Box Mill Lane
These cottages were built on the edge of Abbey Croft Field

Chapter Twenty Three
Cottages at The Wash

There have been cottages along Hedingham Lane, North Street or Hedingham Road for centuries. However only those cottages known to have connections with The Howe are mentioned in this chapter. These cottages and tenements were situated at 'The Wash' or simply 'Wash', and were often described as: *"being in a certain Lane called Hedingham Lane"* on old documents. The majority of these cottages were on the north east side of the road, passed the entrance to Wash Farm. The first row of dwellings were generally referred to as; *"The cottages known by the name, or sign of the Crown"*. This was followed by another row of cottages, which were bought by Edward May and demolished in the early 1870s. Almost opposite these tenements, on the south west side of the road, was a bakery and grocers shop which was leased to tenants by the Hornor and Courtauld families.

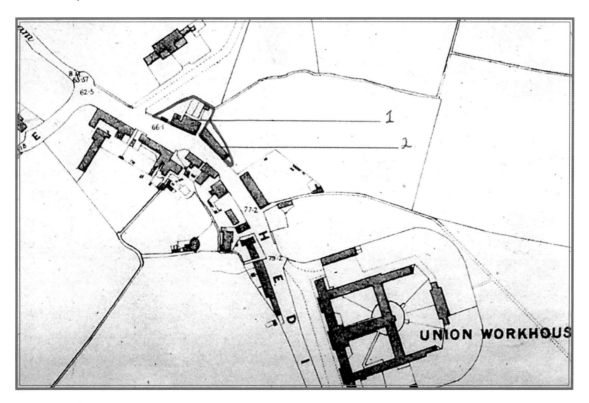

An extract from the map of Halstead surveyed for the Local Board of Health c1855
1. The cottages known by the name or sign of the Crown   2. The cottages purchased by Edward May in 1831

No 1. The cottages known by the name, or sign of the Crown
In 1758 these cottages belonged to John Morley, a gentleman who lived at Little Maplestead, before they were later acquired by John Johnson. Part of this property, which was made up of several cottages was a public house known as the Crown. Licensing records for Halstead confirm that John Johnson held a licence for the Crown from at least 1769, followed by his wife Mary. James Goldstone took over from Mary and was the licensee to around 1800 when the Crown reverted back to residential dwellings.

In September 1838 according to the Tithe Map and Award, the property was divided into two dwellings. John Parker resided in one cottage while the other was unoccupied. James Goldstone, who owned the cottages, lived on the opposite side of Hedingham Lane, in a property which overlooked the River Colne. In 1851 James was a baker, and, with his sister Elizabeth, who was a grocer, they owned a bakery and grocers shop situated at the Wash. Another sister, Mary, also resided with them. When James died at the beginning of 1861 his nephew, Robert James Goldstone, a carpenter from Witham, was his Executor. In his will James instructed Robert to sell his properties at a 'Public Auction'. This included his five freehold cottages and dwelling house, together with his copyhold cottage, formerly the Crown, which was now divided into four dwellings. The auction took place in 1862 at The George Inn, Halstead. Joseph Evans acted as Edward Hornor's agent and purchased the property, known as the Crown, on Edward's behalf for £52 10s 0d. When these cottages were enfranchised by Anne Hornor in 1868/9 the tenants were James Taylor, Robert Rayner, James Basham and Mary Clements.

According to the 1871 census return the four dwellings had been converted back to two cottages. Only Robert Rayner, an agricultural labourer and his wife Mary formerly Williamson, and their seven children, Emma, Emily, Eliza, Timothy, Ruth, George and Edith, born between 1849 and 1871, remained after enfranchisement, as the other cottage was unoccupied. Robert and Mary remained in their cottage, which was numbered 55 North Street in 1891 and renumbered 104 North Street by 1901. Robert died in 1903 aged 78 years. By 1911 the property had been renumbered again, to 130 North Street when Mary with Emma, George, and Edith, lived there. Mary died in 1915 aged 83 years.

Cottages at The Wash early 1900s

In 1869 the centre cottage, once known as the Crown Public House, was divided into four dwellings and occupied by James Basham, Mary Clements, Robert Rayner and James Taylor. The cottage which abutted onto it, on the left hand side, was occupied by Alfred Cook and Thomas Draper.

The cottage which was empty in 1871, was occupied from 1881 through to at least 1911 by James Goodey and his family. James was married in 1871 to Matilda formerly Smith, who was born in Gosfield. In 1881 he was employed as a milkman and Matilda was a silk weaver. Five of their children, James, Mark Silvester, Emma, Herbert and Percy Willie, who were born between 1872 and 1880 resided with them. By 1891 the cottage was numbered 56 North Street and Matilda's mother, Isabella Smith, lived with them. In 1901 the cottage was known as 102 North Street and by 1911 it had changed to 128 North Street. James had also changed jobs during this time being a stockman and a road labourer before he became a general jobbing labourer. James and Matilda's son Mark Silvester was killed in action at Flanders in 1915. Matilda died in 1916 and James died in 1934.

. . . .

Another cottage abutted onto the left hand side of the Crown Cottages. In 1803 Henry Skingley, a brewer from Coggeshall sold the cottage to Thomas Earley of Halstead, a blanket maker. At this time the cottage was rented to Clement Spurgeon, followed by Abraham Shead. Thomas Earley died in 1828 and the property was inherited by his daughter Mary Ann Davey, the wife of Daniel Davey. Mary was admitted the tenant in 1829. Mary died in 1867 and the cottage passed to her eldest son and customary heir Alfred Davey who sold it to Anne Hornor. Anne paid £46 for this cottage together with the other cottages, previously known as the Crown.

Shortly after Anne purchased the cottage in 1869, she was granted an award of enfranchisement when the tenants were Alfred Cook, a general dealer and his wife Emma, a silk weaver. Alfred had married Emma Archer in 1860. In 1871 Alfred's niece, Jane Parker who was a silk winder, William Parker, a bachelor and pensioner, and Thomas Draper an agricultural labourer boarded with the Cook family. Jane Parker left the cottage and married Frederick Bragg in 1874. Their daughter Harriett, who was born in 1875, lived with her great uncle and aunt, Alfred and Emma in the cottage by 1881. Alfred who was now employed as a greengrocer died in 1890 aged 54 years. By 1891 the cottage was known as 54 North Street. Emma died in 1893 aged 56 years.

In 1901 the cottage was numbered 106 North Street and the occupant was Emma Sewell formerly Redgewell, a silk weaver. Emma Redgewell who was born at Sible Hedingham married Alfred Sewell, at Halstead in 1888. Alfred was a private in the 4th Manchester Regiment and they lived at Ashton-under-Lyme, where their first son Alfred was born in 1889. Alfred completed twelve years in the army and was back in Halstead by 1911. He lived with his family at Chapel Hill and worked in the Foundry as a labourer. Alfred junior had been joined by Frederick, Ernest, Annie Elizabeth, Mabel Florence, Lily Ivy and Elsie May who were born between 1891 and 1910. In 1914, when Alfred was 45 years old he joined the Army Reserve Corps for one year as a volunteer.

In 1917 it was noted in The Halstead Gazette that all three of Albert and Emma's sons had enlisted and served in the Royal Fusiliers during the First World War; Alfred was a Corporal, Ernest a Private, and Frederick was a Warrant Officer. Emma died in 1924 aged 56 years and Alfred died in 1937 aged 67years.

In 1911 the cottage was renumbered 132 North Street and was occupied by Emily Mary Rayner formerly Coe, a widow, and her three children. Emily Mary Coe was born in 1870 at Great Maplestead, and she married Herbert Rayner born in 1865, at Halstead in 1895. In 1901 Herbert, a bricklayer's labourer and Emily lived in North Street with their two children Edith Emily and George Albert. Emily's unmarried sister, Ellen, who was a silk weaver, also lived with them.

Another daughter, Elsie May, was born in 1902 shortly before her father Herbert died in 1903 aged 37 years. Emily died in 1950 aged 80 years.

These cottages were demolished around 1925 when SAC replaced them with Courtauld Tudor style houses known as St. Martin's Cottages.

No 2. The cottages purchased by Edward May.
Next door to the right hand side of the Crown was another tenement. It was owned by Thomas Matt, a horse dealer in 1767, and occupied by John Griffin. By 1772 it was in the occupation of Isaac Bull, a blacksmith, before it passed to Robert Miller, a carpenter in 1784.

By 1794 the tenement had been converted into three dwellings and leased to William Parker, Elizabeth Wells and Isaac Hedingham. Robert Miller died in 1801 and in his will he left the three cottages or tenement to his grandson Robert Bragg, the illegitimate son of Susanna Bragg by his son, also called Robert. William Parker continued as a tenant, with 'widow' Goody occupying one of the other cottages. In 1816/17 Robert Bragg sold the tenement to Joseph Maskell, a saddler and horse dealer.

In 1831/2 Edward May of The Howe purchased the cottages for £110, when the tenants were James Binks, John Sargeant and Thomas Edwards. In 1844 when Edward sold The Howe Estate and his other hereditaments, he did not include these cottages in the sale. Instead he kept them for another three years before Aaron Morritt, Edward's former business partner and friend purchased them in 1847 for £200. A newly erected cottage had been built on part of the tenement yards and gardens which was included in the sale. These four dwellings were now occupied by Edward Hostler, William Wickes, John Wright, John Nokes and John Wells.

Bought as an investment the properties were retained by Aaron Morritt after Edward Hornor acquired The Howe Estate. However Land Tax Registers show that Edward Hornor paid tax on these cottages which he rented out to tenants. Edward therefore leased these properties firstly from Aaron and then from Aaron's two executors, John Taylor and Nicholas Walter who administered Aaron's Trust Fund after his death in 1858. Nicholas Walter died in 1862 and in September 1872 John Taylor 'tidied up' everyone's affairs and applied to the Manorial Court to be admitted the tenant of the cottages. This was granted after John confirmed that the loan taken out by Edward May in 1839 to raise funds had been repaid.

Anne Hornor immediately paid John Taylor £110 and bought the cottages which were now occupied by John Wells, Henry Bishop, David Brown, William Last and David Spurgeon. In 1873 the cottages were enfranchised at a cost of £40 5s 3d. By 1874 all but one of the cottages had been demolished as they did not appear on the 1874 Ordnance Survey Map of Halstead. The surviving cottage stood next to the cottages formerly known as the Crown. In 1881 the cottage was occupied by Henry Sturmer and from 1891 until 1925 by Alfred Moule.

The tenants who lived in the cottages bought by Anne Hornor:
David Charles Spurgeon was born in 1840 at Halstead and married Emma Beadle in 1866 and they lived in the end cottage, *(situated at the right hand end of figure 2 on the Local Board of Health Map)*. David, a bricklayer and Emma, a silk throwster, had five children, David Lewis, George James, Charles, Elizabeth and Clara Emily. By 1881 the family had moved to Trinity Square. David died in 1899 aged 59 years and Emma in 1910 aged 70 years.

William Last was born in 1838 at Halstead, the son of James and Sarah Last. In 1851 William lived with his parents and siblings in Hedingham Lane, in a cottage close to the Anchor Public House. By 1861 William, with three other lads from Halstead, William and Thomas Coe and George Spurgeon lodged with Mrs Charlotte Crowe at Castle Bailey, Colchester, while they worked in Colchester as bricklayer's labourers. William returned to Halstead and married Eliza Beckwith in 1863. Eliza who was the daughter of Thomas and Hannah Beckwith was born in 1840. By 1871 William and Eliza lived next door to David Spurgeon with their three children, born between 1864 and 1869, Sarah, Clement and Caroline. Both William and his daughter Caroline aged 2 years, died in 1871.

Sarah, a silk weaver, moved in with her Beckwith grandparents in Hedingham Lane, while Clement lived with his uncle and aunt, Alfred and Caroline Osborne in Thetford, Norfolk. Alfred was a harness maker and Clement was his apprentice. By 1891 Clement had returned to Hedingham Lane where he lived with his grandmother and sister before his marriage to Sarah Ann Cranfield in 1891. They moved to Maldon where he had a harness making business. Sarah married Frederick Root in 1894 and remained in Halstead.

David Brown was born in Sible Hedingham. In 1851 he was a journeyman carpenter and head of the household at a house in Swan Street, where David Hardy and his daughter Pamela were his lodgers. David Brown and Pamela Hardy married in 1852 and by 1861 they lived at The Wash, Hedingham Lane with their three children George, Sarah Ann and Henry William who was born in 1861 and died in 1870. The family had been joined by another son William before they moved to the cottage next to William Last, where Alfred was born in 1871. David worked as a sawyer and by 1881 he and Pamela had moved into a cottage in Box Mill Lane with their two youngest sons:- William who worked as a carpenter, and Alfred, who was unemployed as he was crippled. David's father Thomas Brown also lived with them. In 1891 Pamela worked as a laundress, probably in the laundry which operated from The Howe School House. In 1901 David, a widower and a pauper was a resident at the Union Workhouse. He died in 1909 aged 87 years.

Henry Bishop was born at Little Maplestead and married Sophia Edwards, (who was born in 1837), in 1858, and they had a son Henry who was born about 1860. Henry worked as an agricultural labourer and with his family moved into the cottage next to David Brown. However by 1881 they had left Halstead and moved to Stratford, London, where Henry senior, worked as a plate sawyer.

John Wells who worked as an agricultural labourer for most of his life, lived with Elizabeth and their children in one of the cottages at The Wash. The children Susan, Hannah, Maria, Sarah, Henry and Rebecca were born between 1828 and 1840. By the beginning of 1861 only Rebecca, who worked as a silk throwster, remained at home with her parents. Although by the end of the year she too had left the cottage and married John Chaplin, a journeyman baker. John Wells died in 1878 aged 79 years.

Alfred Isaac Moule was born about 1850 at Hadleigh, Suffolk. He married Sarah Ann Goymer in 1878 and they had a son, John. Sarah died in 1885 and Alfred married Mary Walsh in 1886 and had another son, Herbert. Alfred had various jobs, and over the years he worked as a factors porter, carman, coal carter and general labourer. Alfred and Mary moved into the cottage vacated by Henry Sturmer where they remained until 1923, when, due to their impending demolition,

Alfred, Mary and John were re-housed in one of the cottages on Howe Ground. Alfred and Mary's stay was for a few months only as on the 31st January 1924 they were among the first residents to occupy one of the newly built Courtauld Homes of Rest. John married Jessie Howard in 1924 and they continued to live at Howe Ground until mid 1925. Alfred died in 1930.

. . . .

The south west side of Hedingham Lane, from the Box Mill Lane entrance to opposite the Union Workhouse, was packed with cottages and a public house known as the Anchor. During the mid 1700s and through the 1800s the owners, tenants or occupants were numerous, with the cottages changing hands constantly. One cottage and shop situated in North Street approximately where Clare Cottages, Hedingham Road stand today, was in the Hornor's possession, and was occupied by a succession of flour millers and bakers.

James Porter married Sophia Banbridge at Halstead in 1838 and they had five children Henry, James, Jesse, Cassy and William (Willie). In 1851 James was employed as a silk weaver and lived at Tan Yard with Sophia and their sons, Henry and James. By 1861 James had changed his occupation and, with his wife, they both worked as bakers. They remained at 'Old' Tan Yard until around 1879, when James, Sophia and Willie moved to North Street into the cottage and bakery owned by Edward Hornor. James was the baker while Willie served in the shop. James and Sophia continued to live at the bakery until around the end of the 1880s when Edward Hardy took over the business. When James retired they moved to 1 Bois Field. Sophia died in 1908 aged 89 years and James in 1911 aged 96 years.

Edward Hardy was born in 1845, the son of Thomas, a shoe maker and Catherine Hardy. Edward lived at Toppesfield with his parents and sisters and, in 1861 he worked as an agricultural labourer. He married Mary Ann Wiffen of Sible Hedingham in 1867 and they had a son William Albert born in 1870. Sadly Mary died following the birth of her son. In 1871 Edward and his mother Catherine with William lived at Legerton's Mill in Sible Hedingham where he was the miller.

In 1874 Edward married Ellen Hoy(e) a silk worker from Colne Engaine who was born in 1852. They lived in Head Street, Halstead, although Edward was not at home all the time, as he lodged in Dunmow, where he worked as a corn miller. Edward and Mary moved into the bakery at North Street when James Porter retired. William, who was employed as a gardener lived with them, as did Eliza, Edward's sister. In 1901 the shop was renumbered 117 North Street and the family, along with Edward's father in law John Hoy(e), a widower and shepherd, continued to live there. Edward died in 1906 aged 61 years and Ellen died in 1921 aged 69 years. Following Edward's death the next tenant at the bakery was Edwin Shemming.

Edwin Andrew Shemming was born at Brockdish, Norfolk c1863, the son of Alfred, a basket maker, and Sarah Shemming. Edwin married Hannah Hunt, the daughter of Robert and Virginia Hunt of Walsham le Willows in 1888 in the Stow District. Edwin and Hannah's eldest daughter Charlotte Agnes was born in 1888 at Rattlesden, Suffolk, shortly before the family moved to Colne Engaine where Edwin was employed as a gardener, and resided at Colne Park Lodge, where their second daughter Sarah Jane was born. By 1895 the family had moved to Hall Lodge, Hutton near Billericay, where Edwin worked as a gardener for Arthur Digby-Neave, Lieutenant Colonel of the 3rd Company of the Essex Regiment, who resided at Hutton Hall. Two more children were born; Frederick Alfred and Katherine Elsie. Their daughter Sarah Jane died in

1903 and Charlotte Agnes married Charles Henry Digby in 1906. Both these events took place in Hutton. Edwin and Hannah moved into the shop at North Street in 1906 and ran a grocery and bakers shop assisted by Frederick until he enlisted. During the First World War Frederick was a private in the Army Service Corps, and later transferred to the Kings Royal Rifle Corps and was wounded.

By 1911 Charles and Charlotte Digby and their two sons, Cecil and Edwin, had left Hutton and moved to 95 North Street, near to the Shemming's shop. Charles, however, was not employed in the family business and worked as a tailor.

Edwin and Hannah ran their shop until they ceased trading in around 1922 by which time Samuel Courtauld had started on his 'clean up campaign'. The cottages between Edwin's shop and Box Mill Lane had been demolished to make way for Abel Cottages, which were erected in 1920. The shop and cottage were demolished and replaced by Clare Cottages in 1924 and, in 1926, Edwin and Hannah moved across the road into the newly built, St Martin's Cottages. Hannah died in 1931 and Edwin in 1941.

Edwin and Hannah Shemming outside their shop circa 1908

While Edwin Shemming was running his bakery and grocery business at 117 North Street, Charles Rayner, a builder, who lived close by, erected a pair of cottages which abutted onto the side wall of Edwin's shop. As the cottages were higher than the shop and also jutted out in front of the shop, it was not possible to build them in the same colour bricks from front to back, as there was not enough space. (Note the paler coloured bricks to the left hand side of the shop on the above photograph). The outline of the demolished shop is still visible on the end wall of 115 Hedingham Road today.

Cottages at Doe's Corner circa 1910

Chapter Twenty Four
Cottages at Doe's Corner

Two cottages were situated next to a sharp bend, known as Doe's Corner on the Hedingham Road near to Hepworth Hall and, although they were built within the Halstead boundary, they were sometimes listed under Great Maplestead. They were referred to locally as 'The Cottages, Doe's Corner', and were a pair of small farm cottages built of lath and plaster, which were considered to be very picturesque and consequently they were frequently photographed. Attractive outside, but not so comfortable inside for the inhabitants.

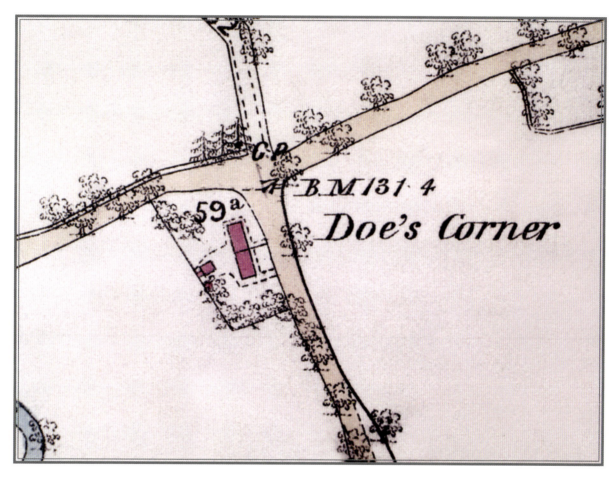

An extract from the 1874 Ordnance Survey Map First edition, shows Doe's Corner and the Cottages. To the north of the map, (number 62) is the drive leading to Hepworth Hall. The road on the east is Dynes Hall Road.

On the 1827 census return, one cottage was occupied by Robert Burkitt, a labourer employed by Mr. Smoothy; either James Smoothy of Hepworth Hall or Thomas Smoothy of Bois Hall, and the second cottage was occupied by Thomas Maythorn(e), born 1762, a gardener employed by James Sperling of Great Maplestead.

The cottages were acquired by Edward May around the late 1820s or early 1830s and appear on the 1838 Tithe Map and Award for Halstead. At this time they were occupied by William Norman who worked for Edward May on the How(e) Estate and John Rayner, who was employed elsewhere.

The left hand side cottage, nearest to Halstead
Henry and Sarah Rayner, both born in 1804 at Halstead and their five children born between 1828 and 1838, John, Sarah, George, William and Elizabeth, occupied the cottage in 1841, with Thomas Maythorn(e) who was born 1820. Henry worked as an agricultural labourer and Thomas was a gardener. By 1851 Henry, Sarah and their family, which now included Alfred born 1843, Eliza 1844 and Frederick 1848, had moved to Chapel Hill with their daughter Sarah, who had married James Barker, and their grand daughter Louisa Barker.

Jonathan Rayner who was born 1820 at Halstead, was also an agricultural labourer. With his wife Ann, who was born 1822 in London, and their children, Susannah, Joshua and Ann they moved into the cottage vacated by Henry and Sarah, where they remained for a number of years. Jonathan and Ann had four more children:- Jonathan, George William, Edward John and Alice. All the children were born between 1843 and 1862. By 1871 the family had left Does Corner and moved into a cottage on Hedingham Road. In the 1890s, Jonathan a gardener and greengrocer, and Ann, with their unmarried daughter Susannah, who worked as a dressmaker, lived at 8 North Street. After Ann died, Susannah looked after her father until he died in 1903 aged 83 years. Susannah moved to Balham House, North Street where she was housekeeper to William Cook and his grandson, William Byford.

The Cottages at Doe's Corner

Abraham Constable, a farm labourer, with his wife Mary Ann and their daughter, Sarah Ann born 1856, lived in the cottage in 1871. Mary Ann died in 1872 aged 54 years and in 1875 Sarah Ann married Henry Abrams whose family lived in the next door cottage. Abraham had left the cottage by 1881 and, in 1891, he lived with his son George and daughter in law Mary Ann and their family in North Street where he received money from the Parish known as 'Parish Relief'. He died in 1891 aged 75 years.

James Wiseman, a farm labourer, born at Sible Hedingham and Harriett Wiseman from Castle Hedingham and their seven children, who were born at Great Maplestead moved into the cottage by 1881. Their children were, Emma, Arthur, Susannah (who was registered blind from birth), John, George, Alice and Agnes. In 1883 it was reported by the Halstead Board of Guardians that; *"The cottage occupied by Mr Wiseman at Doe's Corner was overcrowded as there were six adults and one child living in a space of only 1583 feet, when there should be 1950 feet"*. Orders were therefore issued for the abatement of the overcrowding.

In 1891 the family had been joined by two grand daughters, Edith Wiseman born in 1886 at Halstead, and Celia Ada Wiseman born 1890 at Peckham, London. In 1901 only James, Harriett, Susannah and Celia resided at the cottage until they moved to 8 Box Mill Lane where their daughter Emma also lived. James died in 1911 aged 84 years, Harriett in 1913 aged 83 years, Susannah in 1921 and Emma in 1930. In 1913 Celia married Arthur Eley, a horseman on a farm, who lived at Greenstead Green.

Doe's Corner, with Hedingham Road turning sharp left. Hepworth Hall is just visible in the background. Also note the brick built post box sadly no longer in existence, although a more recent post box still stands nearby.

The right hand side cottage, nearest to Hepworth Hall
Richard Blackwell and his wife, Henrietta formerly Norman, who were married in 1820, and their children Richard and Henry (twins), William, Maria and Ellen occupied the cottage in 1841. After Henrietta died in 1849, Maria took over the house keeping duties, followed by Ellen who married Samuel Disney in 1867 and died three years later in 1870.

Alfred and Emma Cockerton moved into the cottage vacated by the Blackwell family, before they moved to Ilford. They are connected to the Richer family who lived in Howe Cottages. *(See Chapter 18, page 169 for further details relating to the Cockerton family).*

The Cottages at Doe's Corner

The Abrams family from Halstead were the Wiseman's next door neighbours by 1881. Henry Abrams, employed as a gas maker, married Sarah Ann Constable in 1875 and they had four daughters, Edith, Alice, Ethel and Flora. Henry, Sarah and their family moved to Melton Constable in Norfolk, where Beatrice, Jessie, Mildred and Albert were born. By 1901 the family had returned to Halstead and Henry worked as a blacksmith's labourer before he became a blacksmith's striker in a coach building foundry. In 1911 Henry, Sarah Ann and Mildred lived at North Street with Beatrice and her husband Ernest Dorking, a groom, and their daughter Hilda aged one year.

The Chambers family were the next residents after the Abrams. Lewis Chambers, known as Louis, a farm labourer, was born about 1858 at Tilbury Juxta Clare. With his wife Emma formerly Sandford born at North End, Little Yeldham, they lived at Doe's Corner by 1891. They had married in 1883 and their daughter Lizzie was followed by Minnie, Ada, Bessie and Louis. By 1901 the family moved to Head Street and Louis was employed as a road labourer. They had also been joined by two more daughters, Florence and Ivy. In 1911 Louis was a miller's carman, and Minnie, Louis and Ivy who lived at home worked at Courtauld's Silk Mill. Louis died in 1939 aged 81 years.

The Watkinson family moved into the cottage at the end of the 1890s. Henry known as Harry was born in 1855 at Sible Hedingham and his wife Emily, formerly Ellis, was born at Great

Yeldham. They were married in 1878. In 1891 Harry was a general agricultural labourer and lived with his family, Louise, John, and Emily's son, Eli Ellis, aged fourteen years who was born at Sible Hedingham. Lizzie and Alice were born before the family moved to Halstead at the end of the 1890s and another daughter Laura was born in 1899 who died in 1903. Harry died in 1910, aged 54 years and the family moved to 24 Trinity Square. In 1901 Emily worked as a charwoman, John was an ostler at a hotel and Louise, Lizzie and Alice worked at Courtauld's Mill. Eli married Kate Finch in 1899 and in 1901 they lived in Castle Hedingham with their son Arthur.

The cottages at Doe's Corner gradually fell into a bad state of repair and although no proof has been found, it was rumoured that they were hit by a bomb in the First World War and badly damaged. Eventually the cottages were demolished, either because of the war damage, their general disrepair or when the road was widened.

Road works in 1924 were deemed necessary to straighten out the very sharp corner at Doe's Corner and to make the field next to it, which was owned by Samuel Courtauld, more accessible to the public when it was used to hold the Essex Agricultural Show. Over the years Doe's Corner has undergone major roadwork in a quest to make it safer for both vehicles and pedestrians, as well as to prevent the road from flooding when the River Colne burst its banks.

The River Colne in flood near Doe's Corner, with Hepworth Hall in the background

The Wash
With the entrance to Box Mill Lane and the School House on the left hand side
A watercolour by F Fullagar
Courtesy of David and Angela Kerrison

MISCELLANY

(While I was researching The Howe Estate and its owners, I discovered an assortment of interesting little titbits. Some are in the form of anecdotes, some are taken from books and newspapers and some appear in photographic form. By themselves they do not fit into a specific chapter in this book, or their connection to The Howe Estate is sometimes rather 'remote', but together I hope they make an interesting miscellany).

June 1780 - Halstead Association
Whereas several gentlemen have resolved to promote an Association for persecuting felons etc any persons desirous to become subscribers, are requested to pay their subscriptions of half a guinea to Mr Crump at The Kings Arms aforesaid on or before Friday 30th June when a Meeting of Subscribers will be held at the said Kings Arms at Noon to consider such plans that may best promote the purpose of this Association. *(Punctuation evidently did not feature in newspaper reporting in 1780)!*

June 1780 - Halstead Association Against Murders Housebreakers Highway men and every species of Felony.
   1) It was resolved that the number of subscribers to this Association did not exceed 50.
  11) That the benefit of subscriptions take place from the day of paying their subscription money.
111) That all reasonable expenses which may be incurred by apprehending and prosecuting offenders against subscribers of this Association will be paid out of the common stock accounts thereof being laid before a general meeting of this Association and there allowed.
 1V) That a general meeting of the subscribers be held at The Kings Arms in Halstead in the said county on Friday after the Spring and Summer Assizes at Noon at which time and place the Treasurers accounts shall be audited.
   V) That no new rules shall be made or old ones altered but at a general meeting of the Association at the time and place aforesaid.
 V1) That the resolutions of this meeting printed and dispensed in hand bills and published in the Chelmsford Chronicle.
Rand Ekins - Treasurer
PS   Subscriptions to be paid to Mr Crump at The Kings Arms, Halstead aforesaid till the number of subscribers is complete.
(Neighbourhood Watch of yesteryear!)

1786 - Wanted - a good cook for a private family who can be well recommended from her last place. For further particulars enquire of Mr John Crump at The Kings Arms, Halstead.

1786 - Wanted - a single man as a gardener in a private house who will have no objection to the care of two or three horses and to be employed in other occasional business. He must understand the management of melons, cucumbers, mowing grass and all other common works in the garden. A very good character for honesty, sobriety and diligence will be required; For further particulars, inquire of Mr John Crump of The Kings Arms, Halstead.

In 1845 - Charles Walter, who was resident at The Howe for a year, was listed as an annual subscriber to the British Association for the Advancement of Science.

1846 - Great Temperance Demonstration and Rural Fete in The Howe Park. The Members and Friends of the Essex Temperance Association have obtained permission to hold their fete in the beautiful grounds of The Howe courtesy of Edward Hornor. The grounds will be open at 10am, entrance via the Lodge gate. The day will commence with a Ploughing Match to be contested by Teetotal Ploughmen. 1st prize is £2. This will be followed by a Spade Husbandry Match. Marquees will be hired and Temperance Meetings will take place at 3pm and can hold up to 1000 people. Refreshments will be served at 5pm and further addresses will take place on behalf of the Temperance cause. Admission to the Park 3d each and to tea 1 shilling each for adults; Children under 10 years 6d. A Band will play.

Edward Hornor, along with other gentlemen in Halstead was instrumental in introducing 'Penny Readings'. These readings helped to while away the evenings. 'Spelling Bees' was another popular game, where words were given to a number of people to spell. Anyone who failed to spell the word correctly dropped out of the game until there was just the winner left. This game was played by the Hornor children.

The only sweets that the Hornor children were permitted to eat were 'barley sugar'. They would be taken by their nurse to the only sweet shop in Halstead, where this 'treat' was purchased.

As members of the Society of Friends the Hornor family walked to the Meeting House in Colchester Road every Sunday at 10-40am and again during the afternoon in the winter, and at 6pm in the summer.

Girls from a school based in Colchester Road, run by Miss Nott would visit The Howe annually for a picnic, when they always wore their bonnets and sandals which was the school custom.

1851 - Halstead Mechanics Institute. Eighty people attended a meeting held at The Howe and Edward Hornor was unanimously re-elected President.

1852 - Edward Hornor kept 'Down Sheep' on the farm.

1853 - There was a large gathering of young people connected with the Halstead Band of Hope (a Temperance Association) on Tuesday last. Edward Hornor Esquire, with his usual kindness, opened his grounds at The Howe, where tea was served under some lofty elms in front of the mansion. Mr Hornor supplied the party with fruits and in the evening the address was delivered to the young people and company present by the Reverend William Clements. The weather was rather unpropitious.

1853 - Halstead British Schools. Mr Hornor, with his accustomed kindness threw open his beautiful grounds to the children and company. A substantial tea was provided under a row of beautiful trees in front of the mansion and a considerable number of respectable inhabitants of the town promenaded the grounds during the evening watching the children whilst they enjoyed their youthful gambols.

1853 - Wilful damage. George Newman was convicted on the testimony of Abraham Byford, farming bailiff to Edward Hornor of The Howe, Halstead, of wilfully having broken down a hedge by getting on the land where he was discovered trespassing with another man, in search of game. Defendant paid the damage and costs and was discharged.

1853 - Halstead and North Essex Floral Society. The Autumn Show of this society took place at The Howe, the residence of Edward Hornor, Esquire. Owing to the unpropitious state of the weather the company was small, but the exhibition of flowers and fruits was of the most satisfactory character. The Cottagers productions far excelled all others and evinced great care in the cultivation of their gardens. The scene was enlivened by a band of music.

Category: Hot House grapes	3rd place - W West, gardener to E Hornor
Green House plants	1st place - W West, gardener to E Hornor
Specimen Green House plant	2nd place - W West, gardener to E Hornor

1853 - Poultry Stealing. Several depredations of this kind have been made within the last week or two. Edward Hornor, Esquire lost a number of fat turkeys and also several implements of husbandry. Active search is being made by the police to discover the offenders and it is hoped they will yet be detected.

Edward Hornor was elected a member of the Society of Arts in 1853, a position he held until his death in 1868.

1854 - Halstead Police Station. Charge of Stealing clover seed. James Byford of Halstead was bought upon remand charge with feloniously stealing two sacks of clover seed of the value of £18, the property of Edward Hornor, Esquire; and John Butcher and his brother Joseph Butcher, small farmers, living at Gosfield were charged as receivers. The seed was missed from a granary at The Howe in February and was not found until Sunday last when it was discovered in the lake at Gosfield in water about 14ft deep. The seed was lost however by bursting of the sacks………………………………..After a long and patient investigation of six hours duration the bench retired to consult and, on their return stated that there were many very suspicious circumstances bought out against the prisoners, Byford and John Butcher, yet the evidence was not such a nature as to enable them to commit for trial and the prisoners were therefore discharged.

1854 - To the Editor of the Essex Standard
Sir, As an advocate for even-handed justice towards the rich and poor, I trust you will allow me to express a hope that the report which appears in one of the Essex papers respecting certain proceedings at the Petty Session at Braintree on the 12th inst., and the account of what took place at the Police Station at Halstead on the 15th inst., are correct. The report of the proceedings at Braintree states: "Edward Hornor, Esquire, of Halstead, was summoned for cruelty to a horse. The case was privately heard and a fine, it was reported, was imposed." Now I ask if a poor man had ill used his donkey or pony would the case have been privately heard? Would it not have been considered necessary to punish him publicly for the sake of example? There ought not to be, in this country, one law for the rich and another for the poor. I now come to the Halstead case. It seems that a gardener named Byford was charged with stealing some clover seed, the property of Edward Hornor, Esquire. Among the magistrates who are reported to have sat at Halstead Police Station to decide this case, I observe that Edward Hornor is stated to have been present. In the name of common justice, I ask whether this was the prosecutor in the case? If so, some steps should be taken to prevent magistrates assisting to decide their own grievances. The prosecutor in the Halstead case and the person who was "privately" fined by the Braintree Bench I believe to be the same individual. For the credit of our County magistrates I trust some

satisfactory explanations can be given. I am Sir, your obedient servant, 'A Poor Man'.

1854 - Edward Hornor was a trustee of the Halstead District Provident Building Society.

1855-56 Box field which was formerly the property of John Start was leased to James Goodeve Sparrow.

1856 - Town Mission. A meeting was convened at The Howe to promote the object of the town mission.

1858 - John Start owned and rented out a house with yard and meadow situated in Hedingham Road to Samuel Jay Surridge, a farmer, auctioneer and insurance agent who lived at Hepworth Hall.

In 1859 Edward Hornor was the president of an organisation which was formed to ascertain the opening hours of shops in Halstead. It was considered that Monday to Friday closing time should be 7pm and on Saturdays 9pm. This did not please some of the tradesman who wanted to stay open longer, especially on Saturdays; 8pm during the winter months and 10pm during the summer. A solution was agreed upon when Samuel Courtauld and George de Horne Vaizey proposed that if all the tradesmen agreed to close their shops at the earlier time, none would gain an advantage over the others. Also they would all benefit from working shorter hours.

1859 - Zachariah Allen Fitch borrowed £400 from Edward Hornor against a messuage or tenement in Chappell Street now Trinity Street formerly in the tenure or occupation of John Wright, afterwards of Susan Allen widow, with yards, easements, profits or commodities and appurtenances thereto belonging. And also all that messuage or tenement known by the sign of the Half Moon with all the houses, outhouses, barns, stables, curtilages, yards, orchards, hereditaments and appurtenances whatsoever to the said messuage or tenement belonging, or anywise appertaining or with the same occupied or enjoyed or reputed or taken as part parcel or member thereof which said, last mentioned messuage and tenement and premises are situated lying and being in Halstead aforesaid near lands called Pitchards abutting upon the Queens Highway leading from Halstead to Braintree were formerly in the occupation of ? Brown, widow afterwards in the tenure of Joseph Wright deceased and several tenures or occupation of William Winterflood, Oliver Miller, John Kendall, Mary Doe and Martha Clarke or some or one of them. And all that messuage or tenement with yards, gardens and appurtenances were recently in the occupation of Robert Columbus Hughes and now in the occupation of the said Zachariah Allen Fitch and as the same are bounded on the North by premises forming part of the Estate called Pitchards, and now belonging to Mr Robert Ellington Greenwood and in the south by the said street called Trinity Street. On the east by a messuage and premises of the Reverend Duncan Fraser and lately belonging to Mr Robert Skitter in part and by the said premises of Mr Blomfield in the other part. And on the west by a messuage or tenement in occupation of Mrs Cornell lately belonging to Mr Robinson and recently purchased of him by the Colne Valley and Halstead Railway Company. *(Bearing in mind that many people were illiterate, it seems that this document was exceedingly long winded; all he wanted to do was borrow £400)!*

1859 - Halstead Band of Hope. The annual festival was held at The Howe, the beautiful residence of Edward Hornor, Esquire. In the afternoon about 300 young recruits of the cold water army assembled in a meadow near the gas-works, whence they marched, accompanied by the Braintree band, to the park, where a beautiful tea was provided for their enjoyment. Three hundred persons sat down to a public tea provided in the grove during the afternoon, which was spent by the juvenile disciples of Gough in cricketing, football, racing etc. After tea the company, which included friends from Braintree, Coggeshall, Chelmsford, and other places, was largely increased by the free admission of the towns people, nearly 2000 persons being assembled in the park. As darkness approached the band played the National Anthem and the Reverend William Clements, in a short address, moved a vote of thanks to the kind proprietor of the grounds. The vote was carried with three cheers and one cheer for the ladies. The large assembly then quietly dispersed.

1859 - At the 49th Anniversary Meeting of the Colchester and East Essex Auxiliary Bible Society Edward gave £100 in memory of his brother Charles Hornor.

1861 - Thomas Draper was brought up on a warrant for damage done to a certain tree on the estate of Edward Hornor on 19th July. He pleaded guilty. Mr Hornor said the prisoner had gone into his grounds and for the sake of the wood, hacked his trees; and although he did not wish to be hard on the man, he thought it right to let it be known that trespassers could not be permitted to do such things with impunity. Convicted to 1s. damages and 14s. costs or 1 month. The prisoner was committed in default.

1862 - The Essex Agricultural Society Show was held at Sloe Farm in the grounds of Robert Greenwood. Hackney Mare - Commended - Edward Hornor.

1864 - Mr Edward Hornor has joined the board of the Temperance and General Provident Institutions.

1866 - Dunmow Bible Society. The 54th Anniversary of the Dunmow Auxiliary Bible Society was held at the town hall. There was a full highly respectable attendance of Ladies and Gentlemen from the town and neighbourhood and Edward Hornor, Esquire of Halstead presided.

1870 - Floral and Horticultural Society's Fete. This year was held at Gosfield Place.
Geraniums	3rd place	Mrs Hornor, The Howe
Collection of Ferns	1st place	Mrs Hornor, The Howe
Potatoes	3rd place	Mrs Hornor, The Howe
Rhubarb	1st place	Mrs Hornor, The Howe

1870 - An anniversary. It had been arranged to have the annual treat of the children of the High Street Independent Sunday Schools on Thursday week (by kind permission of Mrs Hornor) in The Howe Grounds, but owing to the wet weather Mr Clover kindly lent his Malting for the use of the children, where they amused themselves by singing and various games. About 4-30pm a substantial tea was provided in the Chapel School Room to which about 200 sat down. After tea the children resumed their games and, in the course of the evening, presents, some of which where sent by Mrs Hornor, were distributed.

1872 - Halstead Ragged Schools. The annual outing of the children attending these schools took place at Mr 'Earn' Barritt's Park Hall Farm, Gosfield. The scholars together with about fifty girls from the Halstead Industrial School were conveyed to the farm in wagons kindly lent by Mrs Hornor, Mr John Robert Vaizey and Messrs John and Joseph Blomfield. All heartily enjoyed the trip as well as the substantial entertainment provided in the meadow. Several visitors interested in the two schools were present, including Mrs Hornor and party, Miss Greenwood, Mr and Mrs S Knight, Mr John Collings (superintendent of Ragged Schools) and several of the teachers.

1880 - Vegetable Show at Halstead. Vegetables grown by the holders of allotments on The Howe Estate were exhibited by kind permission of Mrs Hornor in Howe Park. There were about 90 allotment holders and their united productions were a highly creditable display. Two large tables in the grove were covered with the exhibits which included a good share of onions, peas and beans, and potatoes for which the soil in this neighbourhood appears particularly good. The entire show was under the experienced superintendent Mr S Tyler.

1881 - Fine Art and Industrial Loan Exhibition at Halstead. One of the patrons, Mrs Hornor, who was a principal exhibitor at the exhibition, loaned several paintings. There was a fine African Lion's head and skin which was shot by Lewis Hornor. Miss Edith Hornor who had visited Zululand during the war as a nurse, lent a shield taken at Rorke's Drift and a medicine necklace which she had brought home.

1882 - Public Lighting. The Lighting Committee recommended that Mrs Hornor's application for a public lamp to be placed near The Howe Lodge should be acceded to. The lamp would be provided by Mrs Hornor and thereafter maintained by the Board. The report was adopted.

1886 - For Sale. Full sized Brougham, complete with shafts and pole; built by Turrell, Long Acre, *(London),* Price £25; on view at The Howe, Halstead. Apply to George Sturmer, Coachman.

1887 - The American papers give long accounts of the marriage of Miss Hornor of The Howe (late assistant head nurse in a training school for nurses of the Philadelphia Hospital) to General Hawley of Hartford, Connecticut. The Philadelphia Times reports: "General Hawley is a widower. He was president of the National Republican Convention that nominated *(Ullyses S)* Grant in 1868. He was mentioned as a possible US Presidential candidate and was an Editor, General and United States Senator and, had reached the position of one of the foremost men in the country. Miss Hornor belongs to a fine English Yorkshire family. She chose the vocation of nurse and not from necessity for her people occupy a prominent position, but from a desire to help alleviate the sufferings of mankind. In the Zulu War she won unbounded admiration by her bravery and noble self sacrifice. When it was determined to organise trained nurses for the Philadelphia Hospital, Miss Hornor and her friend Miss Fisher were selected to take charge. They have accomplished splendid work. In manner and conversation she is bright and fascinating"

1891 - The Guild of St. Andrew's held its annual social meetings at the Infants School. After tea at 7-30pm there was an interesting lecture on the Indian mutiny.

1891 - Zenana Mission. At The Howe at the invitation of Mrs Hornor, a meeting in connection with the Zenana Mission. 60-70 people attended and Miss Clark related her experience among the Indian women.

1892 - Prizes were given to the scholars of the Girls and Infants Sunday School on the occasion of their annual Christmas Entertainment which took place in January. A most amusing programme was provided for the children through the kindness of the Misses Hornor, and other ladies and gentlemen who assisted them in carrying out a series of 'wax-works'! (?)

1893 - Halstead Boys Football Club. Due to the kindness of Mrs Hornor the boys have enjoyed the privilege of practicing in Howe Park upon all possible occasions and the club has been highly successful.

1893 - Mrs and Misses Hornor gave glove and handkerchief cases to Miss Leonie Clements and Mr Percy Adams when they were married in May 1893.

January 1896 - The success of the District Nurse Fund seems assured at present, many subscribers have helped it forward……………..Mrs Hornor £1, Misses Hornor 5 shillings each.

1902 - A garden party was held at The Howe on Wednesday evening by kind permission of Mrs Hornor. Music was furnished by the Excelsior Quadrille Band, conducted by Mr R Francis. The arrangements were made by Mr W C Sheen.

August Courtauld liked to hunt and rode a pony called 'Pancake'.

April 1919 - Vestry, The Reverend Thomas H Curling presiding:
It was agreed to apply for a faculty for the erection in the Churchyard of a Memorial Cross to be inscribed with the names of all the men belonging to the Parish who fell in the War and which is to be a gift by Mrs Samuel Augustine Courtauld of The Howe, as a token of gratitude for the safe return of her own brothers. Also for a stained glass window to be presented by Mr Harry Harvey Portway, in memory of his son Lionel, killed in France.

In May 1919 after the end of the First World War, a public meeting was called to discuss the possibility of Halstead Cricket Club being reformed. With Frank Vaizey in the chair it was decided to ask SAC to once again become President of the club.

In November 1920 Miss Hornor entertained members of the Mothers Meeting at tea and they had a happy time, thanks to the kindness and hospitality of their hostess and friends.

1924 - Her many friends in Halstead will rejoice to hear that Miss Hornor is making good progress after the severe operation she has recently undergone. We hope she will recover her full health and strength and be able to carry on all the good work with which she has associated herself for so many years.

1924 - The members of Miss Hornor's Mothers Meeting went to Clacton in July for their outing. The only thing to mar their happiness was that Miss Hornor was unable to accompany them. Mrs Vaizey and Mrs G Morton took charge of the party. They had lunch and tea at the Corner House *(Café)*. The latter being provided for them.

SAC would only take his Rolls Royce to Preston and Harry Cooper to be serviced. They had a workshop in Head Street.

When SAC went fishing he used the old fashioned bent-pin method, where a little float bobs on the water. He would take a boy with him to put a worm onto the rod for him.

January 1924 - Members of Courtauld's Sewing Class were entertained to tea and social evening by Mrs S A Courtauld at The Howe. Over 60 enjoyed dancing, games and singing with Mr Dunt at the piano.

February 1924 - The heavy and continuous rain earlier that week has caused the waterways of the district to be greatly swollen causing the River Colne to burst its banks, flooding many acres. In the Halstead area it was considerable, for, on the Hedingham side of the town the main road was flooded near Hepworth Hall, whilst the Box Mill fields were partially submerged and were difficult to negotiate.

April 1924 - Mr S A Courtauld's fine gift.
Samuel Augustine Courtauld, JP of The Howe, Halstead has had erected 20 cottages for the benefit of aged and needy residents in Halstead. They are model cottages built in pairs, in the form of a semi circle, on a very pleasant site formerly occupied by the Workhouse and overlooking the Valley of the Colne. At the extreme ends are two garden houses, facing the main Hedingham Road. The central block contains the Trustees room, over the fine bay window of which is a stone bearing the Essex Coat of Arms and the inscription; *"These Homes of Rest for Halstead people were built and endowed by Samuel Augustine Courtauld. AD 1923"*. Each home is self contained and consists of a living room, bedroom, scullery fitted in an ideal manner embracing every thought for the comfort of the inmates. Gas and fuel will be supplied free by the Trustees, who will pay the rates and taxes, the Homes being entirely free to the occupants, by reason of the endowment of the generous donor. The gardens are laid out in picturesque style. In front of the centre block is a terrace divided from the lawns by a honeycombed wall with steps leading down to the four lawns. Crazy paving is used for the paths.

SAC was very fond of cats and had two Blue Persians, the first one was called 'Breeks' and lived to be seventeen years, this was followed by 'Barts'.

'Barts'

June 1924 - The 62nd Essex Agricultural Show is to be held at The Howe in Hedingham Road. The police have banned parking between Market Hill and down to the rail bridge just past Does Corner.

July 1927 - Mr Courtauld's £40,000 gift.
Prince Arthur of Connaught on Wednesday presided at the laying of the foundation stone of the Samuel Augustine Courtauld Institute of Bio-Chemistry, attached to the Medical School of the Middlesex Hospital. For the erection and equipment of this Research Institute Mr Samuel Augustine Courtauld has given £40,000 and a few years since he gave £20,000 to endow the Chair of Anatomy. Mr Courtauld laid the foundation stone and received from the architect a replica of an ancient Graeco-Roman spatula, and from the builders a fifteenth century Italian bronze pestle and mortar.

1929 - For Sale. Motor lawn mower, (Atco). Good as new, price £20. Apply Victor George Cross, The Howe, Halstead, Essex.

October 1932 - At Chelmsford Cathedral the Bishop of Chelmsford performed the christening on the infant daughter of Major and Mrs Ralph Rayner of Kiplin Hall, Yorkshire. The child was given the names Fleur Revere Courtauld. The Godparents were, Rudyard Kipling, George Courtauld, Squire Winterbotham of Vermont, USA, the Countess of Willingdon, (for whom Rachel Countess of Clonmell was proxy), Mrs Stephen Courtauld and Mrs Tommy Ellis.

January 1933 - An Essex Wedding. Mr A Courtauld and Miss Montgomerie. The marriage took place at Southwark Cathedral of the eldest son of Mr and Mrs S A Courtauld of The Howe and 8 Palace Green and Miss Mollie Montgomerie, elder daughter of Mr and Mrs F D Montgomerie of Great Codham Hall, Braintree. The bride wore a long sleeved gown of ivory panne velvet, the ankle length fluted skirt forming a rounded train at the back. Her long ivory tulle veil was held in place by a narrow wreath of orange blossom and myrtle, and she carried a sheaf of lilies, cream roses and white heather tied with satin ribbon. She was attended by a page, Master George Woode, by two little girls Miss Joanna Rodd and Miss Elizabeth Watkinson, and by five grown up bridesmaids. Miss Pamela Montgomerie, her sister, Miss Billy Royds, Miss Violet Ruggles-Brise, Miss Ursula Bowlby and Miss Jane Adam. The page wore long champagne coloured velvet trousers with a crepe de chine blouse to match and red shoes, and all the maids had long dresses of champagne coloured net, the close fitting bodices having puff sleeves and scarlet velvet sashes tied at the back into bows giving a bussle effect. They had red sheaves and shoes and wore cream gloves. They carried sheaves of scarlet carnations and poinsettias. Mr Guy Wreford-Brown was best man. The reception was held at the Savoy Hotel.

May 1935 - The christening of the infant son of Major Ralph Rayner and Mrs Rayner took place at St. Mark's, Audley Street. The Bishop of Chelmsford and Prebendary W G Pennyman officiated. The child was named Ranulf Courtauld and the Godparents were Major Andrew Holt, Peter Courtauld, Lady (Samuel) Harvey and Miss Betty Vaizey.

1935 - Chrysanthemum show at Bocking. Mr Cross, gardener to SAC was a judge.

May 1936 - The Howe Garden open. Mr SAC, J.P. who is President of the Allotment Association, very kindly opened The Howe gardens to the public on Wednesday. The proceeds going to the funds of the Association. The arrangements were by the secretary (Mr R Bowles, junior) and the committee, and about 100 visitors enjoyed a stroll round the beautiful well-kept gardens, the herbaceous borders, being particularly pretty. The Azaleas and Rhododendrons were also much admired. Assistance at the gate was given by Mr Arnold and Mr C Carruthers.

July 1936 - Scholars attending the Hedingham Road Baptist Sunday School were entertained to their annual summer treat on Saturday and were favoured with fine weather. The youngsters met in the school room at 2-15pm and then marched to The Howe, the grounds of which were again placed at their disposal by Mr S A Courtauld. The children of the Primary Department indulged in their sports on arrival and tea followed. This was served under the supervision of the committee of the Baptists Women's League. The juniors subsequently held their sports which were followed by a cricket match by members of the Young Men's Institute. Several parents and friends visited the grounds in the evening and enjoyed a walk around the gardens. Scrambles for nuts added to the fun and altogether a very happy time was spent. Members of the St. John Ambulance Brigade were present but fortunately their services were not required. The arrangements were carried out by the Sunday School teachers and willing helpers, with E P Wordsworth as School Secretary.

1939 - Miss Ellen Dring died 13th October 1939 aged 85 years. She was the daughter of Jonathan Dring and sister of Henry Dring (who were both gardeners a The Howe). For over 50 years Ellen was employed at Courtauld's factory and had resided at 3 Homes of Rest since they opened.

December 1938 - The Chairman of the Essex Standing Committee, SAC remarked, "*Old age*" - it has been bitterly said, "*when it can no longer set a bad example gives good advice*".

1940 - Situations vacant.
Gardener-Handyman-Chauffeur required at Ashcombe Tower, near Dawlish. Clean licence and good knowledge of general gardening, willing to be useful in any way and preferably over military age; Cottage provided. Application in writing, together with copies of recent testimonials and stating wages required to: Michelmore, Loveys and Sons, Gate House, Totnes, Devon.

1940 - The marriage took place on Saturday at Holy Trinity, Prince Consort Road, Kensington Gore, of Mr Walter Pierre Courtauld of Wethersfield, younger son of Mr and Mrs Courtauld of The Howe, Halstead and Miss Faith Dorothy Caldwell Cook, of Little Batsford, Gerrards Cross, Buckinghamshire. The Reverend J O Hannay and the Reverend Pain officiated. The bride who was given away by her father wore a gown of white and silver brocade, with a white tulle veil and head-dress of pearls. Her ornament was a diamond and sapphire pendant and she carried a bouquet of Madonna lilies. Christopher Courtauld and Ranulf Rayner (nephews of the bridegroom) were pages, and Perina Courtauld and Fleur Rayner (nieces of the bride groom were child bridesmaids. The boys wore pale blue trousers, and white silk shirts and the little girls had dresses of white muslin, finished with blue ribbons, and wreaths and posies of forget-me-nots. Miss Dora Patey and Miss Betty Balance were the grown-up bridesmaids, in dresses of pale blue grosgrain, with pearl Juliet caps, and they carried bouquets of stephanotis. Mr J B Whittingham was the best man, and, like the bride groom was in uniform. The reception was at 8 Palace Green, (lent by Mrs S A Courtauld).

1940 - Gardens in Essex open in aid of Soldiers, Sailors and Airman's Families Association. Wednesday 29th May, S A Courtauld, Esquire, The Howe 2pm to 7pm. Admission 1 shilling.

1949 - Second Gardener required immediately, thorough knowledge inside and out: good cottage provided. Apply Head Gardener, The Howe, Halstead.

One of the Courtauld houses in Hedingham Road, to the left of the footpath leading to the Cottage Hospital had a Spigot Mortar Base in its front garden. (Second World War).

The following relics have been found near to The Howe: A stone age axe on the Howe Estate, Pottery near Does Corner, Elizabethan coin at Fitz Johns Farm.

The Village Hall at Blackmore End endowed by SAC was designed by August Courtauld's father in law Frank Montgomerie.

Another story to emerge as to why the path across The Howe park land, with the path on the other side of Box Mill bridge were both kept in good repair was so that when Betty Rayner visited The Howe, with her children as babies, she could safely push the pram into Halstead, without having to walk along Hedingham Road.

Authors note: Whilst researching the history of the May, Hornor and Courtauld owned cottages in Hedingham Lane/North Street, I discovered that one of the cottages almost opposite St Martin Cottages, was once a bakery and grocers shop. This shop would have been used by The Howe Estate workers and other inhabitants of The Wash and Box Mill Lane, and was situated to the left hand side of the entrance to Valley Yard. Today it is known as 101 and 103 Hedingham Road, the Bake House being number 103.

From at least 1871 John Layzell, with his wife Sarah, ran the bakery and grocery business at the premises. John also owned thirteen houses and cottages in North Street which included a pair of cottages next door to the bakery, which he built in 1888. The initials JL and the date are still visible on them today.

When John died in 1890 the bakery business, houses and cottages were inherited by his son, Edward John Layzell 1851-1919. As Edward, his wife Elizabeth, and their family lived at Hendon, Middlesex, he apparently had no interest in the business and leased the properties to tenants. John's widow Sarah Layzell, moved into one of the nearby cottages where she lived with her nephew Joseph Clarke, a farmer's clerk. After Joseph died in 1902, Sarah, an elderly lady lived by herself until she died in 1912.

Richard Deal, who was born at Cobbs Fenn, Sible Hedingham in 1863 married Mary Evans in 1886. They moved to Tidings Hill, Halstead where their two sons were born Henry William, also known as Harry, in 1886 and Stanley in 1888. Richard was a baker and after John Layzell's death in 1890, the Deal family moved to 103 North Street which they leased from Edward Layzell. Richard continued to run a grocers shop and bakery at the premises, while the next door cottage, 101 North Street, was rented to William Argent, a milkman and his family.

In 1919 both Edward Layzell and his wife Elizabeth Ann died and their two daughters Elizabeth

Mary and Ethel Kate sold 101 and 103 North Street to Richard Deal. Richard ran his grocery and bakery businesses until he retired in 1933. Mary Deal died in 1920 aged 56 years and Richard lived in the cottage until he died in 1945.

Richard and Mary's son Henry, did not enter into the family business but became a carpenter and died in 1911. Their second son Stanley, married Nellie Marie Challis in 1910 in the Risbridge District of Suffolk. They moved into 101 North Street where their eldest son Leonard was born in 1911. He, sadly, died before he reached his first birthday. They had four more children, Sidney, Myrtle, Joan, and Evie. Stanley continued to work as a baker for his father until Richard retired, when he became 'a dealer' who traded in pigs.

Evie Deal, who was born in 1920 married Dennis Sparke in 1947 and the cottages remained within the family until fairly recently, when Barry Sparke, Dennis and Evie's son moved, with his wife Veronica, to Norfolk. Barry can remember the bakery ovens being situated in the basement of number 103 until the 1950s when they were removed to enlarge and improve the living area in the house.

Circa 1924, SAC had intended buying all the cottages on the south west side of North Street, from Box Mill Lane to opposite the Union Workhouse. However, he met with strong opposition when he approached the owners of The Anchor Public House, Richard Deal and Charles Rayner, a builder living at 105 North Street. They resisted SAC's offers and refused to sell their properties as they had no wish to relinquish their businesses and livelihoods. Some of the cottages opposite the workhouse were demolished, but the rest remain to this day; Had they been removed the sites would have been destined for more Courtauld mock Tudor style houses.

Richard Deal
Standing outside their baker's shop in North Street

Nellie Deal with her daughter Evie
Courtesy of Barry Sparke

No. 1 Ernest Evans
No. 3 Charles J Brewer
No. 5 Harry Rayner
No. 7 Walter E Raven
No. 9 Frederick J Potter

No. 2 William D Bright
No. 4 Herbert Plowright
No. 6 Fred C Dixon
No. 8 Ernest H Knight
No.10 George Goodey

Sketches of the Halstead Football players, taken from a booklet printed c1896.

Number 1. **Ernest Evans**. Ernie learnt to play football at Halstead Grammar School and in 1894-95, he played centre half back for the school eleven. He joined the town team in 1888-89 and played regularly for the Excelsiors at Howe Ground in 1893-94. A genial man, Ernie was a popular choice of Captain for the Halstead club when he was elected in 1895. He was an ardent cricketer too, who played for the town club, he was a hard hitter of the ball and a very good bowler.

Number 2. **William Desborough Bright.** William who was born in Coggeshall in 1872, went to Catford Collegiate School, near Lewisham and played under Rugby rules for the school in 1894. The following year he moved to Uckfield Grammar School and played for the school eleven and, as a small built lad he was nicknamed 'The Mite'. His football career included playing for Colchester second eleven and Southend Football Club, formerly known as the Old Rochford Hundred Club, before he played for Halstead. After suffering a leg injury he took on the role of Honorary Treasurer for the club.

Number 3. **Charles J Brewer.** As a small boy Charles kicked a football about in a meadow at Blamsters and became one of the first members of the Old Railway Club during the 1880s. As well as playing for Halstead, Charlie played for Hedingham Football Club. However he returned to Halstead before he took on the role of Honorary Secretary. It was Charlie's efforts too, that helped to bring about the formation of the Second Division within the North Essex League.

Number 4. **Herbert Plowright.** Herbert was born at Kings Lynn in 1868 and learned to play football at school, being the team's captain when he was just thirteen years old. He left school in 1882 playing for the Kings Lynn Star Club and then the Alexandra team, where he obtained his County Colours as one of Norfolk's best players. In 1890 he joined Kings Lynn Town Club before he played for Woolwich Arsenal, Lincoln City Swifts, who were the Lincoln City Reserve team and Warwick County, as well as most of the leading Norfolk Clubs before joining Halstead Town. Herbert was also a talented cricketer.

Number 5. **Harry Rayner.** Harry first appeared in a first eleven match for Halstead in 1889. He was a hard working, quiet member of the team who never tried to gain support from the crowd with 'gallery tricks'. When he was proposed for the position of Captain of the club it was stated that he was giving up football, but four years later he was still playing. He found it impossible to give up football and continued to play when asked to do so.

Number 6. **Fred Candy Dixon.** Fred first played football at his school near Newport before he moved to Hampshire. He was captain of the Solent School Eleven before he went to Hurst College, Sussex, where he played for both the second and first eleven teams. In both the 1891-92 and 1892-93 seasons, the college was in the semi final of the Sussex County Challenge Cup. Fred moved to Halstead in 1893 and played for the town second eleven. He was a very fast player and with his partner Herbert Plowright troubled the opposition's best defences. Fred was a slight man, 5ft 5ins tall and only 8st 6lbs.

Number 7. **Walter Edward Raven.** Walter, known as Wally was a native of Halstead. During the 1893-94 season he played for Halstead Reserves before he joined the First Eleven side in 1894. He rarely missed a match for a couple years until his form seemed to waver, although he was the captain of a team connected with the Halstead Working Men's Club. Wally was also partial to rabbit shooting and once sacrificed a football match for a little 'sporting' enjoyment! He was also Senior Corporal of the local Volunteer Corps.

Number 8. **Ernest H Knight.** Ernest was regarded as the grand old man of local football having played for twenty two seasons; In fact, he played football before the Halstead Club came into existence. Ernest first learnt to play at school in the early 1870s under both Association and Rugby rules, firstly at Ackworth in Yorkshire and then at Hitchin in Hertfordshire. During the 1882-83 season he played for the Foxes (London) and toured with them in Yorkshire. He obtained his county colours playing for Essex in 1886. When the Halstead Club was formed he played for them regularly and seldom failed to make the newspapers, such was his ability to always play well.

Number 9. **Frederick J Potter.** Frederick was born in 1875 and first became connected with Halstead Town Club when he was sixteen years old and engaged in scratch matches. In 1893 due to his powerful kicking he played for the Reserves as a back, a position he disliked as he lacked the ability to successfully tackle his opponents. However, following an injury, Frederick persuaded his captain to let him play in goal and much against his better judgement, the captain agreed; The venture was hailed a great success and Frederick became the club's goal keeper for the rest of the season. The following year, the town goal keeper transferred to the Excelsior team and Frederick took his place and played for the town team.

Number 10. **George Goodey.** George was another popular Halstead forward who kept his place in the team for many years. A good goal kicker, he had scored 13 of the 33 goals achieved in the 1893-94 season. In the last season he divided the credit with Tom Steed, each having six goals. George too, was well known throughout the district for being a good cricketer, a respected batsman and useful bowler.

Glossary

This small glossary relates to terms in this book.

Appurtenance	A right, privilege or property that is considered incidental to the principal property for the purposes such as passage of title, conveyance or inheritance.
Assignee	A person to whom property is transferred by sale or gift.
Copyhold	Originally a tenure dependent upon custom and the lords will. The tenant was protected not by national law but by title written into court rolls. To transfer the property the tenant surrendered to the lord, who then admitted the new tenant. Copyhold tenure was abolished in 1926.
Conveyance of Copyhold Land	The conveyance of copyhold land had to be noted in the manor court rolls. A copyholder 'surrendered' his property, a mortgage of copyhold land was called a conditional surrender. In cases of mortgage the action was recorded in the court rolls but the mortgagee was not admitted to the land. On repayment of the mortgage a warrant of satisfaction was given to the mortgagor.
Customary Freehold	Land held by custom and not by will of the lord. It was abolished in 1922.
Freehold	A free tenure and not subject to the custom of the manor or the will of the lord.
Hereditament	Any kind of property or enclosed area of land adjacent to a dwelling house that can be inherited.
Leasehold	A form of tenure where one party has the right to occupy a dwelling or land for a given length of time. When a lease was for a long periods of time, it was possible for the property to be passed on to an assignee.
Messuage	Dwelling house together with its outbuildings and adjacent land used by the household.
Surrender	A term used to denote 'a yielding up' of copyhold lands.
Tenement	Property such as a building or land that is held by one person and leased to another.

Appendix I

14th November 1930 - Two letters were published in the Halstead Gazette about the renaming of Hedingham Lane, North Street and Hedingham Road.

1. "The Vicarage, Halstead.
7th November 1930
Dear Sir, - The Registers of St. Andrew's Church, Halstead, show the first entry of Hedingham Lane as North Street in April 1863. Then, as though loathe to exchange the old and poetical for the new and prosaic name, the entries alternate between Hedingham Lane and North Street up to 1869. Henceforward North Street succeeds in ousting the sweet assonance of Hedingham Lane and at the same time Parson's Lane, which also becomes Parsonage Street in 1863, is established in the name it still bears. If, as I hope, North Street becomes Hedingham Road, not only shall we escape from the chilly associations which the present name suggests, but shall also come into line with the principle, by which, as it appears, the other principal roads leading out of the town, viz., Braintree, Colchester and Sudbury Roads have been named.
Yours faithfully,
T. H. Curling".

2. "Sir, - I was surprised to read that our Urban District Council had received a letter from Mr. S. A. Courtauld suggesting that 'North Street' should be changed to 'Hedingham Road.' A step backward! I thought he liked improvement and progress - as evidenced by the building of those nice modern houses in the place of old dilapidated cottages - but now he suggests that a main thoroughfare leading from our High Street be changed from a street to a road. Its a nice broad highway, with paths both sides, not generally found on roads. I am ambitious for my native town, and stand for its progress and improvement.

I think the Council came to a too hasty decision - indeed, exceeded their limit - for surely the property-owners and ratepayers who have to pay for the upkeep of the street should have been consulted. The Chairman remembers it being named 'Hedingham Lane;' so do I; also 'Inigam Lane', which probably would soon be revived for old names, like old customs, die slowly.

I think Mr. Krailing's suggestions that 'North Street' remain and continue to the Wash - and from the Wash onward it could be called 'Hedingham Road' - very good and proper.

I don't think Mr. Courtauld would wish to do anything that would lower the prestige of the town, and, perhaps after considering the matter, he will withdraw his suggestions and let things remain as they are.
Respectfully yours,

E. E. Watkinson".

Appendix II

Names of labourers who appeared on the 1827 Census Return for Halstead who lived at How Ground and Does Corner but did not work for Edward May.

Name	Age	Home	Occupation	Employer
Burkitt, Robert	---	Doe's Corner	Labourer	Smoothy
Byford, Phillip	---	How Ground	Sand Carter	Smoothy
Byford, Phillip's son	25yrs	How Ground	Sand Carter	Smoothy
Drury, Thomas	---	How Ground	Broom Maker	None
Maythorn, Thomas	65	Doe's Corner	Gardener	Sperling
Mole, William	---	How Ground	Labourer	Harrington
Parker, John	---	How Ground	Labourer	Sparrow

Mr. Harrington lived in the Parish of Maplestead
Thomas Smoothy lived in the Parish of Great Maplestead
Mr. Sparrow lived in the Parish of Halstead
James Sperling lived in the Parish of Great Maplestead

Appendix III

A letter from Matthew Arnold to Anne Hornor dated 6th October 1872.
Courtesy of The University of Virginia Press.
'The Letters of Matthew Arnold' - Letter reference number V4P131D1

"My dear Mrs Hornor
I send you through the publisher a little book of mine which will perhaps interest you. I send it to show you that you are in my mind at this season when I have so often been coming to Halstead. How beautiful your hills and trees must have been looking in the October sun today: I was always so much struck with the beauty of that Coln(e) valley in autumn. I hope your dear girls are well and that your sons are prospering as you could wish. Beatrice must be almost a young woman - how time passes! She and Edith have never paid that visit to the dentist which was to have bought them to Harrow. And now we are leaving Harrow which has become too sad a place to my wife: we give up our house next March and have taken a cottage in Surrey. My days are filled as usual and I am never able to visit my sister in law at Copford; I think I may promise I will never go there without coming over to Halstead. Let me have a line when you have leisure to tell me how you are all going on; tell me of each and all the girls, and of your daughter Alice and her husband and children. I suppose everything is finished about their new house now; I remember thinking I could live very well in the stables. If you ever see the Gibsons at Walden remember me to them most kindly; the time of my old annual visit to them, as to you, is quite a sad anniversary now; I felt I had such real friends at Walden and The Howe, and there is so little chance of my ever now seeing them. Believe me
most sincerely yours,
Matthew Arnold".

NB.
Matthew Arnold refers to their house in Harrow as 'has become too sad a place to my wife'. This is because their son Trevelen William Arnold had died earlier in 1872 at the age of 18 years.

The Gibson's of Saffron Walden were a well known Quaker family who were initially brewers and later bankers. In 1896 they amalgamated with twenty other private banks to become Barclays and Co Limited, later Barclays Bank.

Appendix IV

Staff who resided at The Howe.

There are no documents available which record every member of staff who worked or resided at The Howe. The list below is compiled using census returns from 1841 to 1911 and electoral registers from 1929 to 1953.

<u>Census Returns 1841-1911</u> (names in the order that they appeared on the Census Returns)

Year	Name	Age	Occupation	Where born
1841	Maxim, James			
	Maxim, Sophia		Housekeeper	Halstead
1851	Corlet, Henrietta		Governess	
1861	Leslie, Isabella	32	Governess	Scotland
	Reeve, Charlotte	42	Cook	Hedingham
	Smith, Sarah	23	House maid	Great Tey
	Wicker, Eliza	19	House maid	Maplestead
	Dedman, Rebecca	23	Nurse	Halstead
	Kendal, Margaretta	21	House maid	Hedingham
	Church, Ann	16	Kitchen maid	Hedingham
1871	Reeve, Charlotte	52	Cook	Castle Hedingham
	Church, Ann	26	Kitchen maid	Castle Hedingham
	Hedges, Emily	24	House maid	Hayes Middlesex
	Fletcher, Emily	17	House maid	Halstead
1881	Woolford, Ellen	33	Cook	Purton Wiltshire
	Padfield, Elizabeth	33	House maid	Holcombe Somerset
	Clarke, Anne	33	Parlour maid	Farnham Surrey
	Downes, Mary	33	Work woman	Attleborough Norfolk
	Scrivener, Anne	20	House maid	Runwell
	Tyler, Eliza	21	Kitchen Maid	Halstead
1891	Woolford, Ellen	44	Cook	Wiltshire
	Padfield, Elizabeth	43	House maid	Somerset
	Vale, Ellen	33	Parlour maid	Felstead
	Miller, Elizabeth	18	House maid	Bury St. Edmunds
	Lorking, Ada	17	Kitchen maid	Colne Engaine
1901	Taylor, Alice M.	37	Cook	Halstead
	Witham, Ellen S.	32	Parlour maid	Langham
	Cracknell, Selena A.	28	House maid	Stambourne
	Stuart, Lizzie	20	House maid	Toppesfield
	Wakeling, Louisa	15	Kitchen maid	Blackmore End

1911	Montgomery, Beatrice	34	Nurse	South America
	Garrity, Ellen	43	Cook	Halstead
	Branch, Lily Emma	26	Parlour maid	Sudbury
	Meadowes, Eleanor	37	House maid	Harwich
	Weston, Edith Eliza	37	House maid	Halstead
	Goddard, Grace Ada	18	Kitchen maid	Halstead
	Norman, Eliza	51	Maid (attendance)	Halstead

Electoral Registers 1929-1953

1929
Gant, Marjorie Isabel Maud
Heath, Minnie Florence
Marriner, Elsie Annie
Peel, Alice Dymond
Powter, Sophia Ann
Shelvey, Stanley Herbert
Souter, Charles Robert

1930
Heath, Minnie Florence
Peel, Alice Dymond
Powter, Sophia Ann
Shelvey, Stanley Herbert

1931
Bright, Rhoda
Powter, Sophia Ann
Seville, Dorothy

1932
Last, Emma J.
Powter, Sophia Ann

1933 & 4
Frost, Alice
Powter, Sophia Ann

1935 & 6
Bartholomew, Edith
Powter, Sophia Ann

1937
Bartholomew, Edith

1938 & 9
Bartholomew, Edith
Box, Florence Maria

1945
Booth, Agnes E.
Hodges, Alice
Keily, Andrew
Watts, Eleanor

1946-1950
Chudley, Harvey
Chudley, Gertrude

1951
Adams, Mabel
Booth, Agnes
Chudley, Harvey
Chudley, Gertrude
Kiely, Andrew

1952
Adams, Mabel

1953
Booth, Agnes
Felton, Alice
Keily, Andrew
Rigby, Frances

Appendix V

Electoral Registers for Noel House, 8 Palace Green, London W8, showing the staff who were in residence. Extracts taken from available registers.

1920   Harding, Arthur
        Saunders, Albert Arthur

1922   Breadmore, Albert Edward
        Plumb, Charles

1923   Lane, Frederick
        Plumb, Charles

1924   Plumb, Charles

1929   Gant, Marjorie Isabel Maud
        Heath, Minnie
        Marriner, Elsie Annie
        Peel, Alice Dymond
        Pope, Ernestine
        Smith, Beatrice
        Shelvey, Stanley Herbert
        Souter, Charles Robert

1930   Bright, Rosina
        Fletcher, Mary Jane
        Grange, Margery
        Groves, Elizabeth
        Howell, Ernest
        Manning, Florence
        Moore, David
        Pope, Ernestina
        Preston, George
        Rodkin, Edith
        Stuart, Elsie

1933   Arthur, George
        Burningham, Mary
        Bush, Jane
        Filler, Edward James
        Lovelock, Marguerite
        Sherwin, Gertrude
        Stevens, Alice

1934   Arthur, George
        Carroll, Edith
        Evans, Mary
        Filler, Edward James

1934   Hovell, Rose
        Lovelock, Margaret
        Stevens, Alice

1935   Arthur, George
        Carroll, Ethel
        Evans, Mary
        Fuller, Edward
        Goodfellow, Mollie
        Hovell, Rose
        Lovelock, Marguerite

1936   Arthur, George
        Edwards, Jack
        Goodfellow, Mollie
        Hewett, Alice
        Lovelock, Marguerite

1938   Alleston, Nellie
        Booth, Elizabeth Mary Agnes
        Fender, Thomas
        Fraser, Christina
        Rogers, Rose Kathleen Dora

1939   Booth, Elizabeth Agnes Mary
        Fender, Thomas
        Fraser, Christina
        McWilliam, James
        Moody, Margaret Ellen
        Stickley, Florence Beatrice

1945   Chudley, Gertrude C.
        Chudley, Harvey J.

1946   Booth, Agnes   1950   Adams, Mabel
        Hodges, Alice   Chudley, Gertrude C.
        Houlton, Nellie   Chudley, Harvey J.
        Kiely, Andrew   Kiely, Andrew
        Slaney, Ann

1947   Booth, Agnes   1951   Adams, Mabel
        Houlton, Nellie   Boothe(sic), Agnes
        Kiely, Andrew   Chudley, Gertrude C.
                                            Chudley, Harvey J.
                                            Kiely, Andrew
                                            Redmond, Rose

After the death of EAC in 1951 Noel House was sold.

Appendix VI

Details of Thelric House, Howe Drive, contributed by Michael Portway.

"**The Plot** comprised the land south of the copse to the left of the drive to The Howe, down to Hedingham road, bordered on the west by a fence, by Hedingham Road to the south and Howe Drive itself to the east. It included the very small copse at the bottom of Howe Drive in the south east corner of the plot. It was purchased from Ralph van Asch in 1956.

The House was designed by Ronald Mobbs ARIBA, it being the first house he designed entirely by himself and was constructed above ground entirely of 'double' lignacite blocks (these being two walled with a cavity between the walls) produced by Lignacite Ltd of Brandon, near Thetford. It had flat roofs, one sloping west to east (living area) and one sloping south to north (sleeping area). Due to the fact the plot sloped up from Hedingham Road and the house was built on the highest point, Mr Mobbs, quite rightly, designed it as a single storey dwelling, spread out from west to east. It was <u>never</u> referred to as a bungalow! The flat roofs were constructed of laminated board, covered in pitch with heavy gauge roofing felt bonded to it, in turn covered with small stones, it was guaranteed for twenty years.

Internally the layout consisted of a small entrance lobby with on the left, a cloakroom (loo and wash basin) and on the right the airing cupboard and a cloaks cupboard in which the telephone was installed. Leading off to the right of the entrance lobby was a door to the dining room, kitchen and living room.

The dining room had a 3 sided window with integral seat and was also the passage way to the living room. On the right hand side was a door to the kitchen, larder and outside covered space. In the kitchen was a coal fired Aga Cooker providing cooking and hot water facilities feeding a towel rail. It had built in cupboards and a let down table at the far end, normal work surfaces and built in cupboards on the internal wall. A wide hatch next to the door gave access to the dining room.

The living room was large with a lofty ceiling, beamed to hold up the flat roof. Along the south side was a large window but, on the west wall was a huge picture window (to make the most of the view across the valley) which was hung in the centre of both sides so it could be reversed and opened inwards in order to clean the interior of the double walled construction. (This before the introduction of sealed units). On the north wall was a fire place beside which was an access door to the coal hole (filled from outside).

To the left of the entrance lobby was a passage off which were the family bathroom and five bedrooms, some with built in cupboards.

The house was constructed by J S Norton, Builders of Halstead and managed by Reg Wishart, whose nickname was 'Weary'! There was no gas main to the site but electricity and main drainage were available.

The Garden. Outside the dining room and living room on the south side was a terrace with a 2-3 foot drop to the ground due to the sloping site. In due course this was met by lawn, with flower beds to the east and west. Later on the west side a swimming pool was constructed by hand. (40 tons of earth being moved over two years and placed around the west and north perimeter of the property).

North of the property was the drive, bordered on its north by a copse of trees and ending at a car port built on to the kitchen. (This was later transformed into a 'granny' flat for the owner's father in law when he was widowed). South of the lawn was a field containing specimen trees which was let to a neighbour to graze horses. This field was also used annually by the neighbours from Ashlong Grove having their bonfire with fireworks display and hot snacks to follow.

Because of its unique construction the house was featured in the 'Ideal Homes Magazine' in the 1960s".

(Over the decades this house has undergone substantial renovation and building work. None of the original outside construction materials or flat roof remain).

NB. Another house was constructed between Halstead and Gosfield opposite Gosfield School, using the same materials as Thelric House, but this too has been demolished and replaced by a brick built house.

Appendix VII

Electoral Register or Street Directory for:

Ashlong Grove	1957-1965/6
Howe Chase	1962-1965/6
Howe Cottage	1956-1965/6
Howe Drive	1957-1965/6
Howe Ground	1954-1965/6
Howe Nursery Holdings	1960-1961

1954 & 1955	Howe Ground		Blackwell, Albert
			Blackwell, Phyllis
			Blackwell, Alec
			Blackwell, Derek
1956	Howe Cottage		Grant, Thomas
			Grant, Elizabeth
	Howe Ground		Blackwell, Albert
			Blackwell, Phyllis
			Blackwell, Alec
			Blackwell, Derek
1957	Ashlong Grove	Fagans	Rippingale, Jack
			Rippingale, Joyce
		Rema	Lacey, Rolfe
			Lacey, Edna
		In t' Veld	Rushbrook, Maurice
			Rushbrook, Kathleen
		April House	Bullivant, Margaret
	Howe Cottage		Grant, Thomas
			Grant, Elizabeth
	Howe Drive	Thelric House	Portway, Michael
			Portway, Mavis
	Howe Ground		Blackwell, Albert
			Blackwell, Phyllis
			Blackwell, Alec
			Blackwell, Derek
1958 & 1959	The Howe		Darrell, Lionel
			Darrell, Ursula
	Howe Cottage		Grant, Thomas
			Grant, Elizabeth
	Howe Drive	Rustlings	Hogarth, Bertram

1958 & 1959	Howe Drive	Rustlings	Hogarth, F. Mary
		Thelric House	Portway, Michael
			Portway, Mavis
	Howe Ground		Blackwell, Albert
			Blackwell, Phyllis
1960	Ashlong Grove	Alney	Hancock, Sydney
			Hancock, Alma
		Le Chene	Youngs, Philip
			Youngs, Eunice
		Chantek	Smith, Eric
			Smith, Beryl
		Perdita	Rayner, Frank
			Rayner, Gem
		Rema	Lacey, Rolfe
			Lacey, Edna
		Oaklea	Rushbrook, Maurice
			Rushbrook, Kathleen
		Fagans	Rippingale, Jack
			Rippingale, Joyce
		Therons	Keeble, John
			Keeble, Lilian
		Ainsdale	Hartley, Donald
			Hartley, Dilys
			Hartley, Elsie
		April House	Bullivant, Margaret
		Number 29	Taylor, Frank
			Taylor, Joan (Roslyn)
		Glenfield	Lockwood, Cyril
			Lockwood, Violet
	The Howe		Darrell, Lionel
			Darrell, Ursula
	Howe Cottage		Osborne, Arthur
			Osborne, Edith
	Howe Drive	Rustlings	Hogarth, Bertram
			Hogarth, F. Mary
		Thelric House	Portway, Michael
			Portway, Mavis
	Howe Ground		Blackwell, Albert
			Blackwell, Phyllis
			Blackwell, Alec

			Blackwell, Neil
	Howe Nursery Holding		Grant, Thomas
1960	Howe Nursery Holding		Grant, Elizabeth
			Grant, Daphne
1961	Ashlong Grove	Alney	Hancock, Sydney
			Hancock, Alma
		Le Chene	Youngs, Philip
			Youngs, Eunice
		Chantek	Smith, Eric
			Smith, Beryl
		Perdita	Rayner, Frank
			Rayner, Gem
		Rema	Lacey, Rolfe
			Lacey, Edna
		Oaklea	Mercer, Noel
			Mercer, Marjorie
		Fagans	Rippingale, Jack
			Rippingale, Joyce
		Therons	Keeble, John
			Keeble, Lilian
		Ainsdale	Hartley, Donald
			Hartley, Dilys
			Hartley, Elsie
		April House	Bullivant, Margaret
		Number 29	Taylor, Frank
			Taylor, Joan Roslyn
	The Howe		Darrell, Lionel
			Darrell, Ursula
	Howe Cottage		Osborne, Arthur
			Osborne, Edith
	Howe Drive	Rustlings	Hogarth, Bertram
			Hogarth, F. Mary
		Thelric House	Portway, Michael
			Portway, Mavis
	Howe Nursery Holding		Grant, Thomas
			Grant, Elizabeth

• • • • • • • • • • • • • • •

During 1962/1963 the properties in Ashlong Grove began to be identified by house numbers instead of by names in the Halstead Directory, published by Victoria Publishing Company, Fleet Street, London EC4.

1963 Publisher's note:
The information given in this Directory is as accurate as it has been possible to make it. Whilst tending apologies for any omissions which may have occurred and any slight errors which may have crept in, we would ask that any amendments be brought to our notice immediately. These will be carefully recorded and incorporated in the next issue, which we hope to make more comprehensive.

To this end we would welcome suggestions and everything submitted will be carefully considered. Many people have helped in various ways in the production of this Directory. To them we extend our thanks in the belief that it will be a very necessary service to the neighbourhood.

Ashlong Grove	1962	1963	1965/66
No. 3	---------	--------	Chaplin, C.F.
No. 4	Hancock, S.W.	Hancock, S.W.	Hancock, S.W.
No. 5	Taylor, F.	Taylor, F.	Taylor, F
No. 6	Lockwood, C.	Lockwood, C.	Whittall, C.
No. 7	Bowen, D.	Bowen, D.	Bowen, D.
No. 8	Wenn, R. D.	Wenn, R.D.	Wenn, R.D.
No. 9	Little, D. J.	Little, D.J.	Pritchard, J.C.W.
No. 10	Wakelin, J.R.	Wakelin, J.R.	Skilton, C.H.
No. 11	Farrant, J.H.	Farrant, J.H.	Farrant, J.H.
No. 12	Croker, C.F.	Croker, C.F.	Croker, C.F.
No. 13	Moore, B.O.	Moore, B.O.	Moore, B.O.
No. 14	Jones, C.M.	Jones, C.M.	Jones, C.M.
No. 15	Howard, G.F.	Howard, G.F.	Howard, G.F.
No. 16	Andrewes, B.A.	Andrewes, B.A.	Andrewes, B.A.
No. 17	Youngs, P.I.	Youngs, P.I.	Youngs, P.I.
No. 18	Smith, E.	Smith, E.	Smith, E.
No. 19	Eagle, R.D.	Eagle, R.D.	Eagle, R.D.
No. 20	Rippingale, J.W.	Rippingale, J.W.	Frankland, R.S.
No. 21	---------	---------	Broughton, J.M.
No. 22	Rayner, F.A.	Rayner, F.A.	Rayner, F.A.
No. 23	Lomas, J.	Lomas, J.	Lofthouse, A.
No. 24	Mercer, N.S.	Mercer, N.S.	Mercer, N.S.
No. 25	Keeble, J.	Keeble, J.	Keeble, J.
No. 26	Langford, G.	Langford, G.	Langford, G.
No. 27	Hartley, D.M.	Hartley, D.M.	Hartley, D.M.
No. 28	Bullivant, M.I.	Bullivant, M.I.	Bullivant, M.I.
No. 29	---------	---------	Mitchell, W.G.
No. 30	---------	---------	Collett, B.F.
No. 31	---------	---------	Laidler, F.R.
The Howe	Darrell, L.D.	Darrell, L.D.	Darrell, L.D.
Howe Cottage	Osborne, A.A.	Osborne, A.A.	Osborne, A.A.
Howe Chase			
Woodlands	Grant, T.W.R.	Grant, T.W.R.	Grant, T.W.R.

	1962	1963	1965/6
Howe Drive			
Rustlings	Hogarth, B.H.W.	Hogarth, B.H.W.	Hogarth, B.H.W.
Thelric House	Portway, M.C.	Portway, M.C.	Portway, M.C.
	Theobald, H.	Theobald, H.	Theobald, H.
Rathearne)	Christie, V.M.	Christie, V.M.	
Renamed: Sandy Lodge)			Ware, H.J.
Howe Ground	Blackwell, A.H.	Blackwell, A.H.	Blackwell, A.H.

· · · · · · · · · · · · · · ·

Please note spelling of names as they appeared on all the Electoral Registers.

Bibliography

August & Rab, A Memoir	by Mollie Butler	1987
The Buildings of England, Essex, 3rd edition	by James Bettley and Nikolaus Pevsner	2007
A Centenary History of Halstead Hospital 1884-1984	by Adrian Corder-Birch	1984
Discover Halstead	by Percy A L Bamberger	1982
The Domesday Book, England's Heritage, Then and Now	by Thomas Hinde	1985
Essex at Work 1700-1815	by A F J Brown	1969
Essex Directories 1839-1937		
Essex Windmills, Millers and Millwrights volume 4	by Kenneth G Farries	1985
Football in Halstead A History of the Town and Excelsior Clubs	reprinted from the East Essex and Halstead Times	c1896
From Construction to Destruction An Authentic History of The Colne Valley and Halstead Railway	by E P Willingham	1989
From Pebmarsh to the Swan A History of One Branch of the Sewell Family of Great Henny Essex c1600-c1940	by Glennis Sewell	2011
Halstead and Colne Valley at War 1939-1945	by Dave Osborne	1983
Halstead and District Local History Society Newsletters		1977 to date
Halstead's Heritage	by Doreen Potts	1989
Halstead Town Football Club	by Dave Osborne	2010
Halstead Directories 1963, 1965-6, 1967-8, 1969		
Hartest, A Village History Researched by the Hartest Local History Group	edited by Clive Paine	1984
The History of Stisted Hall	by Bruce Ballard	1998
Holman's Halstead	by William Holman edited by T G Gibbons MA	1909

Industrial Housing in Essex Comparative Survey of Modern Industrial Sites and Monuments	by Tony Crosby Adam Garwood and Adrian Corder-Birch	2006
A Look Back at Halstead	by Doreen Potts	2003
Man the Ropes	by Augustine Courtauld	1957
Micah Corder (1680-1766) and his Descendants	by Francis Corder Clayton	1885
Old and New Halstead	by William James Evans	1886
People at Work in Halstead and District	by Doreen Potts	1993
Pointers to the Past The Origin of Halstead Street Names	by Michael Bardell	2003
Royal Commission on Historical Monuments (England) Essex North West		1916
Schools and Scholars in Halstead and District	by Mary Downey and Doreen Potts	1986
Some Essex Water Mills	by Hervey Benham	1976
Thomas Cubitt, Master Builder	by Hermione Hobhouse	1971
Wills at Chelmsford, 3 volumes 1400-1858	by The British Record Society	

Essex Record Office
General Family Histories about:
Bentall Family
Courtauld Family
Hornor Family
May Family
Sparrow Family
Start Family
Tweed Family
Vaizey Family
Birth, baptism, marriage, death and burial records for Halstead and surrounding area
Various Electoral Registers for the Halstead area 1860-1963
Land Tax Assessments for Halstead 1866-1922
Manorial Records for the Manor of Abells 1750 to c1900
Manorial Records for the Manor of Hipworth/Hepworth 1725-1745
Monumental Inscriptions
Overseers Rate Books 1829-1845
Rate Books for Halstead, St Andrews, 1831-1861 inclusive

Sale Catalogues of properties in Bocking, Frinton on Sea, Halstead and Ridgewell
Also numerous Conveyances, Deeds, Indentures, Ordnance Survey Maps, Tithe Maps, Wills and a vast array of Miscellaneous items.

Suffolk Record Office
General Title: Weller Poley and Halifax families of Suffolk
Reference: HA 519; Covering dates: 1332-20th Century (1900-1999)
General Family Histories about:
Bentall Estate in Halstead
Poley Family History
Tweed Estate in Halstead and Hartest
Whaley Estates
Also numerous Conveyances, Deeds, Indentures, Ordnance Survey Maps, Tithe Maps, and Wills

Guildhall Library
Worshipful Company of Ironmongers Archive 1767-1848
Holden's Annual London and County Directory 1808, 1811
Johnstone's London Commercial guide 1817
Kent's Directory 1812-1818
Robson's London Directory 1848

London Metropolitan Archives
Various Electoral Registers for Kensington 1910-1950
Deeds relating to the Hornor Family
Photographs of Noel House, Palace Green, London

National Archive Office
Bankruptcy Records for Edward May 1844-51
Documents relating to the Hornor Family
The Law List
Pigots, Whites, Post Office and Kelly's Directories for London

Newspapers
Various issues of:
Chelmsford Chronicle
Essex Newsman
Essex Standard
The Halstead Gazette between 1896 and 1963
Yorkshire Gazette
The Law Journal 1847
The Law Times 1847
The London Gazette 1840s
The Times 1840s
Canada - Nipissing Local Newspaper 1906
Tasmania - Launceston Gazette -various issues

Gentleman's Magazine - various issues

Index

A

Abrams, Henry, 210
Ackroyd, Eileen Rawson, 78
Addison, James, 106
Addlestone, 83,84
Aldwin, Ann, 41
Allen, Robert, 86
Alphamstone, 27
Alston, Frederick William, 126,182
Andrewes, Rev. John Brereton, 72
Argent, Jack, 131
Argent, Sarah, 41
Argent, William, 33
Arnold, Matthew, 65
Ashby, Joseph, 96
Ashcombe Tower, 121,122
Ashen, 92,93
Ashlong Properties Limited, 147,149
Ashworth, Dr. James Henry, 30
Atkinson, Rachel, 26
Attwoods Foot Beagles, 88
Augustine Courtauld Trust, 118

B

Baker and Burton, 147
Balls and Balls, 137,141,142
Barrett, Ernest, 96
Barrett, Richard, 65
Barron, Mary, 186
Basham, Albert, 165
Bean, George, 196
Beckett, Georgette Frances, 51
Beddall, Henry, 95
Bentall, John, 15
Bentall, Katherine, 15
Bentall, Mary, 15
Beridge, Rev. Basil, 86
Bigg, William, 20
Bingham, Edward, 137,138
Birch, Clarence, 149
Birch, Essex, 29
Birdbrook,
  Birdbrook Hall, 50
  Moyns Park, 119
Birkbeck, Alice, 59
Birkbeck William, 59
Bishop, Henry, 203
Blackmore End, 110,118
Blackwell, Albert Harris, 156, 165,193
Blackwell, Richard, 209
Blatch, Ann, 19

Bocking,
  Black Boy, 130
  Little Bradfords, 100,117,119,125
  St. Mary's Church, 108
  Village Hall, 110
Bond, Samuel, 29
Booth, Agnes, 131
Booth, Charles, 52
Borley, 89
Bousfield, Ann, 74
Bowly, Samuel, 61,67
Boxted, Suffolk, 21
Bragg, Alfred, 174
Braintree, 48
Bravo, Ann Morse, 81
Brewer, James, 27
Brewster, Emily Margaret, 27
Brewster, James, 27
Brewster, Mary Anne, 27
Bright, Alexander, 18
Broomhall, John, 65
Brown, David, 203
Brown, Henry (Harry), 131
Brown, John Boyer, 28
Brown, William, 34
Browston Hall, Suffolk, 21
Brunwin, Jane, 33
Brunwin, John, 33
Brunwin, Susanna, 33
Bullard, George, 163
Bullivant, Margaret, 149
Bullock, William, 20
Burder, George, 165
Burroughs, Catherine, 72
Burroughs, Rev. Henry, 72
Burroughs, Sarah, 72
Burt, Frederick, 86,87
Butcher, William, 171
Butler, Richard Austen, 119
Butler, Mollie, 119
Butler, Sydney Elizabeth, 119

C

Caesar, Eleanor, 75
Cameron, Duncan, 151,154
Canham, Bartholomew, 17
Canham, Deborah, 17
Canham, Elizabeth, 17
Canham, Katherine, 15,17
Canham, Margaret, 17
Canham, Mary, 17
Canham, Robert, 17

Canham, Sarah, 17
Carnall, Christopher, 19
Cash, Thomas, 65
Castle Hedingham, 15,17
Catchpole, Elizabeth, 26
Catchpole, Thomas, 25,26
Chambers, Lewis, 210
Childerditch, Essex, 36
Ching, John, 41,42
Ching, Keren Happuch Michell, 41
Ching, Rebecca, 41
Christie, Vic, 152
Christy, James, 65
Chudley, Harvey James, 130
Church, Stephen, 23,36
Clarry, Bertie George, 164
Clarry, Frederick, 164
Clarry, Reggie James, 164
Claydon, Suffolk, 26
Clayton, Allen Francis, 26
Clayton, Francis Corder, 26
Clements, Rev. William, 85
Cockerton, Alfred, 169,210
Cockerton, Emma, 169,210
Coe, Eliza, 179
Coggeshall, 26
    Hornigalls Farm, 25
    Meeting House Graveyard, 27
Colchester,
    All Saints, 20
    Castle Lands, 20
    East Hill, 20
    Holy Trinity Church, 19,21,22
    St. James Parish, 20,21
    St. Mary at the Walls, 20
Coldwell, Coldwell and Courtauld, 104
Coldwell, Edward William, 104
Collar, Robert, 96
Collings, Constance Sewell, 52
Collings, Gertrude May, 52
Collings, Harold William, 52
Collings, Rev. William, 52
Collings, William Knibb, 52
Colne Engaine, 28
    Colne Park Lodge, 204
    Rook Tree Farm, 28
Colne Valley and Halstead Railway, 50,62,63,75
Colne Valley Railway Preservation Society, 145
Constable, Abraham, 208
Constable, Edward, 67,68
Constable, Henry James, 163
Cook, Faith Dorothy Caldwell, 122,134
Corder, Alfred, 25,26

Corder, Ann, 25,26
Corder, Charles, 25,26
Corder, Elizabeth, 25,26
Corder, Emmaretta, 25,26
Corder, George, 25,26
Corder, Gladys, 170
Corder, James, 24-26
Corder, Mary, 25,26
Corder, Phoebe, 26
Corder, Richard, 25,26
Corder, William John, 87
Corder, William Start, 25,26
Corlet, Henrietta, 61
Coudert, Adelaide, 81
Coudert, Ann Morse, 81
Coudert, Joseph Hawley, 81
Coudert, Louis Leonce, 81
Coudert, Alice Marian, 81
Coumbe, Albert Thomas, 51
Courtauld, Augustine, 14,100,117-119,197
Courtauld, Augustine Christopher Caradoc, 117
Courtauld, Edith Anne (EAC), 100,106-108,
    111-114,116-119,125,134,135,197
Courtauld, Edith Elizabeth (Betty), 100,119-122,
    127,134
Courtauld, Elizabeth, 116
Courtauld, Faith Dorothy, 122,134
Courtauld, George, 86,99,106,126,129,130
Courtauld, Jeanne, 121
Courtauld, John Sewell, 104
Courtauld, Jonathan Louis, 123
Courtauld, Julia Elizabeth, 123
Courtauld, Julien, 117
Courtauld, Katherine Mina, 99
Courtauld, Martha Jane, 123
Courtauld, Mollie, 117-119
Courtauld, Perina, 117
Courtauld, Richard Savill, 123
Courtauld, Samuel, 116
Courtauld, Samuel Augustine (SAC), 13,14,69,
    98-102,104,106-108,110-113,116-119,125-135,
    137-139,157,167,170,173,193,195-197,205,211
Courtauld, Sarah Louise, 123
Courtauld, Serena, 129
Courtauld, Simon Pierre, 123
Courtauld, Stephen Napier, 117,130
Courtauld, Susanna, 99
Courtauld, Susanna Ruth, 117
Courtauld, Sydney Elizabeth, 119
Courtauld, Sylvia, 123
Courtauld, Walter Pierre (Peter), 100,119,122,123,
    134
Courtauld, William Montgomerie, 117

Courtaulds Limited, 99,116,122,123
Cross, Kathleen Dorothy, 128
Cross, Victor George, 127
Crump, Elizabeth, 33
Crump, Jane, 33-35
Crump, John, 11,17,24,33-36,167,183,198
Crump, Mary Ann, 33,167
Crump, Susanna, 33,34
Cubitt, Thomas, 42
Currie, Ann Girdlestone, 51
Curling, Canon Thomas Higham, 74
Cutts, Rebecca, 33

D

Darrell, Lionel (Dudley), 152
Darrell, Ursula, 152
Day Samuel, 26
Day, Sarah Tayspill, 26
De Horne, John, 33
Denham Park, Denham, Buckinghamshire, 59,61
Desborrow, Jane, 17
Digby, James, 43,190
Digby, William, 189-191
Doggett, Eric, 198
Doggett, Dorothy, 198
Draper, Thomas, 194
Dring, Eliza, 169,170
Dring, Ernest George, 169,170
Dring, Florence Louisa, 169, 170
Dring, Henry, 169,170,182
Dring, Sidney Walter, 169,170
Drury, Janet, 131
Durward, Ada Hilda, 178

E

Earls Colne, 26
   The Blue Boar, 20
Earls Colne Brass Band, 85
Eastry, Frinton on Sea, 133,135
Eastry, Kent, 112,135
Edgbaston, Birmingham, 26
Edgware Estate, 19
Elford, Jonathan, 15
Elkins, Randolph, 18
Ellis, Emily, 37
Ellis, Sir William Charles, 59
Emberson, Samuel, 173
Essex Agricultural Society Show, 106,211
Essex County Hospital, 106
Essex Regiment, 76,85
Essex Volunteer Battalion Brass Band, 87

Evans, William, 11
Evans, Jacob, 187
Evans, Joseph, 187,200

F

Fairbank, Stanley Ernest, 193
Farrington, Dora, 51
Feering Bury Manor, 24-26
Felsted School, 106
Finchingfield, 18,19
Firman, James, 18
Fisher, Helen Sophia, 21
Fitzgilbert, Richard, 11
Flood, Charles William, 125
Fookes, John, 17
Forster, Deborah, 65
Forster, Robert, 13
Forster, William, 65
Foyster and Company, 30
Frost, William, 96
Fry, Elizabeth, 25
Frye, Alfred Thomas, 166
Fuller, Edith, 193
Fuller, George, 193
Fuller, Phyllis, 193
Fuller, Winifred, 193

G

Gardiner, James Spalding, 89
Garrad, Gertrude Mary, 78
Garrod, Samuel, 168
Gaymer, Mary, 163
Gedding, Suffolk, 15
Gee, Osgood, 20
Gepp, Mary Ann, 27
Gestingthorpe, 12
Gibson, Phoebe, 26
Gilbin, Charles, 89
Gilby, Richard, 18
Gilling, John, 86
Gissing Hall, Diss, Norfolk, 11,24,29
Gladstone, Ernest, 83
Goodman, William, 163
Gorham, Elizabeth, 61
Gorham, Ruth, 61
Gosfield,
   Cut Hedge, 86,99,126,129
   Gosfield Hall, 120
   Gosfield Place, 86
   Park Cottages, 126

St. Catherine's Church, 108,119
Gosset, Louisa, 56
Gosset, William, 13,45,55,56,61,167,191
Gould, Mary Ann, 37
Grant, Thomas William Richard, 145,181
Great Maplestead, 36
    Dynes Hall, 86
    Fitz Johns Farm, Dynes Hall Road, 14,36,110
Great Yeldham,
    Spencer Grange, 117,118
Great Yeldham United Football Club, 118
Great Waltham, 19
Greenstead Green,
    Gladfen Hall, 41
    Greenstead Hall, 86
    Three Horse Shoes, 18-20
Greenwood, Lucy, 64,65
Greenwood, Thomas, 23,189,190
Gretna Green, 49
Grubb, Jonathan, 67

H

Hadley, Louisa, 51
Hall, Benjamin, 21
Halstead,
    Abel Cottages, 103
    Anchor Public House, 204
    Ashford Lodge, 86,127
    Ashlong Grove, 39,139,141,145,146,149-151, 167,173
    Attwoods, 73,75,76,77
    Bentalls Farm, 76
    Beridge Road, 101,110
    Black Boy, 17,19,20
    Blackenham Bridge, 14
    Blackenham Street, 14
    Blamster's Farm, 64
    Bois Field, 44,64
    Bois Hall, 24,36
    Box Mill, 23,28,43,189-191
    Box Mill Lane, 12,33,43,45,64,100,101,103, 108,188-196,198,205,212
    Brook Street Farm, 14
    Causeway, 17,34
    Chapel Street, 17
    Cock, 17,20
    Colchester Road, 50,61,62,65,69,75,82,101, 108,110
    Cottage Hospital, 82,101,106
    Courtauld Homes of Rest, 74,77,101,105,106, 113,120,127,128,177,193,204
    Courtaulds Mill, 76
    Crow Bridge, 19
    Crown Public House, 101,199-202
    Doe's Corner, 12,17,38,106,157,163,206-211
    Gatehouse Yard, 19
    George Inn, 28
    Globe Yard, 29
    Grammar School, 65,73
    Greenwood School, 65
    Head Street, 36
    Hepworth Hall, 11,14,17,20,110,207,209,211
    Hepworth Hall Bridge, 62
    High Street, 15,17,18,23,27,30,36
    Holy Trinity Church, 75
    Kings Road, 162
    Lyndhurst, 76
    Mallows Field, 101,110
    Manor of Abells, 17,34,43,190,194
    Manor of Hepworth, 155
    Market Hill, 85
    Memorial Cross, 113-115
    Mill Chase, 101,110
    Nether Priors, 64,86
    New Congregational Church, 50,65,75,85
    North Street Baptist Church, 85
    Parsonage Lane, 15
    Parsonage Street, 75
    Prospect Place, 163
    Quaker Meeting House, 61,62,65
    Red Cow Public House, 190,193-195,198
    Red House, 69,82,140
    Sloe House, 86
    St. Martin Cottages, 103,202,205
    Stanstead Hall, 116
    Tan Yard, 194
    The Angel, 18-20
    The Bear (or White Bear), 17,20
    The Bricklayers Arms, 197
    The Bull (or Black Bull), 17,19,20
    The Cedars, 86
    The Chase, 36
    The Chequers, 17,19,20
    The Croft, 86
    The Dolphin, 18-20
    The Globe, 29
    The Howe School, 64,73,81,196-198,202,212
    The Kings Arms, 17,20,33,64
    The Kings Head, 20
    The Red Lion, 17,33
    The Swan, 17
    The Three Feathers, 18
    The Wash, 12,55,56,102,199,200,212
    Three Crowns, 17,19,20
    Three Pigeons, 17

Thrift's Hill, 12, 167,168
Tidings Hill, 194
Town Street, 15,17,18,30
Townford Bridge, 17,23
Townford Mill, 17
Trinity Street, 163
Two Brewers, 17,19,20
Union Offices, 75,103
Union Workhouse, 44,82,83,102,104,203,204
Wash Farm, 12,14,23,24,33,36,67,101,104, 110,189,198
Wash Hill, 13,167,168,193
White House, 15,30
Halstead and District Nursing Association, 74,82
Halstead Board of Guardians, 44,73,75,82,104,209
Halstead District Advisory Committee, 76
Halstead District Provident Building Society, 61
Halstead Excelsiors Football Club, 67,68
Halstead Golf Club, 157
Halstead Local Board of Health, 199
Halstead Local Volunteer Fire Brigade, 87
Halstead Summer Garden Parties Organisation, 86
Halstead Temperance Society, 85
Halstead Town Band, 87
Halstead Town Football Club, 87,107
Halstead Urban District Council, 14,139,140,147
Hamilton, Archibald, 37
Hamilton, Emma, 37
Hardy, Edward, 204
Harkstead, Suffolk, 20
Harper, Edward, 59
Harrington, Herbert, 87
Harris, Frank, 86
Harris, George, 64
Hartest, Suffolk, 15,16
   Brick House Farm, 21
   Cooks Farm, 15,18,19,21
   Cooks Parmenters, 18
   Hartest Farm, 21
   Hartest Lodge, 21
   Hedgefield, 18
   Hill Farm, 21
   Kew Gardens Farm, 21
   Manor of Hartest, 21
   Potches (Potts), 18
   Sorrells Farm, 15,18,19,21
   Thatchers, 19
   The Place Farm, 21
Hartington, Marquess of, 56
Harvey, Joseph Jarrom, 166
Hawke, Ambrose Lansdale, 79
Hawke, Ethel Caroline, 79
Hawley, Alice Marian, 80,81,83

Hawley, Edith Anne, 80,81
Hawley, Edith Josephine Roswell, 80,81,83
Hawley, Harriett, 80
Hawley, Joseph Roswell, 80,81
Hawkedon, Suffolk, 21
Healey, Tim, 87
Hines, Dr. James, 30
Hogarth, Bertram, 146,147
Hogarth, Mary, 147
Holman, William, 14
Hoole, Henry Elliott, 46
Hooper, Alfred, 30
Hooper, Ann, 30
Hooper, Emily, 30
Hooper, James Hill, 29,30
Hooper, Joseph, 29,30
Hooper, Mary, 30
Hooper, Rachel, 29
Hooper, William Start, 30
Hornor, Alice, 59,61,73,161
Hornor, Allan Moline, 61,78,79
Hornor and King, 59
Hornor and Turner, 59
Hornor, Anne, 13,59,61,64,65,67-70,72,79,81, 83,86,87,89,90,95,96,126,155,167,170,192, 194,201,202
Hornor, Beatrice, 61,83,196
Hornor, Benjamin, 59
Hornor, Caroline Christian, 78,79
Hornor, Catherine, 72
Hornor, Charles Birkbeck, 59,61,64
Hornor, Charles Ernest, 61,72,79
Hornor, Dora Lily Jane, 79
Hornor, Edith Anne, 61,79,80
Hornor, Edward, 13,14,50,56,58-67,69-72,75, 79,81,83,89,90,102,161,167,170,183,187, 191,192,194,196,200,202,204
Hornor, Ethel Caroline, 79
Hornor, Francis Birkbeck, 61,72
Hornor, Florence, 61,69,73,81-83,196
Hornor, George Edward, 79
Hornor, Lewis, 61,72,83,156
Hornor, Maud Mary, 79
Hornor, Sarah Jane, 59
Howard, Leonard, 125,195
Howe, Thomas, 26
Howe, William, 30
Howlett, Maria, 29
Howlett, Samuel, 29
Hughes, Henry George, 175
Humfrey, Nicholas, 18
Humphries Silk Weaving Company, 128
Hustler, Orbell, 34

Hutchinson, Elizabeth Susannah, 35
Hutchinson, John, 35

I

Iver, Buckinghamshire, 13,59-61,64

J

Jarman, Arthur, 165
Jarvis, George, 193
Johnson, John, 199
Jordan, Dr. George Robert Leslie, 30
Joscelyne, Charles Walter, 37
Joscelyne, Emma Elizabeth, 37
Joscelyne, Elizabeth, 37
Joscelyne, Mary Ann, 37
Joscelyne, Samuel, 36,37

K

Keatinge, Maurice, 28
Kedington, Suffolk, 82
Kelsey, Jane Florence, 51
Kelsy, Elizabeth, 116
Kelvedon, 25
Kent, Charles, 23
Ker, Dr. William Percival, 30
Kerrison, David, 128
Kersey, Elizabeth, 26
Kiely, Andrew, 130
King, John, 59
Kirkham, William, 28

L

Lacey, Richard, 47,48
Lacey, Rolfe, 149
Lacey, Sarah, 47
Lamarsh, 27
Lancaster, Caroline Susan, 52
Langley, Madelon Katie, 52
Last, William, 203
Laver, James Henry, 171,179
Lawrence, Albert, 87
Lawrence, Eliza Maria, 50
Layzell, James, 162
Legerton, Frederick, 191
Legerton, Horace, 191
Leslie, Isabella, 61
Levington, Suffolk, 26
Lewis, Marian, 51
Lewis, Robert, 55

Lister, Arthur Venning, 116
Lister, Edith Anne, 100,112
Lister, Henry Reid, 115
Lister, James Solly, 116
Lister, Lucy, 112
Lister, Walter Kendrick, 116
Lister, Walter Venning, 112
Little Maplestead, 36
    Little Maplestead Hall, 50
Little Yeldham, 27,89,90
Lockwood, Adelaide, 81
London,
    Charlotte Street, Cavendish Square, 26
    Newgate Prison, 25
    Oxford Street, 20,44,47
Long, Ronald, 140
Long, Sir James, 33

M

MacNair, Caroline Christian, 78
Macnamara, Arthur, 13,45,55,56,61,167,191
Macnamara, Elizabeth Lee, 56
Maidwell, Thomas Hustler, 169
Maldon, Essex, 26
Marriage, James, 26
Mathews, Morton, 189
Mathews, William, 65
Maxim, James, 44
Maxim, Sophie, 44
May, Abraham, 41,47
May and Morritt, 42-44,55
May, Augusta, 42,47,48,53
May, Caroline Susan, 52
May, Edward, 12,36,39,41-50,52,53,55,56,156,
    157,167,173,183,191,199,202,207
May, Edward John, 42,48,52
May, Emily Ching, 42,47,48,53
May, George, 48
May, George Lacey, 46-48
May, Isaac, 41
May, John, 34,41
May, Keren Amelia, 42,44,45,49,50
May, Keren Happuch, 42,45,47-49,52,53,55
May, Mary, 41
May, Samuel, 41
May, Sarah, 41
May, William, 41,48
Mayne, Ellen Flora, 28
Mayne, Emily, 28
Mayne, John, 27,28
Mayne, John Augustus, 28
Mayne, John Thomas, 27

Mayne, Margaret, 28
Mayne, Sarah, 28
Mobbs, Ronald, ARIBA., 146
Moger, Stanley, 130
Moline, Anne, 61
Moline, Elizabeth, 61
Moline, John, 65
Moline, Robert, 13,61
Monk, Elizabeth, 174
Monk, Martha, 174
Montefiore, Claude Goldsmid Joseph, 133
Montgomerie, Frank Douglas, 119
Montgomerie, Esme, 119
Montgomerie, Mollie, 117-119
Morland, Thomas, 13
Morley, John, 199
Mornington, Rt. Hon. William, Earl of, 194
Morritt, Aaron, 42,44,55,56,202
Morritt, Ann, 56
Morritt, Elizabeth, 55,56
Morritt, Hester, 56
Morritt, Nicholas, 55,56
Morton, Gerard Sinclair, 82
Morton, Violet, 82
Moul, Anthony, 33,167
Moul, John, 167
Moul, Stephen, 167
Moule, Alfred Isaac, 203

N

Napier, Esme, 119
Nash, George, 24
Nash, Jonathan, 28
National Temperance League, 65,66
Nevill, Sir Thomas, 11
Newman, Emma, 27
New Zealand, 153
Nicholson, Thomas, 46
Nightingale, Florence, 80
Norden, George, 95
Norden, William, 95
Noel House, Palace Green, Kensington, 106,119,
   125-127,133-135
Norman, Arthur, 185,186
Norman, Charles, 185,186
Norman, Christopher, 194,195
Norman, Edward, 185
Norman, Eliza, 186,187
Norman, Hannah, 174,185,195
Norman, Henry, 174,183-185,195
Norman, Herbert, 185,186
Norman, James, 183,187

Norman, Jane, 187
Norman, Martha, 167,171,185,193,195
Norman, Mary Ann, 187
Norman, Sarah, 183,187
Norman, Sarah Ann, 185,186,193,195
Norman, Susanna, 183
Norman, Susannah, 187
Norman, Thomas, 46,183,186,187,194
Norman, William, 33,183-186

O

Oakley, Rev. Edwin, 83
Osborne, Arthur (Mick), 145,181
Osborne, Edith, 145
Osborne, Ray, 145
Overall, Emma, 196
Owen, Hugh, 65
Oxford, Earl of, 11

P

Paflin, Charles, 170,174
Palmer, Charles Ingelby, 51
Parker, John, 158
Parker, William, 168
Parks, Catherine, 72
Parks, Luther, 72
Parks, Sarah Tilden, 72
Parr, Charles, 186
Parr, Eliza, 186
Parr, George, 185
Parr, Hannah, 185,186
Parr, Mary, 185,186
Partridge, William Freeman, 169
Patrick, George, 196
Paxman, James Noah, 197
Paylen, Margaret, 196
Peapell, Nelson, 126
Pebmarsh, 18,27
   Moat Farm, Cross End, 27
   Sparlings Farm, 27
   St. John the Baptist Church, 27
   The Cottage, 27
Penny, Amelia Lucy, 51
Penny, Edith, 51
Perry, John, 11
Peto, Harold Ainsworth, 132
Peto, Sir Samuel, 132
Phelps, Edward John, 80
Phillips, Mary Ann, 33
Piper, Edward, 36

Piper, John, 36
Plant, Robert, 173
Plumb, Charles, 129,130
Plumb, Rhoda, 76,77
Plumbe, William, 17
Poley, George Weller, 21,22
Poley, Rev. John Weller, 21
Poole, Elizabeth, 36
Porsenna vase, 138
Porter, Harriett Sarah, 51
Porter, James, 204
Portway and Son, 162
Portway, Charles, 86,156
Portway, Harriet Amy, 83
Portway, Harry Harvey, 156
Portway, Mavis, 146
Portway, Major Michael, 146,156
Potter Henry, 15
Potter, Katherine, 15
Powter, Sophia Ann, 131
Pratt, Charles, 17
Priestman, David, 25
Prior, James, 168
Purleigh, Essex, 26

Q

Quilter, James, 48

R

Rae, Dr. Archie Herbert, 30
Rae, Robert, 65
Rainham, 19
Ramsey, Frederick, 171
Raven, Edward, 161,162
Raven, Walter Edward, 162
Raven, Walter William, 161
Rayment, George, 163
Rayner, Andrew Piers Courtauld, 121
Rayner, Lady Betty, 120-122,127
Rayner, Charles Edwin, 113,175
Rayner, Charles Henry, 174-176,178
Rayner, Dennis Edwin, 177
Rayner, Dennis Henry, 175-178
Rayner, Fanny, 175
Rayner, Fleur Revere Courtauld, 121
Rayner, Frank, 88
Rayner, Rev. George, 119
Rayner, Henry, 208
Rayner, Jonathan, 208
Rayner, John, 23
Rayner, Marcel John, 177

Rayner, Nicholas Courtauld, 121
Rayner, Brig. Sir. Ralph Herbert, 119-122,127
Rayner, Ranulf Courtauld, 121
Rayner, Sarah, 208
Rayner, Sheila, 121
Reeve, Charlotte Ann, 171
Richards, Dr. Sybil Muriel, 30
Richardson, Charles, 46
Richer, James, 169
Rickman, Beatrice, 83,84
Rickman, Thomas Apsley, 83,84
Ridgewell, 27,89-96
   Green Farm, 89
   Hill Farm, 62,67,89-96,187
   Pannells Farm, 89
   Ridgewell Hill Farm, 89
Rippingale, Jack, 149
Risbridge Union Workhouse, Kedington, 104
Roberts, Ann, 41
Roberts, Elizabeth, 41
Roberts, Henry, 161
Roberts, John, 41,42
Rodgers, Derwick, 181,182
Root, John, 33
Ruffle, John, 190
Runnacles, Harcourt, 174
Rushbrook, Michael, 149

S

Salmon, Jack, 130
Samuel Courtauld and Company Limited, 99
Sargent, Sir Malcolm, 116
Saunders, Albert, 126,167,171
Sayells, Elizabeth, 169
Sayells, Emma, 169
Sebag-Montefiore, Cecil, 197
Servier, Elizabeth Docker, 51
Sewell, Alleine, 50
Sewell, Amy Constance, 50,52
Sewell, Arthur Edward William, 51
Sewell, Benjamin Leonard, 51
Sewell, Charles Bertie, 51
Sewell, Decimus, 44,49-51
Sewell, Decimus Reginald, 51
Sewell, Edith, 50
Sewell, Edith Lucy, 51
Sewell, Edward May, 50,51
Sewell, Elizabeth, 50,52
Sewell, Eliza Maria, 50
Sewell, Ernest Aveling, 51
Sewell, Florence, 51
Sewell, Harriett Amelia Blanche, 51

Sewell, Harriett Sarah, 51,52
Sewell, Helen Elizabeth, 50
Sewell, Isaac, 189,190
Sewell, John, 50,190
Sewell, Lionel Isaac, 51
Sewell, Mark Luke, 51
Sewell, Maud Daisy, 51
Sewell, May, 51
Sewell, Percy, 50-52
Sewell, Percy Servier, 51
Sewell, Reuben John, 51
Sewell, Rhoda Susannah, 51
Sewell, Robert Claude, 51
Sewell, Thomas, 28
Sewell, William, 189
Shalford, Great Codham Hall, 119
Shemming, Edwin Andrew, 204,205
Shewell, Joseph, 13,65
Shewell, Joseph Talwin, 13
Shewell, Richard Bevington, 13
Shewell, Robert, 13
Sible Hedingham, 17
   Cut Maple, 191
   Hole Farm, 191
   Manor of Prayors Glasscocks, 15
   Sparrows Farm, 14,110
   Swan Street, 191
Sibley, Alice, 196
Sibley, George William, 179,196
Sinclair, Dr. Duncan, 30
Smith, Beatrice, 131
Smith, Edward, 163
Smith, Ernie, 145
Smoothy, Elizabeth, 50
Smoothy, Thomas, 24,36,198
Snowden, Ernest Arthur, 108,128
Somerton, Suffolk, 21
Southampton, 26
Sparrow, Elizabeth, 36,37
Sparrow, James Goodeve, 28,33
Sparrow, Jeremiah, 36
Sparrow, John, 11,12,24,35,36,43,183
Sperling, Charles, 86
Sperling, James, 207
Spiers, Dora Lily Jane, 79
Spiers, James, 79
Springett, Bertram James, 164
Spurgen, Sarah, 15
Spurgeon, David Charles, 202
Spurgeon, Martha, 183
Stanstead, Suffolk, 21
Stansted Mountfitchet, 26
Start, Ann, 23,29

Start, Augusta Sarah, 27
Start, Charles William, 27
Start, Ellen Jane, 27
Start, Elizabeth, 23,29
Start, Emma, 27
Start, John, 23,26,27,29
Start, John Creswell, 27
Start, John Creswell Newman, 27
Start, Louisa Emma, 27,29
Start, Maria Sophia, 29
Start, Mary, 23,26,29
Start, Mary Anna, 26,29
Start, Samuel, 29
Start, Sarah, 27
Start, Sarah Fulcher, 26
Start, William, 11,20,23,24,26,28,29,33,35,36
Steed, John, 124
Stisted,
   Gowers Farm, 48
   Stisted Hall, 197
Sturmer, George, 159,160
Sturmer, Susanna, 159,160,170
Sturmer, Walter, 160
Sturmer, William, 159,160,170,183,187
Suckling, Ronald, 108
Suiter, Joseph, 27
Surridge, Joseph, 28

T

Tayler, Elizabeth, 86,127
Taylor, John, 44,48,55,56,65,202
Teffont Evias, Wiltshire, 27
Tenner, Catherine, 18
Thirkettle, James, 182
Tibble, George, 131
Tilbury Juxta Clare, 27,90-93,95
   Tilbury Green, 90,96
   Tilbury Hall, 75,76,90
Tilden, Sarah, 72
Tisseau, Sarah, 72
Tivetshall, Norfolk, 24,29
Tortoise Iron Works, 162
Totman, Abraham, 36
Totman, Elizabeth, 36
Tunbridge, Benjamin, 167
Turkentine, Bernard, 130,145
Turkentine, Lily, 131
Tweed, Ann(e), 15
Tweed, Jane, 11,17-19,23
Tweed, John, 15,17
Tweed, Katherine, 15,17
Tweed, Mary 15

Tweed Ralph, 15
Tweed, Robert, 11,15-20,23
Tweed, Sarah, 15
Tweed, Spurgen, 15
Tyler, Edith, 76,77
Tyler, George, 67,68
Tyler, James, 161

U

Underwood, John, 95,96
Underwood, Robert, 96

V

Vaizey, Alice, 73-78
Vaizey, Alice Lilian, 73,78,87
Vaizey, Ann, 74
Vaizey, Eleanor, 75
Vaizey, Francis Arthur (Frank), 67,73,76,77,
   87,176,177
Vaizey, George de Horne, 194
Vaizey, John, 73
Vaizey, John Leonard, 73,77,78
Vaizey, John Robert, 73-75,77,78,90
Vaizey, Robert Edward, 73,75-77,95
van Asch, David, 153,154
van Asch, Jula, 153,154
van Asch, Ralph Gerrit, 14,118,139,141,142,
   145,147,149-154

W

Wade, Alice Lilian, 78
Wade, Alice Margaret, 78
Wade, Eileen Rawson, 78
Wade, Gertrude Mary, 78
Wade, Henry Oswald, 78
Wade, John Leonard, 78
Wade, Marjorie Helen, 78
Wade, Mary, 78
Wade, Dr. Oswald Tetley, 78
Wade, Sarah, 78
Walford, Jane, 17
Walford, John, 17
Walford, William, 18
Waller, Alice, 59
Waller, Robert, 59
Walter, Ann, 56
Walter, Charles, 13,55,56
Walter, Elizabeth, 56
Walter, Ellen, 56
Walter, John, 56

Walter, Mary, 56
Walter, Nicholas Thomas, 55,56,202
Walter, Thomas, 55
Walter, William, 56
Walton, 15,17
Ware, Hugh, 152
Warner, Robert, 65
Watkins, Gino, 118
Watkinson, Henry, 170,210
Wayman and Long, 150
Webb, Frederick Thomas, 197
Wells, John, 203
Westminster, Marquess of, 56
West, William, 160
West Yorkshire Regiment, 78
Wethersfield, 18,110
Whaley, Ann, 19,21,22
Whaley, Charles, 19
Whaley, Charles Blatch, 19
Whaley, Jane, 19,21,22
Whaley, John Blatch, 11,19-22,24,33,167
Whatley Hill & Co., 141,142
Wheeler, Thomas, 159
Wilding, Stanley, 151
Wilkinson, William, 78
Williams, Stephen, 46
Willoughby, Capt. B.D., 121
Wilson, Rebecca, 161
Wilson, Rev. Thomas Given, 65
Wink, Dr. Charles Stewart, 30
Winterflood, William, 24
Wiseman, James, 209
Worthington, Edward, 35
Worthington, Elizabeth, 35
Worthington, Leonard, 35
Worthington, John, 35
Wyatt, Susanna, 56

Y

York, 59
Younge, Robert, 17
Younge, Sarah, 17

Z

Zboinska Countess, 72

The Author –
Pam Corder-Birch

Pam born in Lancashire has spent most of her life in the South East of England. After living and working for many years in London, Pam returned to the Essex/Suffolk border where she met and married Adrian. As a member of the Essex Family History Society, Bradford, Lancashire and Sussex Family History Societies, Pam enjoys all aspects of genealogy. A keen interest in her family's history led to her writing her first book, 'Accolade to an Artist, The Life and Work of William Woodhouse 1857 - 1939' as the artist has a family connection. Pam also shares Adrian's love for local history, being a member of the Halstead and District Local History Society. Following many years in the legal profession Adrian is now employed in local government and is a respected local historian and the author of several books. As a keen gardener, much of her spare time is spent working in their woodland garden.

Other Books by Pam and Adrian Corder-Birch

Accolade to an Artist - The Life and Work of William Woodhouse 1857 - 1939
by Pam Corder-Birch
(A Lancashire artist renowned for painting animals, especially horses and dogs as well as land and seascapes).   £12-95
*Remittance in English Pounds Sterling should be made payable to **Pamela Corder-Birch** for £12-95 plus £3-50 postage and packing.*

• • • • • • • • • • • • • • •

Our Ancestors were Brickmakers and Potters - A History of the Corder and related families in the clay working industries
by Adrian Corder-Birch (with photographs and illustrations by Christine Walker)   £14-95

*Remittance in English Pounds Sterling should be made payable to **Adrian Corder-Birch** for £14-95 plus £3-50 postage and packing.*

• • • • • • • • • • • • • • •

A Centenary History of Halstead Hospital (1884 - 1984)   £1-95
A Pictorial History of Sible Hedingham -   £4-75
A History of Great Yeldham   £6-95

The above three books were written by Adrian Corder-Birch and published by Halstead and District Local History Society.

*Remittances in English Pounds Sterling to **Halstead and District Local History Society**. Appropriate postage and packing should be added to the above amounts.*

• • • • • • • • • • • • • • •

ALL the books listed above are available from Pam and Adrian Corder-Birch, Rustlings, Howe Drive, Halstead, Essex CO9 2QL.
Any *enquiries to: Pam and Adrian Corder-Birch, email:* corder-birch@lineone.net